MARITIME LAW AND POLICY IN CHINA

KX Li
BSc, LLM, MSc, PhD (Wales)

CWM Ingram
MA (Cambridge)

Routledge
Taylor & Francis Group
LONDON AND NEW YORK

First published 2002 by Cavendish Publishing

2 Park Square, Milton Park, Abingdon, Oxon OX14 4RN
711 Third Avenue, New York, NY 10017, USA

Routledge is an imprint of the Taylor & Francis Group, an informa business

First issued in hardback 2016

Transferred to digital printing 2009

British Library Cataloguing in Publication Data

Li, KX

Maritime law and policy in China

1 Maritime law – China

I Title II Ingram, Colin

343.5'1'096

ISBN 978-1-85941-739-3 (pbk)
ISBN 978-1-138-16048-4 (hbk)

PREFACE

In December 2001, commissioned by the International Maritime Organization (IMO), Mr Colin Ingram and I undertook an advisory mission to Vietnam to assist the authorities in updating their maritime code and legal system. Before and during the mission, we reviewed various maritime codes and conventions. Maritime law in China was among those examined.

We agree with Dr Hazelwood's comments on the Chinese Maritime Code that: 'The PRC is to be congratulated on its international and forward looking perspective. The Code has been some 40 years in the working but has done, at a stroke, what other leading maritime nations have been struggling to achieve in a piecemeal fashion over many decades. In adopting many international maritime conventions, the PRC puts a number of so called leading maritime nations to shame.'[1] This systematic approach could, at least, be an alternative form of maritime legislation, and is recommended for developing maritime nations in establishing or updating their maritime legal systems.

However, we found that there are few publications available, especially in the English language, on Chinese maritime law. Instead of engaging in a comprehensive analysis, our aim is to provide an introduction to the Chinese maritime legal system and a more accurate English translation of maritime-related laws. In some important areas, comparisons are made to English law and international conventions.

On 11 December 2001, China officially became the 143rd member of the World Trade Organisation (WTO). China's accession to the WTO was a significant event to the world as well as to China. We hope this work can be of assistance to those who want to know more about the Chinese maritime legal system.

Thanks go to Mr Owen Tang JD, Researcher in Law at the Department of Shipping and Transport Logistics, Hong Kong Polytechnic University, for his valuable assistance in preparing this work.

Dr KX Li
17 July 2002

---

1 Steven Hazelwood, 'New Maritime Code – maritime insurance', a Paper for the International Conference on Maritime Law, 11–14 October 1994, Shanghai Maritime University, at p 4 in the 9th Paper.

CONTENTS

TABLE OF CASES

TABLE OF LEGISLATION

TABLE OF INTERNATIONAL INSTRUMENTS

TABLE OF ABBREVIATIONS

ADB	Asian Development Bank
ASG	Admiralty Solicitors Group
BHS	Bureau of Harbour Superintendency
CLC	International Convention on Civil Liability for Oil Pollution Damage
CMI	Comité Maritime International
COSCO	China Ocean Shipping (Group) Company
GATT	General Agreement on Tariffs and Trade
GDP	Gross Domestic Product
HIPH	Hutchison International Port Holdings
ILO	International Labour Organisation
IMO	International Maritime Organization
MOC	Ministry of Communications
MOL	Mitsui OSK Lines
MPL	Maritime Procedure Law
NPC	National People's Congress
NSC	National Supreme Court
PICC	People's Insurance Company of China
PLA	People's Liberation Army
PRC	People's Republic of China
PSC	Port State Control
RMB	Ren Min Bi
SDR	Special Drawing Rights
UNCTAD	United Nations Commission on Trade and Development
WTO	World Trade Organisation

PART 1

MARITIME POLICY AND LEGAL SYSTEM IN CHINA

1 INTRODUCTION

China has emerged as one of the major maritime nations in the last two decades. In 1980, China had only 955 ships totalling 6 million gross tons (gt). By 1990, this had increased to 1,948 (13 million gt), and by 1998, to 3,175 (16 million gt).[1] The annual growth rate is about 13% in number of ships and 7.7% in tonnage, which is much higher than the world average of 1.1% and 1.3% respectively.[2] According to *Lloyd's List*,[3] the population of China was 1.28 billion in July 2001. Gross Domestic Product (GDP) based on purchasing power parity was estimated at US$ 4.5 trillion, and the GDP real growth rate was estimated at 8%. Chinese GDP was composed of 50% industrial, 35% services and 15% agriculture. Its industries included iron and steel, coal, machine building, armaments, textiles and apparel, petroleum, cement, chemical fertilisers, footwear, toys, food processing, motors, consumer electronics and telecommunications. China's foreign trade is predicted to be worth about US$ 550–600 billion by 2005, up from US$ 320 billion in 1998.[4] Studies reveal that, after meeting its own domestic needs, China could supply as many as 91,000 officers and 150,000 ratings, exceeding the Philippines as the top maritime labour supplier.[5] Studies show also that China maintains one of the best quality fleets in the world.[6]

1 Lloyd's Register: World Fleet Statistics and Statistical Tables (*annum*). Ships referred to are those being more than 100 gt and registered in China. Ships registered outside the countries are not included. China had 378 ships (above 1,000 gt) registered under open registry (UNCTAD: *Review of Maritime Transport*, 1997).

2 Li, KX and Wonham, J, 'Who is safe and who is at risk: a study of 20-year-record on total accident loss in different flags' (1999) 26(2) Maritime Policy & Management 137–44, at 139.

3 *Lloyd's List* (2001): China Special Report, 17 October 2001.

4 'Battling agencies block industry growth' (2001) *South China Morning Post*, 19 November.

5 Li, KX and Wonham, J, 'Who mans the world fleet? A follow-up to the BIMCO/ISF manpower survey' (1999) 26(3) Maritime Policy & Management 295–303, at 297, 298.

6 Li, KX and Wonham, J, 'Who is safe and who is at risk: a study of 20-year-record on total accidental loss in different flags' (1999) 26(2) Maritime Policy & Management 137–44, at 142. Li, KX and Wonham, J, *The Role of States in Maritime Employment and Safety: A Legal and Economic Study*, 2001, Dalian, China: Dalian Maritime University Press. From 1977 to 1996, the average total loss rate (total loss number of ships/per thousand) for the Chinese fleet was 1% and aggregated total loss rate was 0.78% compared with the world average of 3.97% and 3.91% respectively (Li and Wonham, 2001, pp 252 and 268). According to Alderton, T and Winchester, N, 'Flag states and safety: 1997–99' (2002) 29(2) Maritime Policy & Management 151–62, Table 1, the casualty rate is 0.67% for the Chinese fleet, which is much lower than the world average of 1.6%.

Maritime related cases accepted by the Maritime Courts reached 5,166, representing a 20% average annual growth from 1990 (Table 1). To cope with increasing pressure from shipping and trade, China has passed more than 20 maritime-related laws, the most significant being the Maritime Code 1992 and the Maritime Procedure Law (MPL) 1999. China has also ratified most of the maritime conventions, in particular those adopted by the International Maritime Organization (IMO) (Table 2). As a whole, it constitutes a complete maritime legal system in line with the general international practice.

One of the pillars of this legal system is the Maritime Code, adopted on 7 November 1992, at the 28th Meeting of the Standing Committee of the 7th National People's Congress of the People's Republic of China (PRC), and entered into force on 1 July 1993. It was a milestone for China in completing its maritime legal framework. The history of the drafting of the Maritime Code reflects China's economic, political and legal development. The drafting originated in the early 1950s, just a few years after the founding of the new China, at a time when most of its fleet had moved to Taiwan and shipping facilities had been seriously damaged or destroyed. The new government took a series of policy decisions and measures in an attempt to keep the maritime transportation system in survival. Establishing a maritime law framework was one of these measures. The drafting of the Maritime Code began with the study and translation of the Russian Maritime Law. A drafting committee was established by the Ministry of Communications (MOC) consisting of law professors, lawyers and shipping practitioners from governmental agencies, shipping companies and maritime universities, and the first official draft was finished in 1963.

In 1966, China began the 'Cultural Revolution' and the drafting was therefore stopped for political reasons, and was not resumed until 1981. The Maritime Code was at last completed after more than 40 years' work, a milestone in regulating its maritime industry and in forming its maritime policy. At the time, it was one of the longest codes in China in terms of the number of Articles. During the discussion in the National People's Congress, it was widely accepted that the Code had been very well drafted in terms of policy-making and structure as well as wording. It was passed with an overwhelming majority, 98 votes in favour out of a total of 101 votes, which was rare in Chinese legislation. The success of the drafting may be attributed to the following factors:

(1) China has a group of professional maritime law experts who are familiar with both international maritime law and the Chinese legal system;

(2) government accords a top priority to the maritime industry and the drafting of the Code;

(3) the pressure arising out the development of economy and trade;

(4) the assistance from international organisations and foreign maritime law experts;[7]

(5) a long germination period. The fact that it was drafted over a 40 year period meant that there was enough time to collect information, to develop new policy, to get comments and to undertake revisions.

To implement the Maritime Code, China has also promulgated a series of Regulations in accordance with its Maritime Legislative Plan. These include the Ship Registration Regulations which were promulgated on 2 June 1994 and came into force on 1 January 1995. The MOC, in pursuance of Articles 210(2) and 211(2) of the Maritime Code, approved by the State Council of the PRC, promulgated two special Regulations on 15 November 1993, the Provisions Concerning Limitation of Liability for Small and Coastal Ships (the Coastal Provisions) and the Provisions Concerning Limitation of Liability for Passenger Ships Sailing between Chinese Ports (the Passenger Provisions). Both entered into force on 1 January 1994.

The Maritime Procedure Law (the MPL) of the PRC is another important piece of legislation. It represents a significant step in achieving a cohesive maritime legal system. Passed on 25 December 1999 by the 9th National People's Congress (NPC) and entering into force on 1 July 2000, the MPL consolidates previous laws and practice, and adopted the substantial provisions of the International Convention on Arrest of Ships 1999 (the 1999 Convention).[8] The MPL is expected to have a great impact on maritime practice in China.

The MPL consists of 12 chapters, on General Principles, Maritime Preservation, Jurisdiction, Maritime Injunctions, Preservation of Maritime Evidence, Maritime Security, Service, Trial Procedure, Constitution of Limitation Funds, Registration and Payment of Claims, Maritime Lien and Addendum (coming into force). However, this Part focuses on maritime jurisdiction and arrest of ships, which are the key elements of the new law.[9] The MPL is a specific law on maritime procedure under the general principles set out in the Civil Procedure Law of the PRC (the Civil Procedure Law)

7 It is worth mentioning that during the drafting of the Maritime Code, international maritime organisations such as the IMO, Comité Maritime International (CMI) and others gave a great amount of help in providing information, comments and suggestions to the draft. Maritime experts from these organisations or other countries also went to China to give lectures concerning the new development of international maritime law and conventions. To the knowledge of the authors, the following scholars in maritime law have been to China giving lectures or comments on the draft of the Maritime Code: Prof Alex L Parks; Prof Allan Philip; Prof David J Sharpe; Prof David Steel; Prof Edgar Gold; Mr Emery W Harper; Prof Francesco Berlingieri; Mr Gordon W Paulsen; Prof Jan C Schultsz; Mr Kaj Pineus; Prof Piet Jan Slot; and Prof Robert Force.

8 International Convention on Arrest of Ships 1999, 6B Benedict on Admiralty Doc No 8-1A (7th rev ed, 1999) (not in force).

9 For the position before the MPL, see Tang, Z, 'Maritime jurisdiction of the People's Republic of China: legal framework, recent developments and future prospects' (1994) 25(2) JMLC 251–78.

1991.[10] The MPL is to prevail where there is a difference between the Civil Procedure Law and the MPL (Article 2).[11]

The enactment of the Maritime Code, the MPL and other maritime-related laws and regulations was also a sign of establishing a comprehensive legal framework for the Chinese maritime industry. Previously, Chinese maritime polices relied largely on administrative decisions and documents – the so called Red Title Document – which could be changed according to political and social events. This resulted in criticism concerning the lack of stability and openness in Chinese shipping administration and policy-making.

The 'open door' policy and the fast development of foreign trade and the shipping industry required a long term maritime policy. In this sense, the publication of the Maritime Code and regulations is a very important step in maritime development and reform of the country. These legislative maritime policies, some of which have been practised for a long time and others which are new philosophies, will influence the Chinese shipping industry in the future for the long term.

China had been seeking GATT/WTO membership since 1986. After 15 years of negotiation with trading partners, China officially became a member of the World Trade Organisation (WTO) in November 2001. China's accession to the WTO was a significant event to the world as well as to China. WTO membership will compel China to change its current commercial laws and practices to conform to WTO rules. Trade disputes would be resolved through the WTO adjudication procedures rather than through bilateral bargaining. This has already had a dynamic effect in drawing the Chinese maritime legal system toward openness and transparency.

---

10 Laws and Regulations of the PRC Governing Foreign-related Matters (1991–92), 297; the English text can also be found at http://www.qis.net/chinalaw.

11 Under the Chinese legal system, there are three levels of law. At the top, the Constitution; second, the principal laws, eg, the General Principles of Civil Law, the Civil Procedure Law; third, the specific laws, eg, the Maritime Code and the MPL. For detailed discussion on this topic, see Jin, ZG and Weng, ZM, *China Maritime Litigation*, 1993, Shenzhen: Haitian Press, pp 44–51, written in Chinese. Laws of the first and second levels are passed by the NPC whilst laws of third level are passed by the Standing Committee of the NPC. Laws of the lower levels in principle must not conflict with those in the higher levels. However, a specific law will be applied where the principal law has no detailed provisions. For example, the Contract Law, as a principal law, in Article 123 provides 'if there are provisions as otherwise stipulated in respect of contracts in other laws, such provisions shall be followed': 2000, Beijing: China Legal System Publishing House, at 59.

2 THE ROLE OF THE MOC UNDER THE MARITIME CODE

During the period of planned economy in China, administrative decisions and State interventions were the main measures used to regulate industry and its activities. With the economy developing and reforming, administrative measures have been largely scaled down in many industries, including the maritime transport sector.

The MOC plays a vital role in Chinese shipping administration. It lost its function as a 'Ministry of Transportation' in 1975 when it became no longer responsible for railways and civil aviation transport. It covers only sea, waterway and highway transportation. Key features in achieving this include maritime strategy-making and maritime policy-making. The MOC also exercises other duties as law or regulations authorise. Under the Maritime Code, for example, the MOC has the following functions:

(1) to give permission to foreign ships to engage in the maritime transport or towage services between the ports of the PRC (Article 4);

(2) to prohibit and fine any illegal flying of the national flag of the PRC (Article 5);

(3) to work as a general administrator of the national shipping industry, to develop specific regulations concerning its administration and to implement these after they have been submitted to and approved by the State Council (Article 6);

(4) to issue Seaman's Books and other relevant certificates (Article 33);

(5) to work out the limits of liability of carriers with respect to the carriage of passengers by sea between the ports of the PRC (Articles 116, 211);

(6) to work out the limits of liability for ships with a gross tonnage not exceeding 300 tons and those engaged in transport services between the ports of the PRC as well as those for other coastal works (Article 210);

(7) to perform or control salvage operations (Article 192).

According to Article 8 of the Ship Registration Regulations of the PRC, the Bureau of Harbour Superintendency (BHS) of the PRC under the MOC is the competent authority in charge of ship registration. The Harbour Superintendency Administrations at various ports are the designated agencies conducting the registration of ships. The scope of their authority shall be defined by the BHS. From the above discussion, one can see that the MOC not only is a maritime rule and policy-maker and a maritime administrator, but also plays an important role in implementing the Maritime Code.

3 INTERNATIONAL STANDARDS

It is one of the guiding principles of China's foreign policy to work within the confines of international law and to respect the commonly accepted international practice. As one of the main drafters of the Maritime Code, the adviser of the Standing Committee of the People's Congress, Guo Riqi, pointed out: 'The Maritime Code has been drafted strictly according to international standards, either from a general point of view or from specific points of view.'[12] For example, in Chapter 2, concerning maritime mortgages and liens, it adopts the provisions of the 1967 Convention on Maritime Liens and Mortgage. Concerning contracts of carriage of goods by sea in Chapter 4, it adopts the substantial provisions of the Hague-Visby Rules with due consideration to the Hamburg Rules. Concerning contracts of carriage of passengers by sea in Chapter 5, it adopts the substantial provisions of the 1974 Athens Convention. In Chapter 8, concerning collision at sea, it adopts the substantial provisions of the 1910 Collision Convention. In Chapter 9, concerning salvage, it adopts the substantial provisions of the 1989 International Convention on Salvage. In Chapter 10, concerning limitation of liability for maritime claims, it adopts the substantial provisions of the 1976 Convention on Limitation of Liability.

There are several reasons for China to adopt international maritime conventions and practices. First, since China adopted its 'open door' policy as a long term strategy to accelerate its ambitious modernisation programme, foreign trade with more and more countries and regions has grown dramatically. Over 90% of China's international trade is transported by ships and passes through its ports. To meet the needs of its steadily developing foreign trade, China needs not only an expansion of its fleet, but also a globally recognised maritime legal system. As Article 1 of the Maritime Code provides:

> This Code is enacted for the purpose of regulating the relations arising from maritime transport and those pertaining to ships, securing and protecting the legitimate rights and interests of the parties concerned, and promoting the development of maritime transport, economy and trade.

Second, an attractive environment for foreign investors has to be established, not only in terms of its foundation, but superstructure as well. To achieve this, laws and regulations concerning foreign investment, particularly joint-ventures, taxation and technology transfer are important. Shipping-related laws and regulations also constitute a very important component of China's economic legislation.

---

12 Guo Riqi, 'An introduction to the legislation of the Maritime Code', in the Ministry of Communications (ed), *The Essentials of the Maritime Code*, 1993, Beijing: People's Communications Press, p 2.

Third, the implementation of international conventions has to be given priority for both economic and political reasons. As is widely recognised, one of the existing problems in the world maritime industry is that conventions adopted by international organisations have not been implemented adequately, properly and identically by its member countries, especially by less developed countries. In answering the question: 'What do you think will be the major challenge for the world maritime community for the remainder of the century?', Mr William A O'Neil, the Secretary General of the IMO replied, 'Making sure that the conventions and other regulations that have been adopted by the IMO over the years are properly implemented'.[13] The measures introduced by the IMO during the last 30 years have provided a framework for maritime safety and reduced maritime pollution from ships. If all of these measures were vigorously applied, the problems would be reduced dramatically. States which are parties to maritime conventions need to implement them through domestic legislation. However, it is for the individual State to decide how to undertake their international obligations. As a member country of the IMO, it is also in China's interest to properly implement these conventions through its maritime legislation.

Last, it is an attempt to unify international maritime law and practice. Shipping is an international business, operated and to some extent regulated internationally. There is no doubt that international action is generally more effective than national action, especially in the context of prevention of marine pollution. This means that every country should enforce the same rules. As Prof F Berlingieri pointed out:

> There are various degrees of uniformity in maritime law and various ways of reaching it. The ideal solution is that the same provisions should exist in the national legal systems and that such provisions should be interpreted in the same manner in all countries.[14]

There are still a number of areas of maritime law where there are no international conventions, such as charter-parties, contracts of sea towage, general average and maritime insurance. However, in these areas there are rules and standard contracts which are generally accepted by the shipping industry as sources of law and implemented by incorporating them into bills of lading or charter-parties. The drafters of the Maritime Code carefully examined these rules and standard forms and adopted them according to the Chinese reality, as observed by Dr S Hazelwood:

13 IMO, *Questions to Mr O'Neil*, 1995, London: IMO Publications, p 2.

14 (1987) 18(3) Journal of Maritime Law and Commerce 317.

> The drafters of the new Chinese Code went on a 'window-shopping' exercise with a view to selecting the best products that they saw from jurisdictions around the world for incorporation into their shopping basket. We can see that from a review of Chapter 6 which deals with charter-parties (there is no international convention on charter-parties) it would appear that the Chinese Code has taken bits and pieces of charter-party law from around the world and produced its own recipe on charter-parties. Marine insurance is not covered by any international convention. This is so in law but there is almost a *de facto* international marine insurance regime in that so many countries around the world have followed the English model. In a survey conducted by the United Nations in 1982, it was found that something like two-thirds of the world's marine insurance markets followed the English system of marine insurance.[15]

In addition to charter-parties and marine insurance, a chapter deals with general average, respecting which there are no international conventions to deal with either, but only generally accepted rules – the York-Antwerp Rules – which originally date from 1864 and were revised or amended in 1890, 1924, 1950, 1974 and 1990. The chapter on general average in the Maritime Code was adapted from the 1974 version, which was approved by the conference of the CMI in Hamburg.

4 DIFFERENT REGIMES FOR INTERNATIONAL TRADE AND DOMESTIC TRADE

China has a quite different economic and political system from most other countries. This is reflected also in its maritime administrative and legal system. But in international maritime trade, it has to keep in line with international practices and customs. This results in two different regimes in the country, one for its 'domestic trade' and one for 'international trade',[16] although the difference has been reduced dramatically since the adoption of the open policy. During the drafting of the Maritime Code, there was very strong lobbying by the domestic carriers in favour of unification of the two systems, as it was felt that their interests may be better protected under international practices. However, their voices were not strong enough. The

15 Steven Hazelwood, 'New Maritime Code – maritime insurance', a Paper for the International Conference on Maritime Law, 11–14 October 1994, Shanghai Maritime University, at p 9.

16 'International trade' means maritime transportation between a Chinese port and a foreign port or between foreign ports. 'Domestic trade' means maritime transportation between Chinese ports, also called coastal or domestic transportation. See China Maritime Code, Articles 2 and 4.

Maritime Code still adopted different regimes for international trade and domestic trade that may be justified as follows.

First, international trade linking to other parts of the world is a market-oriented economy with little or no intervention from the government. In principle, international trade is open to foreign flag ships. Back in 1988, an important reform measure was adopted which completely opened up Chinese international trade to the outside world. According to this, the government would neither assign the carried amounts of foreign trade cargo to any domestic or foreign carriers nor impose any cargo share on the national ships through administrative measures. Carriers and cargo owners were encouraged to have direct talks with respect to the carriage of cargo based on normal commercial practices. Since then, in its international trade, China has phased out cargo reservation policies. These measures marked the emergence of Chinese maritime transportation services, to a large extent, from governmental intervention to free competition; although the abandoning of the practice of cargo reservation also meant a great loss to national shipping companies. China Ocean Shipping (Group) Company (COSCO) alone lost a security of about 255,000 tons of cargo every day.[17] Actually, China's accords of 1991 with the US, of 1992 with the European Community and of 1993 with South Korea have encouraged the container majors to move directly into the Chinese market, running their own feeders, booking their own cargoes and marketing their own services. More and more big liner operators, such as APL, Hapag-Lloyd (together with its alliance: NYK line, Neptune Orient Lines and P&O Containers Ltd), Maersk Line/Sea-Land, Mitsui OSK Lines (MOL), Nedlloyd Lines, Orient Overseas Container Lines and MISC make direct calls at Chinese ports. A comment from a foreign liner executive noted that China is becoming a freight market like any other country. The international trade is governed by the Maritime Code.

In port services, foreign flag ships used to have to pay higher port dues than national flag ships when calling at Chinese ports. This practice was changed on 1 April 1992. Since then, there has been no discriminatory treatment of foreign flag ships in international trade.

While domestic trade is governed by the Law of Contracts, the Administration Rules of Waterway Transport and the Enforcement Details of Contracts of Waterway Transport, under which contracts must guarantee the fulfilment of the National Plan, any contract that violates the National Plan is deemed 'null and void'. The domestic trade is still under the influence of the planned economy and reserved for the national flag ships. However, the proportion of planned transportation has recently decreased dramatically, but transportation of strategic materials, energy materials and materials for disaster relief remains under State control.

17 Liu Guo, 'A brief analysis on China's shipping' (1992) *Maritime China*, spring issue, Beijing.

Second, carriers have different liabilities in different trades. Article 2(2) of the Maritime Code provides that 'the provisions concerning contracts of carriage of goods by sea contained in Chapter 4 of this Code shall not be applicable to the maritime transport of goods between the ports of the People's Republic of China', but only applicable to international trade. Article 51 in the Chapter, which was adopted from Article 4(2) of the Hague Rules, provides that a carrier shall not be liable for the loss of or damage to the goods arising or resulting from any of the following causes:

(1) fault of the Master, crew members, pilot or servant of the carrier in the navigation or management of the ship;

(2) fire, unless caused by the actual fault of the carrier;

(3) *force majeure* and perils, dangers and accidents of the sea or other navigable waters;

(4) war or armed conflict;

(5) act of the government or competent authorities, quarantine restrictions or seizure under legal process;

(6) strikes, stoppages or restraint of labour;

(7) saving or attempting to save life or property at sea;

(8) act of the shipper or owner of the goods or their agents;

(9) nature or inherent vice of the goods;

(10) inadequacy of packing or insufficiency or illegibility of marks;

(11) latent defect of the ship not discoverable by due diligence; or

(12) any other cause arising without the fault of the carrier or his servant.

However, international carriers are liable for delays in delivery of the cargo carried. Article 50(2) of the Maritime Code provides that the carrier shall be liable for loss of, or damage to, goods caused by delay in delivery due to the fault of the carrier. This provision is adapted from Article 5 of the Hamburg Rules. Thus, it may be concluded that the carrier's liability under the Maritime Code was based on the principles of the Hague Rules but greatly influenced by the Hamburg Rules in some aspects.

In domestic trade, under the Enforcement Details of Contracts of Waterway Transport, a carrier undertakes strict liability for the carried goods. This means he is liable for all the losses of and damages to goods carried to the full extent without package limitation, excepting only losses and damages caused by '*force majeure*, inherent vice of goods and acts or negligence of the shippers or consignees'. But domestic carriers are not liable for any delay in delivery.

Third, carriers enjoy different global limitations of liabilities. For international trade, limitation of liability for maritime claims is governed by Articles 204–15 in Chapter 11 of the Maritime Code. These provisions were adapted from the 1976 Limitation Convention. For domestic trade, under the Special Limitation Provisions, limits of liability are lower than those in international trade. The reasons for this were given by the Director of the Division of Law of the MOC, Xu Qingyue (1994) as:

> Such ships, which are smaller in size and burdened heavily with planned transport, have lower levels of capability for compensation, especially ships engaging in works other than transport services, which are sometimes managed by a government agency or carry out works by governmental orders. Hence if the limited amount was too high to most of them, then the purpose of the regime of limitation of liability would not be reached.[18]

From the above, one can see that concerning the liability of domestic carriers, the new provisions in the Special Limitation Provisions are inconsistent with those of old ones under the Enforcement Details of Contracts of Waterway Transport. This is because the latter was made under the strong influence of planned economy, under which cargo was recognised as State property that should be well protected. Thus, the carriers should pay great attention to loading, to handling, to carriage, and to taking care of the cargo, so they should compensate the damage or loss of the cargo without application of package limitation. But when the Special Limitation Provisions were drafted, the philosophy changed to how to protect the poor domestic carrier. With continuing development of the economy, the provisions concerning the two kinds of carriers may become closer and even unified. With China's accession to the WTO and further openness of its economy, this dual system has to move gradually toward one system.

5 LIMITATION OF SHIPOWNER'S LIABILITY

The Several Regulations on Average Claims 1959 (1959 Regulations), issued by the Ministry of Communications of the PRC, formed the first piece of maritime regulation relating to limitation of the shipowner's liability. Although simple, it contains the important doctrine of limitation of liability. It stipulates in Article 4 that 'the liability of the shipowner is limited to the total amount of the ship's value, plus freight revenue and the compensation to the ship'. This is known as the ship's value system. Obviously, under this system, if the ship is a total loss, the claimant will get nothing from the shipowner. This principle was confirmed by the Regulations on Carriage of Goods by Waterways of the PRC in 1979.

18 Xu Qingyue, 'Special provisions on limitation of liability for maritime claims for ships of less than 300 tons and those engaging in the coastal trades', a Paper for the International Conference on Maritime Law, 11–14 October 1994, Shanghai Maritime University, at p 14.

The Maritime Code changes the principles of limitation of the shipowner's liability from ship's value system to tonnage system. The relevant provisions are in Chapter 11, 'Limitation of Liability for Maritime Claims' (Articles 204–15) in the Maritime Code, which adopted the principles and the substantial Articles of the 1976 International Convention on Limitation of Liability for Maritime Claims (the 1976 Convention). However, some differences exist and will be discussed in the following parts.

The provisions concerning the limitation of liability in the Maritime Code are only applicable to international sea-going ships[19] exceeding 300 gross tons (international limits).

In pursuance of Articles 210(2) and 211(2) of the Maritime Code, approved by the State Council of the PRC, the MOC promulgated two special regulations on limitations regarding coastal vessels and passenger vessels, namely, the Coastal Provisions and the Passenger Provisions. The two special regulations apply the same principles as the Maritime Code but with different limits. Under these two regulations, the limits of liability for ships sailing between national ports or those engaging in coastal works are about 50% below the international limits. The reason was that given by Xu Qingyue on the previous page.[20]

It had also been considered that, on the other hand, if the limits were too low, they would tend to benefit foreign ships when claims were brought against the ships in Chinese jurisdiction. In this situation, the claimants, who would probably be Chinese, would be disadvantaged because of the relatively low compensation limits.

5.1 Claims subject to limitation

The claims that are subject to limitation are listed in Article 207 of the Maritime Code:

(1) claims in respect of loss of life or personal injury or loss of or damage to property including damage to harbour works, basins and waterways and aids to navigation occurring on board or in direct connection with the operation of the ship or with salvage operations, as well as consequential damage resulting therefrom;

19 An 'international ship' means any sea-going ship sailing between a Chinese port or ports and a foreign port or ports, but does not include ships sailing on inland waterways.

20 See fn 18 above.

(2) claims in respect of loss resulting from delay in delivery in the carriage of goods by sea or from delay in the arrival of passengers or their luggage;
(3) claims in respect of other loss resulting from infringement of rights other than contractual rights occurring in direct connection with the operation of the ship or salvage operations;
(4) claims of a person other than the person liable in respect of measures taken to avert or minimise loss for which the person liable may limit his liability in accordance with the provisions of this Chapter, and further loss caused by such measures.

It is provided further that all such claims, however lodged, may be entitled to limitation of liability. As regards remuneration set out in item (4), however, the person liable has to pay the amount as agreed in the contract, and he may not invoke the provisions on limitation of liability of this Article. Categories (d) and (e) of Article 2(1) of the 1976 Convention, relating to claims for wreck and cargo removal, were not repeated in the Maritime Code. This does not mean that China is out of the international maritime community. Under Article 18 of the 1976 Convention, any State may reserve the right to exclude the application of these two categories. Other countries, for example, France, Germany and Japan, have made a similar reservation.

5.2 Claims excepted from limitation

According to Article 208 of the Maritime Code, the following claims are not covered:

(1) claims for salvage payment or contribution in general average;
(2) claims for oil pollution damage under the International Convention on Civil Liability for Oil Pollution Damage to which the People's Republic of China is a party;
(3) claims for nuclear damage under the International Convention on Limitation of Liability for Nuclear Damage to which the PRC is a party;
(4) claims against the shipowner of an nuclear ship for nuclear damage;
(5) claims by the servants of the shipowner or salvor, if under the law governing the contract of employment, the shipowner or salvor is not entitled to limit his liability or if he is by law only permitted to limit his liability to an amount greater than that provided for in this Chapter.

Item (2) means the Maritime Code does not cover claims for oil pollution damage. In other words, a party is unlikely to limit his liability for oil pollution under the Maritime Code. China is a Member State of the 1969 International Convention on Civil Liability for Oil Pollution Damage (CLC). This treaty governs limitation for oil pollution claims. Pursuant to the CLC, only shipowners are entitled to limit liability for oil pollution claims. This means there is no law in China which provides any right of limitation where pollution claims are brought against a party other than a shipowner. As discussed above, the shipowner includes only the charterer and operator in the Maritime Code (Article 204). Thus, salvors and other parties may not limit their liabilities for oil pollution claims. There appears a discrepancy between Article 3(b) of the 1976 Convention and the CLC 1969. This drawback, however, could have been solved by extending the application to other parties, in addition to the shipowners, in domestic legislation.

5.3 The loss of the right to limit

The Maritime Code provides in Article 209 that: 'A person liable shall not be entitled to limit his liability in accordance with the provisions of this Chapter, if it is proved that the loss resulting from his act or omission done with the intent to cause such loss or recklessly and with knowledge that such loss would probably result.' This is an adoption of Article 4 of the 1976 Convention.

With regard to contracts of carriage of goods by sea and contracts of carriage of passengers by sea, the carrier loses the right to limit his liability if the loss, damage or delay in delivery of the goods, or the death of or personal injury to a passenger or the loss of or damage to his/her luggage resulted from 'an act or omission of the carrier done with intent to cause such loss, damage or recklessly and with knowledge that such loss or damage would probably result'.[21]

It was the first time that the expression of 'an act or omission done with intent to cause such loss or recklessly and with knowledge that such loss would probably result' appeared in Chinese law. The degree of fault involved in 'recklessly and with knowledge' is less than 'intention' and greater than 'negligence', which is similar to 'culpable negligence' in Chinese law. The incorporation in the Convention of the concept of 'intention', which was commonly accepted in other jurisdictions, was to avoid the use of ambiguous words.

Respecting Articles 204, 205 and 206, 'a person liable' could be the shipowner, manager, salvor or their servants or an insurer. It is clear that a person liable can limit liability automatically unless evidence produced proves the person is guilty of conduct barring limitation. The burden of proof is on the claimant. In practice, it is extremely difficult for a claimant to break the limit, thus, it is sometimes called an unbreakable system of limitation of liability.

21 Articles 59 and 118 of the Maritime Code.

If the party is guilty of conduct barring limitation, he may lose the benefits of insurance as well as the benefits of limitation according to Article 242 of the Maritime Code, which provides that the 'insurer shall not be liable for the loss caused by the intentional act of the insured'.

5.4 The limits of liability

Both the Maritime Code and the 1976 Convention contain three separate limits in respect of the following categories:

(1) claims for loss of life or personal injury;

(2) other claims;

(3) claims for loss of life or personal injury to passengers.

The limits for the first two categories in the 1976 Convention are to be calculated according to the ship's gross tonnage calculated in accordance with the tonnage measurement rules contained in Annex I of the International Convention on Tonnage Measurement of Ships (1969).[22] It is the same under the Maritime Code; although it is not provided expressly, that can be deduced from:

(1) using the term 'gross tonnage' in the Maritime Code; and

(2) the fact of China being a Member State of the International Convention on Tonnage Measurement of Ships 1969.

The limits for claims for loss of life or personal injury to passengers are to be calculated according to the number of passengers which the ship is authorised to carry according to the ship's relevant certificate.[23]

5.5 Limits for claims for loss of life or personal injury

Under Article 3(1) of the Coastal Provisions and Article 210(1) of the Maritime Code, the limits in respect of claims for loss of life or personal injury relating to an international ship (international limit) shall be calculated as follows:

(1) 54,000 SDR for a ship with a gross tonnage exceeding 20 tons and up to 21 tons;

(2) for a ship with a gross tonnage exceeding 21 tons and up to 300 tons, 1,000 SDR for each ton in excess of 21 tons in addition to 54,000 SDR;

(3) 333,000 SDR for a ship with a gross tonnage ranging from 300 tons to 500 tons;

22 Article 6(5) of the 1976 Convention.

23 Article 211 of the Maritime Code.

(4) for a ship with a gross tonnage exceeding 500 tons the following sums are be added to 333,000 SDR:

for each ton from 501 to 3,000 tons: 500 SDR;

for each ton from 3,001 to 30,000 tons: 333 SDR;

for each ton from 30,001 to 70,000 tons: 250 SDR;

for each ton in excess of 70,000 tons: 167 SDR.

Concerning the limits for coastal trade, Article 4 of the Coastal Provisions provides that the limits in respect of claims for loss of life or personal injury shall be 50% of that for the same tonnage of an international ship. These limits are illustrated in Figure 1.

According to Article 3(2) of the Coastal Provisions and Article 210(2) of the Maritime Code, the limits of claims *other than* for loss of life or personal injury (other claims) should be calculated as follows:

(1) 27,500 SDR for a ship with a gross tonnage exceeding 20 tons and up to 21 tons;

(2) for a ship with a gross tonnage exceeding 21 tons and up to 300 tons, 500 SDR for each ton in excess of 21 tons must be added to 27,500 SDR;

(3) 167,000 SDR for a ship with a gross tonnage ranging from 300 tons to 500 tons;

(4) for a ship with a gross tonnage in excess of 500 tons, the following amount shall be added to 167,000 SDR:

- for each ton from 501 to 30,000 tons: 167 SDR;
- for each ton from 30,001 to 70,000 tons: 125 SDR;
- for each ton in excess of 70,000 tons: 83 SDR.

Also, according to Article 4 of the Coastal Provisions, the limits for other claims concerning a coastal ship shall be 50% of that for the international ships. These limits are shown in Figure 2.

The Maritime Code provides separate limitation amounts for the two categories of claim. Where the amounts for payment of claims for loss of life or personal injury are insufficient, the unpaid balance of those claims shall rank rateably with other claims against the fund established for other claims.[24]

It also provides that claims in respect of damage to harbour works, basins and waterways and aids to navigation shall have priority over other claims, but without prejudice to the right of claims for loss of life or personal injury.[25]

For a salvor who is 'not operating from any ship or for any salvor operation solely on the ship to, or in respect of which, he is rendering salvage

24 Article 210(3) of the Maritime Code; Article 6(2) of the 1976 Convention.

25 Article 210(4) of the Maritime Code; Article 6(3) of the 1976 Convention.

services', the limitation of liability shall be calculated according to a gross tonnage of 1,500 tons.[26]

5.6 Claims for loss of life or personal injury to passengers

Article 211 of the Maritime Code relates claims for loss of life or personal injury to passengers carried by sea. It provides that limitation of liability of the shipowner shall be 46,666 SDR for each passenger, up to the number of passengers the ship is authorised to carry, with a maximum amount of 25,000,000 SDR.

According to Article 4 of the Passenger Provisions, regarding domestic passenger transport, the limitation of liability of the shipowner (domestic limit) shall be Ren Min Bi (RMB) 40,000 multiplied by the number of passengers which the ship is permitted to carry, but shall not exceed RMB 21,000,000. This provision is applicable to ships sailing in both coastal and inland waters. These limits are shown in Figure 3.

5.7 Contradictions between Chapters 5 and 11

Adopting so many different conventions in different chapters within one code is a new method of implementing international conventions. Different conventions have different systems and concepts, and gaps or contradictions may even exist among the provisions of conventions. Great efforts were made to codify them into the Maritime Code. However, this phenomenon may still exist among different chapters of the Maritime Code.

For example, Chapter 5 (covering passenger claims), which adopts the 1974 Athens Convention, should be read together with Chapter 11 (regarding limitation of liability of maritime claims).

According to Article 117(1) of Chapter 5, the limit of 46,666 SDR is applicable to a 'per passenger' scenario. Therefore, the total limit of liability of a carrier tends to vary depending on the number of claims submitted by the passengers involved in the relevant casualties. If this number is less than the passengers the ship is certified to carry, the amount of the limit calculated according to Article 117 will be less than that under Article 211. It is clear from the words that the shipowner is entitled to limit his liability to the lower level. However, a question arises when a ship is heavily overloaded with passengers, for example, in the cases of the *Dona Paz* disaster in the Philippines in 1987 which claimed nearly 4,400 lives, and the Haiti ferry

26 Article 210(5) of the Maritime Code; Article 6(4) of the 1976 Convention.

disaster in 1993 which claimed 1,800 lives.[27] In such situations, the number of people dead or injured is much greater than the number of passengers the ship is authorised to carry. In this case, of course, the carrier would probably be guilty of conduct barring limitation and would lose the protection of both limits. The point is that if the carrier is allowed to limit his liability in such a situation, should the limit be calculated on the number of passengers actually carried, or on the number the ship is authorised to carry?

Article 19 of the Athens Convention provides: 'This Convention shall not modify the rights or duties of the carrier, the performing carrier, and their servants or agents provided for in international conventions relating to the limitation of liability of owners of sea-going ships.' As China has ratified the Athens Convention, the above provision, which does not appear in the Maritime Code, will be applied together with the Maritime Code. It becomes clear that if the total amount payable to all claimants after application of the limitation provisions under Chapter 5 exceeds the global limitation fund, calculated in accordance with Article 213 of Chapter 11, the latter will be applied. The same rule would apply if China were to ratify the 1990 Protocol to the Athens Convention and raise the limit per passenger to a maximum of 175,000 SDR per carriage.

Another contradiction relates to the concepts of 'each contract of carriage' and 'any given occasion' in Chapters 5 and 11. Article 117(1) in Chapter 5 refers to the limitation of liability being governed by 'each contract of carriage', the whole period during which the passenger is being transported. However, the limitation of liability in Article 212 in Chapter 11 refers to the aggregate of all claims that may arise on 'any given occasion'.[28] If a passenger is injured several times during the course of a voyage, according to Article 117, the limitation of liability would only apply once, while limitation of liability set out in Article 212 would probably apply several times as there would be several 'given occasions'. One of the main drafters, an adviser of the Standing Committee of the People's Congress of the PRC, Guo Riqi, pointed out that there is a conflict between the two provisions.[29] In our opinion, Article 19 of the Athens Convention will also govern this situation, thus, Article 212 appears to be the paramount clause to apply, although such incidents may rarely occur.

27 *Lloyd's List International*, 'Haiti ferry disaster claims up to 1,800' (1993) LLP Ltd, 19 February.

28 It was expressed as 'on any distinct occasion' in Article 7(1) of the 1976 Convention.

29 Guo Riqi, 'An introduction to the legislation of the Maritime Code', in the Policy and Law Department of the Ministry of Communications and the Legal Affairs Centre of Communication (eds), *The Essentials of the Maritime Code*, 1993, Beijing: People's Communications Press, p 26.

5.8 Bar to other actions and counter-claim

Article 214 of the Maritime Code provides that where a limitation fund has been constituted by a person liable, the claimant may not exercise any right against the assets of the person liable. Where any ship or other property belonging to the person constituting the fund has been arrested or attached, or, where a security has been provided by such person, the court without delay shall order the release of the arrested ship or the attached property or the return of the provided security. This Article derives from Article 13(1) and (2) of the 1976 Convention.

If a person, entitled to limitation of liability under the Maritime Code, has a counter-claim against the claimant arising out of the same occurrence, their respective claims are to be set off against each other and the provisions of the Maritime Code shall only apply to the balance.[30]

6 CABOTAGE RESERVATION

'Cabotage' is a nautical term derived from Spanish, literally denoting navigation from cape to cape along the coast without going into the open sea. Cabotage, used as a legal term, here refers to the right to transport goods or passengers between ports of a country.

It is understandable that developing countries adopt the practice of cabotage or other policies to improve the development of their national shipping industry, although it is surprising to find out that almost all the traditional maritime nations, except the UK, adopt this policy.[31]

The first adoption of the cabotage policy in Chinese legislation dated back to 1963 in the Temporary Customs Law, which provided that no foreign ship was allowed to engage in Chinese coastal transport. One who knows a little about modern Chinese history will not be surprised about the Chinese adopting this policy. There are generally three arguments for such a policy – national security, economic security and promotion of a national merchant fleet. The arguments were still strong enough to overcome the pressures from free international competition in domestic markets at the time when the Maritime Code was being drafted. Eventually, this appeared in Article 4 of the Maritime Code as follows:

30 Article 215 of the Maritime Code; Article 5 of the 1976 Convention.

31 According to Ademuni-Odenke, *Protectionism and the Future of International Shipping*, 1984, Dordrecht, Netherlands: Martinus Nijhoff Publishers, p 96, the following countries are practising cabotage policy: Australia; Canada; Denmark; Finland; France; Germany; Greece; Iceland; Italy; Japan; the Netherlands; New Zealand; Norway; Portugal; Spain; Sweden; Switzerland; and the United States.

> Maritime transport and towage services between the ports of the People's Republic of China shall be undertaken only by ships flying the national flag of the People's Republic of China, except as otherwise provided for by laws or administrative rules and regulations.
>
> No foreign ships may engage in the maritime transport or towage services between the ports of People's Republic of China unless permitted by the competent authorities of transport and communications under the State Council.

In the first paragraph, it is provided that only ships flying the Chinese flag are allowed to engage in domestic transport, but those with foreign interests, such as ships of a company in joint-venture with a foreign partner or with foreign investment, shall be permitted by the MOC under the regulations concerned. The second paragraph reinforces the policy that foreign ships are forbidden to engage in domestic trade with the exception that the MOC has the right to give specific permission to foreign ships for domestic transport or towage service, for example, if the transport or towage service needs special technology or skills that are not available among the national companies.

According to Article 2 of the Ship Registration Regulations of the PRC, ships owned by Chinese-foreign joint-ventures, whose principal places of business are located in China, and whose investment proportion of registered capital contributed by Chinese investors is not less than 50%, are entitled to register as Chinese ships, and thereby fly the Chinese flag. However, according to the 1995 Temporary Regulations on the Direction of Foreign Investment, transportation by waterways (domestic) is classified under the items restricting foreign investment, which means the investment programme shall be approved by the MOC.[32] Therefore, foreign investors may access Chinese coastal transportation either through a joint-venture with Chinese partners or by seeking permission directly from the MOC.

In July 1992, the MOC, in addition to reconfirming Chinese policy on opening up its international trade to the outside world, proclaimed the decision to extend the open policy to certain maritime auxiliary activities. Foreign investors were allowed to operate cargo handling, storage and warehousing, packing and unpacking services, in the form of joint-ventures with domestic partners. This policy applied even to internal waterways and road transport. Earlier in the same year, the shipping agency services were also opened to foreign operators. By the end of 1993, China had 190 shipping companies engaged in international maritime transportation, of which 56 were Sino-foreign joint-venture companies; there were also 121 international shipping agency companies and three branches of foreign shipping

32 Article 10(2) of the 1995 Temporary Regulations on the Direction of Foreign Investment. Under these regulations, foreign investment is divided into three categories – projects encouraging foreign investment, projects restricting foreign investment and those forbidding foreign investment (1995) *People's Daily Overseas Edition*, 1 July, p 2.

companies.[33] There are also successful joint-venture programmes in port constructions and operations. For instance, Hutchison International Port Holdings (HIPH), which runs the Hutchison Whampoa Ltd's terminal in Hong Kong, is a partner on a 50/50 basis in the Shanghai Container Terminals joint-venture with Shanghai Port Container Development Co, leads a consortium with a 70% stake in Yantian International Terminals, has a 50% stake in Nanhai Container Terminals in San Shan Port, and has signed a joint-venture agreement to develop two container berths in Zuchi Port in Shantou.[34] Nedlloyd has also recently announced its interest in investing in terminal facilities in Shanghai because of its conviction that, eventually, these ports will attract market share and international carriers.[35] According to Mr Paul H Sullivan, the vice president (East) of the Asian Development Bank (ADB), of the estimated US$ 233 billion investment required for infrastructure in China over the ninth five year plan (1996–2000), around US$ 111 billion will be required for transport (road, rail, sea and their equipment).[36] This provides foreign investors with a huge stage to perform on.

7 STRICT CONDITIONS FOR SHIP REGISTRATION[37]

The PRC is a signatory of the UN Convention on the Law of the Sea and approved the Convention on 15 May 1996. The Convention is generally accepted as being an accurate statement of current international law concerning this issue. Article 91(1) of the Convention provides that every State shall fix the conditions for the granting of its nationality to ships. For the registration of ships in its territory and for the right to fly its flag, there must exist a genuine link between the State and the ship. Accordingly, China has adopted a strict policy for the granting of its nationality to ships in its maritime legislation. Only ships which belong to the following categories can register as Chinese ships and have the right to fly its flag:

33 According to the Minister of the MOC, Mr Huang Zhendong, on 23 June 1994, News Conference, Beijing.

34 Monie, GD, 'The relationship between technological innovation, privatisation, competition and subsidisation in ports', Seminar on Reforms and New Port Policies in Latin America, Barcelona, 28 March 1995, p 14.

35 Brevetti, F, *Seatrade Review*, March 1996.

36 Sullivan, PH, a Paper prepared for the China Infrastructure International Conference, 10–12 July 1995, organised by the Academy of Macroeconomics Research, the State Planning Commission of the PRC and the Institute for International Research.

37 For a comparative study on the conditions of more than 86 ship registers, please see Li, KX and Wonham, J, 'New development of ship registration' (1999) 14(1) International Journal of Marine and Coastal Law 137–54.

(1) ships owned by citizens of the PRC whose residences or principal places of business are located within Chinese territory;
(2) ships owned by enterprises which are legal persons established under Chinese laws and whose principal places of business are located within Chinese territory; if foreign investment is involved, the proportion of the registered capital contributed by the Chinese investors shall not be less than 50%;
(3) ships owned by the Chinese government and public organisations;
(4) other ships for which the BHS of the PRC deems the registration to be necessary.[38]

Nonetheless, the procedures to establish a Chinese-foreign joint-venture and complete the PRC registration are complicated but attractive. An application to set up a joint-venture shipping company with investment exceeding US$ 30 million has to be approved by both the MOC and the Ministry of Foreign Economic and Trade. But with the help of good maritime lawyers, it is not very difficult to get through all these procedures.

It is also worth noting that the Ship Registration Regulations of the PRC adopt the principle of single nationality. In other words, a ship shall not have more than one nationality; ships registered in foreign countries shall not be granted Chinese nationality unless the foreign registration has been deleted or suspended.[39] Ships granted Chinese nationality must be manned by Chinese Masters and crew unless otherwise permitted by the BHS.[40] To meet the new tendency of international demise charter business, there are special provisions in the regulations (Chapter 5) dealing with demise charter registration.

8 MARITIME COURTS AND JURISDICTION

To cope with the increasing number of maritime disputes, China established the special Maritime Courts system to deal exclusively with maritime cases aiming to increase efficiency and quality of handling of maritime cases which require special knowledge and expertise. The China Maritime Court system was established in 1984 by a decision of the Standing Committee of the People's Congress. There are nine Maritime Courts located in port cities – from north to south, they are: Dalian; Tianjin; Qingadao; Wuhan; Shanghai; Ningpo; Xiamen; Guanzhou; and Haikou (see Figure 4).

Maritime Courts have the same status as intermediate courts in the Chinese legal system. Their Appeal Courts are the relevant provincial

38 Article 2 of the Ship Registration Regulations of the PRC.
39 Article 4 of the Ship Registration Regulations of the PRC.
40 Article 7 of the Ship Registration Regulations of the PRC.

Supreme Courts. Appeal judgments are final. Maritime cases do not go to the National Supreme Court (NSC) unless a special review or supervision process is being invoked under the Civil Procedure Law.[41] Maritime Courts usually have three divisions: the Maritime Commercial Division; the Admiralty Division; and the Enforcement Division. Maritime Courts have jurisdiction over any maritime cases defined by the NSC.[42] The jurisdiction of Maritime Courts covers any maritime dispute, including: (a) maritime tortious claims, for example, collision and marine pollution; (b) maritime contractual claims, for example, carriage of goods or passengers, employment of crew, port operation, and marine exploitation, etc; (c) execution of judgments and arbitration awards in maritime cases; and (d) applications for preservation measures.

An application to arrest a ship should be made in writing and in Chinese with supporting documents providing evidence that the arresting party has a *prima facie* claim against the shipowner. Foreign arresting parties must provide their Chinese lawyers, who make the arrest application, with a Power of Representation, which must be notarised and legalised by a Chinese Embassy or Consulate (Articles 241 and 243 of the Civil Procedure Law). To commence legal proceedings, the first step is to choose the court that has jurisdiction over the case.

8.1 International jurisdiction

Its international jurisdiction empowers the Maritime Courts to deal with cases involving foreign parties or elements. According to various laws, Chinese courts have jurisdiction over cases where:

(1) the contract was signed or performed within Chinese territory (Article 243 of the Civil Procedure Law);

(2) the defendant has distrainable property or its representative office in China (Article 243 of the Civil Procedure Law);

(3) the tortious action was committed in Chinese territory or territorial sea (Article 243 of the Civil Procedure Law);

(4) Chinese courts have exclusive jurisdiction over maritime joint-ventures established in China (Article 24 of the Civil Procedure Law);

41 Article 177 of the Civil Procedure Law of the PRC.

42 *The Decision on the Scope of Cases to Be Handled by Maritime Courts*, issued by the SPC in 1989. See Supreme Court Bulletin 31 (1989) (in Chinese). See also Mo, JS, *Shipping Law in China*, 1999, Hong Kong: Sweet & Maxwell Asia, p 369.

(5) the collision occurred on the high sea between Chinese ships or involving a Chinese ship;[43]

(6) the collision was between foreign ships outside the Chinese territorial sea, but the first port of arrival is a Chinese port;[44]

(7) both parties agreed to the jurisdiction of Chinese courts, unless the law provides otherwise (Article 8 of the MPL);[45]

(8) the defendant raises no objection to the jurisdiction of a Chinese court and responds to the action by making his defence (Article 245 of the Civil Procedure Law); or

(9) the arrest of a ship by itself can establish the jurisdiction of Chinese courts (Article 19 of the MPL).[46]

If there is any difference between national laws and international treaties concluded or acceded to by China, the latter shall be applied.[47]

8.2 Regional jurisdiction

Each Maritime Court has its 'jurisdictional territory'.[48] This division is achieved by the fact of the location of the accident, or the property, or the port, or the place where the defendant is domiciled, which links the case to the

43 An action for collision occurring between sea-going ships can only be introduced 'before the court where the defendant has his habitual residence or a place of business': Article 1(1) of the International Convention on Certain Rules concerning Civil Jurisdiction in Matters of Collision, to which China is not a party, but which can be accepted by the courts as generally accepted international rules and customs.

44 In the collision case of *Trade Quicker Inc Monrovia Liberia v Golden Light Overseas Management SA Panama*, both ships were registered in Panama. The Chinese court took the jurisdiction and applied Chinese law as both parties were unable to provide evidence of Panamanian law at the time of trial. Reported in *Selected Cases of the People's Courts (Chinese)*, by the Supreme People's Court (SPC), 1993, Beijing: Publishing House of the People's Court, at 157–63.

45 Also Article 244 of the Civil Procedure Law; Article 269 of the Maritime Code. In the case of a 'jurisdiction clause' in a bill of lading, the Chinese Maritime Courts are ready to exercise their jurisdiction if so chosen in the bill of lading, eg, in the case of *Aix-en-Provence*, reported in P&I International, May 2000, at 118–19. However, Chinese courts may overrule a 'foreign forum clause' in a bill of lading and take over jurisdiction on the basis of a 'closer connection' with Chinese interests and on the basis that a 'foreign forum clause' is not a real agreement in the absence of receiver's consent. (P&I International, May 2000, at 118–19.)

46 Also Article 243 of the Civil Procedure Law. In the case of *Harbour Grain* (translated from its Chinese name), the applicant was an Italian supplier and the defendant was a Hong Kong shipowner. Apart from the ship being anchored at a Chinese port, Dalian, there was no other link to China. The Dalian Maritime Court awarded the arrest, and thereby obtained jurisdiction over the case: Jin and Weng, *China Maritime Litigation*, 1993, Shenzhen: Haitian Press, p 408.

47 Article 268 of the Maritime Code; Article 238 of the Civil Procedure Law.

48 Section two, 'Regional Jurisdiction' (Articles 22–35) and section three, 'Transferred Jurisdiction and Designated Jurisdiction' (Articles 36–39) of the Civil Procedure Law.

court that has jurisdiction over it. However, there have been some grey areas about which the court should have jurisdiction over certain types of cases. The MPL now details the courts which have jurisdiction in each situation that in the past led to confusion and conflicts of jurisdiction among different courts. These can be categorised as follows:

(1) maritime tort actions: the court of the port of registration (Article 6(1) of the MPL), as well as the court of the place where the tort was committed or of the place where the defendant is domiciled (Articles 29–31 of the Civil Procedure Law);

(2) maritime contract actions: the court of the port of transshipment (Article 6(2) of the MPL), as well as the court of the place of departure, destination or of the place where the defendant is registered (Article 28 of the Civil Procedure Law);

(3) actions based on charter-parties: the court of the ports of delivery, redelivery, registration, or the court of the place where the defendant is domiciled (Article 6(3) of the MPL);

(4) actions based on marine insurance contracts: the court of the location of the property insured, or of the location of the accident, or of the place where the defendant is domiciled (Article 6(4) of the MPL);

(5) actions based on contracts of crew employment: the court of the place of residence of the claimant, or of the place where the contract has been concluded, or of the ports where the crew embarked or disembarked, or of the place where the defendant is domiciled (Article 6(5) of the MPL);

(6) actions based on maritime security (including mortgages): the court of the location of the property, or of the place where the defendant is domiciled (Article 6(6) of the MPL);

(7) actions based on mortgages: the court of the port of registration domiciled (Article 6(6) of the MPL);

(8) actions based on maritime liens, ownership, possession, and usage of ships: the court of the location of the ship, or of the port of registration, or of the place where the defendant is domiciled (Article 6(7) of the MPL);

(9) a lawsuit instituted for expenses of maritime salvage shall be under the jurisdiction of the court where the salvage took place or where the salvage ship first docked after the disaster (Article 32 of the Civil Procedure Law);

(10) the court of the port has exclusive jurisdiction over conflicts arising from port operations (Article 7(1) of the MPL);

(11) for actions relating to marine pollution from ships, the court at the place where the pollution or the damage occurred, or where prevention measures should be taken has exclusive jurisdiction over such a case (Article 7(2) of the MPL);

(12) as to actions relating to marine exploitation and activities within Chinese territorial sea and other administrative sea areas, the court of the place where the contract is performed has exclusive jurisdiction over the case (Article 7(3) of the MPL).

9 SECURITY BEFORE JUDGMENT

There is no action *in rem* procedure available in Chinese law. Rather, pre-judgment security can be obtained by action *'in personam'* combined with 'custody of property' where the execution of a judgment would become impossible or difficult because of the acts of either party or for other reasons (Articles 92–99 of the Civil Procedure Law). According to Chinese legal theory, laws only deal with legal relations between (among) persons (natural or legal), but not between persons and property (*rem*). The name of the respondent must be specified when filing the application. Such practice has often caused difficulties to the applicants.[49] Also, bearing in mind the often urgent nature of the arrest of ships, the MPL now provides that an application is allowed where the identity of the defendant is unknown to the arresting party (arrester) (Article 25 of the MPL). However, in these situations, the action would theoretically still be brought against the unnamed owners, not the offending ship itself. The application for an arrest should be made in writing and in Chinese, specifying the objective and purpose of the application, the name of the ship and quantum of security required with supporting evidence (Article 15 of the MPL).

The purpose of the arrest of ships under the MPL is mainly to obtain security before trial (Article 18), and is a preservative measure in nature. The concept of 'arrest' in the MPL (Articles 12 and 22) means any detention or restriction on removal of a ship by order of the court to secure maritime claims. It is worth noting that the ship under such court arrest may, with the arrester's agreement, continue to trade under restriction on sale or mortgage (Article 27 of the MPL). Apparently, the definition of arrest in the MPL is less strict compared with that in the Arrest Convention 1999, which provides that 'arrest means any detention or restriction on removal of a ship' (Article 1(2)).

The term 'arrest' as defined in the MPL does not include detention of ships by government authorities based on the Law of the Territorial Sea and the Contiguous Zone 1992 (Article 8),[50] the Maritime Traffic Safety Law 1983 (Article 19)[51] and the Port State Control (PSC) Programmes to prevent

49 Jin and Weng, *China Maritime Litigation*, 1993, Shenzhen: Haitian Press, p 398.

50 Laws and Regulations of the PRC Governing Foreign-related Matters (1991–92), at 345.

51 Laws and Regulations of the PRC Governing Foreign-related Matters (1949–90), at 1,268.

maritime accidents and pollutions at sea. However, the MPL applies to enforcement of judgments and arbitration awards (Articles 22 and 42 of the MPL).

As to the scope of the MPL, it does not spell out its coverage in terms of the type and size of ships. Chinese law does not differentiate between a ship and a vessel. Ships referred to in the MPL should be deemed the same as those defined in the Maritime Code (Article 3), which refers to 'sea-going ships and other mobile units', but does not include ships or craft to be used for military or public service purposes. However, military and public service ships can be subjected to arrest where they are engaged in commercial activities.[52] Cases relating to inland ships sailing in areas that are not covered by the jurisdiction of Maritime Courts are still subject to the jurisdiction of local People's Courts. Apparently, however, the MPL applies to inland ships where it is appropriate.

10 MARITIME CLAIMS

Whether arrest of ships should be permissible in respect of any type of claim or whether it should be limited to specific types of claims is always at the core of an arrest law.[53] Shipowners would understandably prefer to see a definitive and closed list of claims that can lead to the arrest of ships, whilst claimants would like to have an open list of claims for arrest. China's legislator finally adopted a closed list of claims as set out in Article 21 of the MPL.

However, compared with previous court practice in China, the MPL has expanded maritime claims to include claims in respect of damage to the environment (Article 21(4)), removal of wrecks (Article 21(5)), unpaid insurance premiums (notably including Club calls) (Article 21(17)), commissions, brokerages and agency fees (Article 21(18)) and contracts for the sale of ships (Article 21(22)). These items are not included in the traditional claims list for arrest of ships as defined in the Regulations on Arrest of Ships Prior to Litigation[54] and the Arrest Convention 1952.[55] In this respect, the MPL is substantially in line with the 1999 Convention (Article 1(1)). However, the wording in sub-paragraphs (2), (3), (6), (7), (12), (15) and (21) is slightly

52 In the case of *Beituo 604*, a PLA (People's Liberation Army) ship, after its colliding with a fishing ship during a commercial transport on 10 May 1992, was verified an arrest by a Maritime Court at the request of the fishing company. See Jin and Weng, *China Maritime Litigation*, 1993, Shenzhen: Haitian Press, pp 400–01.

53 Gaskell, N and Shaw, R, 'The arrest convention 1999' (1999) LMCQ 470–90, at 473.

54 Article 1(1)–(20) of the Regulations on Arrest of Ships Prior to Litigation issued by the SPC in 1986 (Chinese) (quoted in Guangzhou Maritime Court, *Practice of Maritime Courts*, 1992, Shenzhen: Haitian Press, at 335), which was repealed by the MPL.

55 International Convention Relating to the Arrest of Sea-going Ships 1952, 6B Benedict on Admiralty Doc No 8-1 (97th rev ed, 1999) (entered into force in 1956).

different. The Chinese text apparently allows a greater degree of flexibility for interpretation.

Under the MPL, a maritime claim is a pre-condition of an arrest. It leads to an arrest only if other conditions set by law are met at the same time. The MPL requires a close link between the ownership at the time when an arrest is effected and at the time when the claim arose. According to Article 23 of the MPL, an asserted maritime claim is given a right of arrest in the following situations:

(1) where the person who was the owner or demise charterer of the offending ship at the time when the maritime claim arose and was liable for the claim is the owner or demise charterer of the ship when the arrest is effected;

(2) where the person who was the demise charterer of the offending ship at the time when the maritime claim arose and was liable for the claim is the owner or demise charterer of the ship when the arrest is effected;

(3) where the claim is based upon a mortgage or a charge of the same nature on the ship (see, eg, Articles 11–20 of the Maritime Code);

(4) the claim relates to the ownership or possession of the ship (see, eg, Articles 7–10 of the Maritime Code);

(5) lastly, a right of arrest exists where the claim is against the owner, demise charterer, manager or operator of the ship and is secured by a maritime lien (see, eg, Articles 21–30 of the Maritime Code).[56]

11 SISTER-SHIP ARREST AND OTHER PERMISSIBLE ARRESTS

Sister-ship arrest was another topic for debate at the drafting stage of the MPL. Many argued that the proliferation of single-ship companies often means that in practice, there is no possibility of arresting a sister-ship. Therefore, a proposal was made to introduce the concept of an 'associated ship', which includes any ship that is beneficially owned by the same person as the offending ship. However, this argument was not adopted in the new law. Article 23(2) of the MPL provides that only other ships 'owned by', but not 'associated with' the same owners, demise charterers, time charterers and voyage charterers as the offending ships can be arrested as sister-ships of the offending ship. With the development of container trade, the practice of slot or cell share among liners has become common. Instead of chartering the whole or part of a ship, a container operator (a slot charterer) will instead regularly book a set number of container units of a ship of another operator. In the

56 According to Article 26 of the Maritime Code, a maritime lien shall not be extinguished by virtue of the transfer of the ownership of the ship unless it has not been enforced within 60 days of a public notice being made by the court at the request of the transferee. As to the form of a public notice, Articles 32 and 39 of the MPL do not spell out which newspapers should be used, but for foreign readership, *People's Daily Overseas Edition* (Chinese) and *Chinese Daily* (English) are the two major sources.

Tychy case, the English Court of Appeal held that a slot charterer was within the expression 'the charterer' in s 21(4) of the Supreme Court Act 1981, whose other ships could be arrested as sister-ships.[57] However, Article 23(2) of the MPL and Article 3(2) of the Arrest Convention 1999 do not specifically mention 'slot charterer', which has left a grey area to the courts for further clarification.

The MPL does not spell out in detail the meaning of 'owned by', which apparently only refers to 100% ownership. The courts are unlikely to permit arrest of a ship that is joint-owned (Articles 10 and 16 of the Maritime Code) by a third party who is not at fault regarding the claim concerned. There are different views on arrest of a ship co-owned by a third party without fault, which have been left to the courts for further clarification. However, no clarification is needed in the case of cargo arrest. Shipowners will only be allowed to arrest of cargo that is owned by the charterer who has not paid for the hire or freight.[58] This principle should be applied in the case of a sister-ship, that is, the sister-ship cannot be arrested if it is jointly owned by an innocent third party. However, for such a defence, the joint ownership shall be registered in accordance with Article 10 of the Maritime Code.

Claimants under English law have a wider choice regarding which ship to arrest, either the offending ship or any other ship of which the relevant person is the beneficial owner in respect of all the shares in the sister-ship. In the case of action *in personam*, one may execute against any of the defendant's property including all his ships. Or, once an appearance is entered in an action *in rem*, the action proceeds as though it were *in personam* and the final judgment may be satisfied against all the property of the defendant. However, in an *in rem* action where no appearance is entered, the action is against the ship only, not against the owners *in personam*. Logically, there can be no execution against the owner's other property, that is, no other sister-ships of the same owners can be arrested.

Under the MPL (Articles 44–50), cargoes, bunkers and supplies on board a ship can be subjected to arrest provided that they are owned by the debtors. These provisions cover carrier's lien on cargo for unpaid hire and freight, contributions in general average, demurrages payable to shipowners, as defined in the Maritime Code (Article 87), and unpaid hire or other sums of money due to shipowners by charterers as defined in the Maritime Code (Article 140). The arrester is entitled to arrest the property or obtain security in amount up to the value of his claim. The documents needed for filing an application to arrest cargo and bunkers may include the relevant charter-party and proof of the outstanding hire. Courts can order the bunkers to be discharged and stored ashore upon the arrester's request and at his cost.

---

57 [1999] 2 Lloyd's Rep 11, which was reviewed in (2000) LMCLQ (May) 129–31.

58 Jin and Weng, *China Maritime Litigation*, 1993, Shenzhen: Haitian Press, pp 412–13.

12 WRONGFUL ARREST AND COUNTER-SECURITY

It was appreciated by China's legislators that the obtaining of security in support of a claim by the arrest of the ship is a powerful weapon which can put shipowners under oppressive commercial pressure. Therefore, the new law puts a strict obligation on the applicant for arrest to prevent the facility from being abused and to protect shipowners' interests. Under the MPL (Article 16), when an arrest application is filed, the court may require the arresting party to provide sufficient counter-security for wrongful arrest.[59] However, the MPL does not spell out in more detail in which circumstances courts may require such counter-security. Courts have usually required such a security where: (a) the applicant lives or is domiciled abroad; (b) the applicant's financial position is unstable or unclear to the court; and (c) the evidence for arrest is not strong.[60] Courts will not usually require a security where the applicant is a well known and financially strong national company and the evidence for arrest is clear and strong.

The MPL does not specify the form of counter-security. As a result, it leaves this to the courts to decide (Article 75). Courts would usually require foreign claimants to provide counter-security in the form of a Bank Guarantee issued by a Chinese bank, for example, the Bank of China, or Letters of Undertaking issued by Chinese insurers, for example, China P&I Club, PICC (People's Insurance Company of China). As to the amount of counter-security, theoretically, it is the value of the damage or losses that could be caused to shipowners as a result of the wrongful arrest. A wrongful arrest exists where: (a) the applicant has no maritime claim for arrest; or (b) the owners of the ship arrested are not liable for the maritime claims; or (c) security demanded by the applicant is unreasonably high.[61] The exact amount is left to the court to decide, and is usually calculated based on a 30 day period of hire of the ship in question, as the arrest period is 30 days under the MPL (Article 28). The amount of counter-security can be ordered to be the same amount as the security demanded from the shipowner.[62] If the claimant's claim ultimately fails and constitutes a wrongful arrest, the shipowner can bring a claim against the claimant for wrongful arrest and losses caused thereof, which can be secured by the counter-security provided by the claimant.[63]

The security for wrongful arrest is a useful device that can inject greater equity into ship arrest and may greatly affect a creditor's choice of whether

59 Also the Civil Procedure Law, Article 93.

60 Jin and Weng, *China Maritime Litigation*, 1993, Shenzhen: Haitian Press, p 405.

61 *Ibid*, pp 405–06.

62 In the case of *Tianwei* (translation from its Chinese name), the court ordered a counter-security from the applicant of US$ 400,000, ie, the amount of security demanded from the shipowner. Guangzhou Maritime Court, *Practice of Maritime Courts*, 1992, at 292–93.

63 Article 254 of the Civil Procedure Law.

and where to arrest the ship. The MPL (Article 78) provides that the arresting party can also be held liable for commissions and interest arising from the demand for excessive security as well as losses of freight or hire due to delay. These provisions would significantly reduce the chance of arrest in China and demands for excessive security by claimants.

Under English law, wrongful arrest may result in a condemnation of the arrester in damages only when the court is satisfied that the arrest was motivated by *mala fides* (bad faith) or *crassa negligentia* (gross negligence) as defined in *The Kommunar (No 3)*.[64] Counter-security is only sometimes ordered at the court's discretion as in *The Tjaskemolen*.[65] Merely unjustified or erroneous arrest would not normally entitle the defendant to claim damages, although he may be able to recover costs arising therefrom.[66] It is not usual for English courts to impose requirements on the arrester to put up counter-security to secure the defendant against losses which may be incurred as a result of the arrest. The arrester can, however, be held liable for damages for having demanded excessive security under s 34 of the Australian Admiralty Act 1988.

It was understood by delegates at the 1999 Diplomatic Convention on Arrest of Ships that counter-security for an arresting ship is a device that can inject greater equity into ship arrest.[67] The matter, however, has been left to the discretion of national law and the courts concerned. The 1999 Arrest Convention does not spell out in more detail what kinds of circumstances courts should take into account. In particular, there is no definition of 'wrongful or unjustified arrest' referred to in Article 6, but it may include a situation where, although the arrest was reasonable at the time of arrest, it later proves to be unjustified because the claims ultimately fail on their merits.

13 RE-ARREST AND MULTIPLE ARREST FOR THE SAME CLAIM

Chinese legislators have been convinced that a ship should not be re-arrested and subjected to multiple arrest.[68] First, as public policy, re-arrest for the same

64 *The Kommunar (No 3)* [1997] 1 Lloyd's Rep 22.

65 *The Tjaskemolen* [1997] 2 Lloyd's Rep 476.

66 *The Dudora* (1879) 4 PD 208.

67 Thomas, R, 'Towards a new arrest convention' (1998) *Lloyd's List*, 24 June, at p 7.

68 Sing gives four situations covering re-arrest and multiple arrest: (1) arrest of a ship after she has been released upon provision of security; (2) arrest of a ship after a sister-ship has been released upon provision of security; (3) arrest of a ship after security has been furnished to prevent her arrest; and (4) arrest of a ship after an earlier arrest of another ship. Sing, TK, *Admiralty Law and Practice*, 1998, Singapore: Butterworths Asia, p 179. However, the MPL (Article 24) and Arrest Convention (Article 5) expressly cover only the first situation.

claim should not be encouraged in order to prevent a ship from being repeatedly arrested in one port after another. Further, it has long been established in other jurisdictions[69] that the security represents the ship; the ship being thereby released, and which cannot be re-arrested for the same cause of action. Lastly, re-arrest and multiple arrest of ships are not permissible under the 1952 Convention. The MPL (Article 24) therefore adopted the principle that a ship cannot be re-arrested in respect of the same maritime claim where the ship has been arrested and released.

In line with the stand of the Arrest Convention 1999, the MPL allows exceptions to this general principle. First, where the nature or amount of the security provided is inadequate (Article 24(1)). Secondly, where the person who has provided the security is unlikely to be able to fulfil some or all of his obligations (Article 24(2)). Lastly, where the ship arrested or the security previously provided was released either with the consent of the claimant acting on reasonable grounds; or because the claimant could not, by taking reasonable steps, prevent the release (Article 24(3)).

It is understood that the initial amount should be considered 'inadequate' only where it was calculated erroneously or based on wrong information. Normal deviation cannot be regarded as 'inadequate' for re-arrest. These provisions are principally in line with Article 5(1) of the Arrest Convention 1999, which has its roots in English law.[70] However, in *The Hero*,[71] an English court allowed an application before judgment was obtained to increase the quantum of security, as the initial security provided was too low owing to a clerical error. In the case of *The Arctic Star*, the Court of Appeal allowed a re-arrest of the ship as the court found the person who had already provided the security was unlikely to be able to fulfil his obligation.[72]

It is worth pointing out that from a practical point of view, the security provided by owners, by means of either Bank Securities or Letters of Undertaking issued by P&I Clubs,[73] will normally state that the condition of the provision of the security is based on the arrester's 'releasing and/or refraining from arresting or otherwise detaining the [ship's name] or any other ship or property in the same or associated ownership, management,

69 It is stated in *The Wild Ranger* that 'bail given for a ship in any action is a substitute for the ship; and whenever bail is given, the ship is wholly released from the cause of action, and cannot be arrested again for that cause of action' (1863) Br & L 84, at 87; 167 ER 310, at 312.

70 *The Wild Ranger* (1863) Br & L 84.

71 *The Hero* (1885) 10 PD 141.

72 *The Arctic Star*, Court of Appeal, delivered 29 January 1985, reported in *The Times* on 5 February 1985.

73 Li, KX, 'Acceptability of P&I Club letters as security' (2000) 2 International Journal of Shipping Law, 76–86.

possession or control for the purpose of obtaining security'.[74] It is clear, therefore, that the acceptance of the security by the arresting party concludes a separate contract between the arresting party and the shipowners, thereby the arrester has abandoned the right to re-arrest the ship or to arrest other ships.[75]

14 RELEASE FROM ARREST

Under the MPL (Article 18), the arrested ship should be released immediately after the shipowner provides security, or after the arresting party acting on reasonable grounds withdraws his application for arrest. The arrested ship should also be released or the security provided should be returned if the arresting party has not commenced legal proceedings or arbitration proceedings within 30 days (Article 28).

There is a change in the MPL regarding provisions of security for release of an arrested ship compared with Chinese practice in the past. Under the Regulations for Arrest of Ship Prior to Litigation, to lift an arrest, a 'reliable and sufficient' security had to be provided for the court (notably not for the arresting party).[76] After filing the case in court, the parties have no opportunity to negotiate the form and terms of a security. The issue will thus be decided by the court. Usually, courts require a Bank Guarantee issued by a Chinese bank or Letters of Undertaking issued by a Chinese insurer. Chinese courts will not usually respect Letters of Undertaking issued by foreign insurance companies or P&I Clubs which have no attachable assets within the jurisdiction.[77]

It is noted under the MPL (Articles 75 and 76) that the parties can now negotiate on 'the form and amount of security' at any stage; the court will intervene only when the parties cannot reach an agreement. If a shipowner or his Club can persuade the arresting party to accept Letters of Undertaking issued by foreign issuers (P&I Clubs), the court will allow the ship to be released. With more experience in dealing with P&I Clubs, Chinese claimants have realised that most P&I Clubs are financially strong and stable, and are keen to safeguard their credibility and to see their Letters of Undertaking being honoured. It is expected that more and more claimants in China will be

74 Admiralty Solicitors Group (ASG), *Standard Wording of ASG Collision Undertaking*, 1994, London: Author.

75 Li, KX, 'Acceptability of P&I Club letters as security' (2000) 2 International Journal of Shipping Law 76–86; Sing, TK, *Admiralty Law and Practice*, 1998, Singapore: Butterworths Asia, pp 179–80.

76 Regulations for Arrest of Ship Prior to Litigation, Article 3(4).

77 Li, KX, 'Acceptability of P&I Club letters as security' (2000) 2 International Journal of Shipping Law 76–86.

ready to accept Letters of Undertaking issued by P&I Clubs, especially those issued by the 13 members of the International Group of P&I Clubs.

It is worth pointing out that provision of security for releasing the ship from arrest by shipowners shall neither be construed as an acknowledgment of liability nor as a waiver of any defence or any right to limit liability.[78] As to intervention on the wording of security, under the MPL (Article 75) courts will not vary the form or terms of security, which is considered a private agreement between the parties.[79] However, it is appreciated that arrest of a ship is a strong weapon against shipowners. Chinese courts, therefore, can exercise judicial discretion to vary the wording of the security to protect the legitimate right of the defendants. As to the amount of security, the court has the right to decide according to the evidence. The principle for setting the amount is that the claimant is entitled to sufficient security to cover the amount of his claim with interest and costs according to the *prima facie* evidence. These practices are in line with the common law as set out in *The Bulgaria* and *The Moscanthy*.[80] As to a completed comparison of relevant provisions on arrest of ships in China with English law and international conventions, please see Table 3.

15 JUDICIAL SALE

The Chinese courts have a conservatory jurisdiction of 30 days following an arrest (Article 28 of the MPL), during which period substantial proceedings must be commenced, in absence of which the arrested ships will have to be released.[81] If the owner of the ship has not provided security as required within the period, the arrester, following the commencement of formal proceedings, may apply to a court for sale of ship (Article 29 of the MPL). Judicial or forced sale is the final stage of the arrest. However, not every arrest case ends up with a judicial sale. Many ships are released against securities provided by owners as discussed previously.

78 Article 3(5) of the Regulations on Arrest of Ships Prior to Litigation, which was consolidated and replaced by the MPL. Similarly, that a P&I Club stands as surety for a member to release an arrested ship does not imply any acknowledgment or admission of the club's liability to cover the claim. Hazelwood, SJ, *P&I Clubs: Law and Practice*, 3rd edn, 2000, London: LLP, p 297.

79 Hazelwood, SJ, *P&I Clubs: Law and Practice*, 3rd edn, 2000, pp 285–87; Li, KX, 'Acceptability of P&I club letters as security' (2000) 2 International Journal of Shipping Law 76–86.

80 *The Bulgaria* [1964] 2 Lloyd's Rep 524; *The Moscanthy* [1971] 1 Lloyd's Rep 39, at 44.

81 In this situation, the security obtained may, and upon request, shall be returned to the owner. *Weigao Success* (translated from its Chinese name) in Jin and Weng, *China Maritime Litigation*, 1993, Shenzhen: Haitian Press, p 404.

The court should notify the judicial sale through newspapers or the press, or where a foreign ship is involved, through overseas edition newspapers, less than 30 days before the auction.

Judicial sale confers on a purchaser a 'clean' title free from all charges and encumbrances, including maritime liens (Article 29(2) of the Maritime Code). Therefore, any person having a maritime lien must exercise his right or register his claim in the court within 30 days of public notice on the transfer of the ownership made by the court.[82] The security for judgment obtained by a claimant through arrest is finally reflected in the funds from the sale. The value of the security will be affected by other claims and the priority order of such claims.

The legal costs and expenses of enforcing maritime liens and judicial sale, of preserving and selling the ship, and of distribution of the proceeds of sale and other expenses incurred for the common interests of the claimants, shall be deducted and paid firstly from the proceeds of the judicial sale (Article 24 of the Maritime Code). Under Chinese law, maritime liens have priority over possessory liens, which in turn have priority over ship mortgages (Article 25 of the Maritime Code). Claims for crew wages, loss of life or personal injury, taxes and port dues, salvage payments and damage to property resulting from tortious acts are protected by maritime liens (Article 22 of the Maritime Code). If the fund is insufficient for all claims in the same rank, the claimants will then be paid in proportion.

A claimant having a low ranking claim should be careful when deciding to arrest a ship. Where the ship's value (market value) is lower than the quantum of higher ranking claims, he may not recover anything from the proceeds of the sale of the ship, but may only pick up legal costs if the owner decides not to provide security for the claim.

16 MARITIME INJUNCTION

Although Chinese courts have the power to order a party to perform or not to perform certain legal actions, the Maritime Injunction introduced by the MPL is a new concept in Chinese law. The Maritime Injunction is defined by Article 51 of the MPL as 'a coercive measure granted by a Maritime Court, upon the request of a claimant, by means of an order requiring a respondent to do or refrain from doing something, so as to prevent the legitimate rights and interests of the claimant being infringed'.

82 It should be noted that the period of public notice for judicial sale is 30 days (Article 32 of the MPL). However, the period of public notice for assertion of a maritime lien is 60 days (Article 26 of the Maritime Code; Article 124 of the MPL).

The MPL sets out three conditions upon which a Maritime Injunction can be granted: (a) the applicant of a Maritime Injunction should have a specific maritime claim; (b) the respondent violates laws or contracts; (c) without a Maritime Injunction as a matter of urgency, damage will occur or be exacerbated. The purpose of a Maritime Injunction is to prevent the interests of the applicant from being infringed by the action or non-action of another party. Courts may require security from the applicant for a Maritime Injunction (Article 55 of the MPL). The defendant is entitled to an indemnity from the applicant for any loss or damage occurring as a result of a wrongful injunction (Article 60 of the MPL).

It appears that the Maritime Injunction under the new law is similar to the Mareva Injunction under English law.[83] However, there are some differences worth noting. First, the basic criteria governing the grant of a Mareva Injunction under English law appear stricter, under which the claimant must show: (a) a cause of action against the defendant in the jurisdiction at the time of application;[84] (b) a strong *prima facie* case;[85] (c) that the defendant has assets within the jurisdiction;[86] (d) that the defendant is likely to frustrate judgment by removing his assets from the jurisdiction;[87] and (e) the balance of convenience favours issue of a injunction.[88] However, counter-security is usually not required for application of a Mareva Injunction.

Secondly, the Mareva Injunction applies not only to the assets within the English jurisdiction to prevent the defendant from transferring or dissipating those assets out of the jurisdiction, but also to those assets situated outside the jurisdiction, by the so called 'Worldwide Mareva Injunctions', requiring the assets located outside the jurisdiction to be transferred to a jurisdiction where the Mareva remedy will be recognised.[89] On the other hand, the Maritime Injunction under Chinese law applies only to the assets within the jurisdiction.

Lastly, the Mareva Injunction applies only to assets (tangible, non-tangible, real or personal, including, *inter alia*, ship, cargoes, bunkers, proceeds of sale and bank accounts). A Maritime Injunction appears to have a wider scope, giving remedies not only against assets, but also in the form of an order for specific performance against the defendant.

---

83 The Mareva Injunction is now known as a 'Freezing Injunction' under the Civil Procedure Rules 1998 (SI 1998/3132).

84 *The Siskina* [1978] 1 Lloyd's Rep 1, at 6; *Mercedes Benz AG v Leiduck* [1995] 2 Lloyd's Rep 417, at 424.

85 *Nippon Yusen Kaisha v Karageorgis* [1975] 2 Lloyd's Rep 137, at 138.

86 Tetley, W, *Maritime Liens and Claims*, 1998, Canada: Les Éditions Yvon Blais Inc, p 987.

87 *The Genie* [1979] 2 Lloyd's Rep 184, at 189; *The Niedersachsen* [1983] 2 Lloyd's Rep 600, at 617.

88 *Rasu Maaritima SA v Pertamina* [1977] 2 Lloyd's Rep 397, at 405.

89 *Babanaft International Co SA v Bassatne* [1988] 2 Lloyd's Rep 435.

17 CONCLUSION

Two main decisive factors motivated China in introducing its present reform of its maritime policy and legal system. First, since China adopted its 'open door' policy as a long term strategy to accelerate its ambitious modernisation, foreign trade with more and more countries and regions has grown dramatically. Over 90% of China's international trade is transported by ships. Sustaining the development requires not only an expansion of China's fleet, but also a consistent, enforceable and globally recognised maritime policy and legal system.

Secondly, as maritime transportation is an international undertaking, anyone who would like to join the game should apply the existing rules – the international maritime conventions and customs.

Recognising the importance of adequate, proper and identical implementation of the international maritime conventions by less developed countries, the way of drafting the Maritime Code could also serve as a model for developing countries in their maritime legislation.

Figure 1 Limitation of liability for personal injury claims[90]

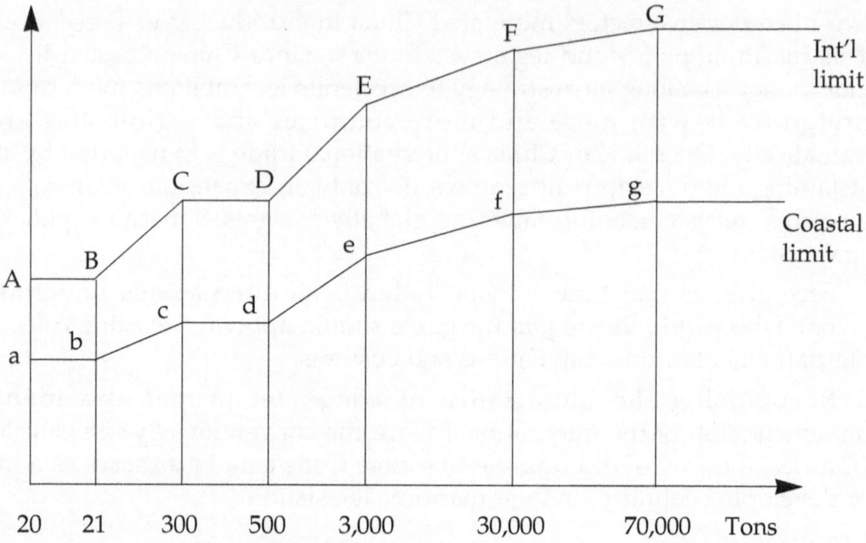

Where:

A=B=54,000 SDR

C=D=(300-21)*1,000+540,000=333,000 SDR

E=(3,000-500)*500+333,000=1,583,000 SDR

F=(30,000-3,000)*333+1,583,000=10,574,000 SDR

G=(70,000-30,000)*250+10,574,000 SDR=20,574,000 SDR

a=b=1/2A=27,000 SDR

c=d=1/2C=166,500 SDR

e=1/2E=791,509 SDR

f=1/2F=5,287,000 SDR

g=1/2G=10,287,000 SDR

90 Li, KX, 'The Chinese law on global limitation of liability' (1996) 3 Lloyd's Maritime and Commercial Law Quarterly (Aug) 400.

Figure 2 Limitation of liability for other claims[91]

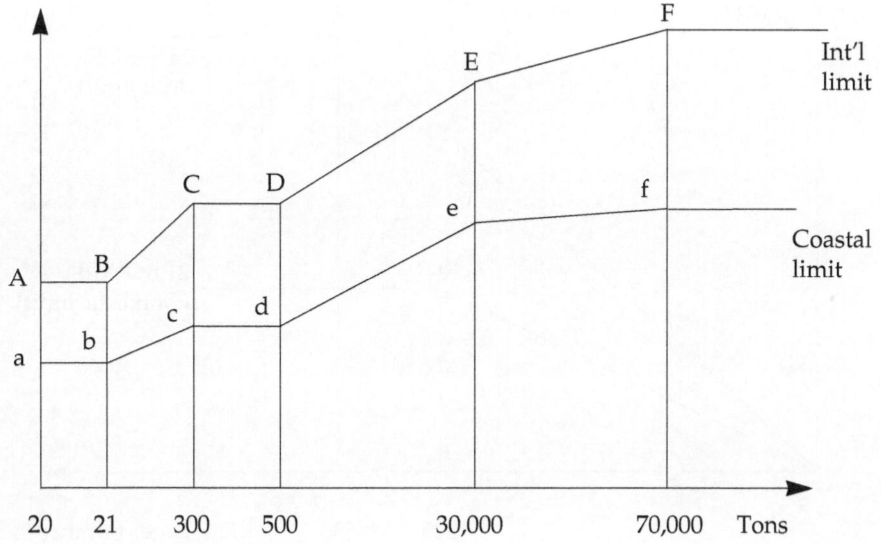

Where:
A=B=27,500 SDR
C=D=(300-21)*500+27,500=167,000 SDR
E=(30,000-500)*167+167,000=5,093,500 SDR
F=(70,000-30,000)*125+5,093,500=10,093,500 SDR
a=b=1/2A=13,750 SDR
c=d=1/2C=83,500 SDR
e=1/2E=2,546,750 SDR
f=1/2F=5,046,750 SDR

91 *Ibid,* at 401.

Figure 3 Limitation of liability for passenger injury claims[92]

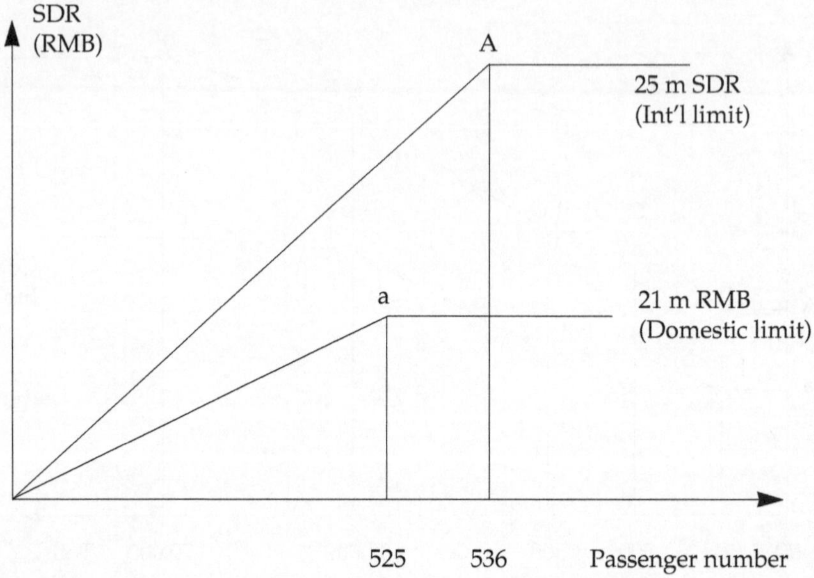

Where:
A=25 m SDR for international carriage
a=21 m RMB for domestic carriage

92 *Ibid*, at 402.

Figure 4 Locations of Maritime Courts in the People's Republic of China

Table 1 First-trial cases heard by People's Courts and Maritime Courts (1990–98)

Year	Criminal	Civil	Economic	Administrative	Maritime	Total
1990	459,656	1,851,897	591,462	13,006	753	2,916,774
1991	427,840	1,880,635	566,592	25,667	951	2,901,685
1992	422,991	1,948,786	650,601	27,125	1,654	3,051,157
1993	403,267	2,089,257	892,580	27,911	1,830	3,414,845
1994	482,927	2,383,764	1,051,742	35,083	1,959	3,955,475
1995	495,741	2,718,533	1,275,959	52,596	2,847	4,545,676
1996	618,826	3,093,995	1,515,848	79,966	3,945	5,312,580
1997	436,894	3,277,572	1,478,822	90,557	4,534	5,288,379
1998	482,164	3,375,069	1,450,049	98,350	5,166	5,410,798
Total	4,230,306	22,619,508	9,473,655	450,261	23,639	36,797,369

Source:

National Bureau of Statistics of China, the PRC: China Statistic Yearbook (1999)

Table 2 China ratified maritime conventions

Conventions adopted by UN (Source: UN, 2001/02)	Parties	Into force	China	HK	Macao
UN Convention on a Code of Conduct for Liner Conferences, 1974	85	06/10/83	23/09/80	28/06/85	–
UN Convention on the Carriage of Goods by Sea (Hamburg Rules), 1978	28	01/11/92	–	–	–
UN Convention on the Multimodal Transport of International Goods, 1980	7	–	–	–	–
UN Convention on the Law of the Sea (UNCLOS), 1982	138	16/11/94	07/07/96	07/07/96	07/07/96
UN Convention on Conditions for Registration of Ships, 1986	9	–	–	–	–
UN Convention on the Liability of Operators of Transport Terminals in the International Trade, 1991	1	–	–	–	–
International Convention on Maritime Liens and Mortgages, 1993	5	–	–	–	–
International Financial Leasing, 1988	6	01/05/95	–	–	–
Conventions adopted by IMO (Source: IMO, 2002)	**Parties**	**Into force**	**China**	**HK**(1)	**Macao**(1)
Convention of the International Maritime Organisation	162	17/03/58	V(2)	V(2)	V(2)
International Convention for Safety of Life at Sea, 1974 1978 Protocol 1988 Protocol	146 99 59	25/05/80 01/05/81 03/02/00	25/05/80(3) 17/03/83(6) 03/02/00	25/05/80(4) 01/05/81(7)	07/02/84(5) 07/02/84(8)
International Convention on Load Lines, 1966 1988 Protocol	149 58	21/07/68 03/02/00	05/01/74 03/02/00	21/07/68	22/03/70
International Convention for Safe Containers, 1972	72	06/09/77	23/09/81(9)	08/03/79(10)	22/10/86

Conventions adopted by IMO (Source: IMO, 2002)	Parties	Into force	China	HK[1]	Macao[1]
International Convention on Standards of Training, Certifications and Watchkeeping for Seafarers, 1978	141	28/04/84	28/04/84[11]	28/04/84[12]	30/01/86
International Convention on Maritime Search and Rescue, 1979	73	22/06/85	24/07/85[13]	22/06/85[14]	29/11/85
Special Trade Passenger Ships Agreement, 1971	17	02/01/74	–	27/10/81	–
Convention on the International (Maritime) (Mobile) Satellite Organisation, 1976	88	16/07/79	16/07/79[15]	16/07/79[16]	16/07/79
Convention on Facilitation of International Maritime Traffic, 1965	91	05/03/67	17/03/95[17]	24/09/70[18]	05/10/90
International Convention for the Prevention of Pollution from Ships, 1973/1978					
Annex I/II	121	02/10/83	02/10/83[19]	02/10/83[20]	22/01/88[21]
Annex III	103	01/07/92	13/12/94	–	–
Annex IV	87	–	–	–	–
Annex V	108	31/12/86	21/02/89	–	–
Annex VI	5	–	–	–	–
Convention on the Prevention of Marine Pollution by Dumping of Waste and Other Matters, 1972	78	30/08/75	03/09/7[22]	17/12/75[23]	14/05/78[24]
International Convention Relating to Intervention on the High Seas in Case of Oil Pollution Casualties, 1969	77	06/05/75	24/05/90[25]	06/05/75	15/05/80
1973 Protocol	44	30/05/83	24/05/90[25]		
International Convention on Civil Liability for Oil Pollution Damage, 1969	49	19/06/75	29/04/80[26]	19/06/75	24/02/77
1976 Protocol	55	08/04/81	28/12/86[27]	08/04/81[28]	02/04/86
1992 Protocol	86	30/05/96	05/01/00[29]	05/01/00	–
Convention on the Establishment of an International Fund for Compensation for Oil Pollution Damage, 1971					
1976 Protocol	33	22/11/94	01/07/97[30]	22/11/94[31]	–
1992 Protocol	80	30/05/96	05/01/00[32]	30/05/96[33]	22/11/94
Convention Relating to Civil Liability in the Field of Maritime Carriage of Nuclear Materials, 1971	16	15/07/75	–	–	–

Conventions adopted by IMO (Source: IMO, 2002)	**Parties**	**Into force**	**China**	**HK**(1)	**Macao**(1)
Convention Relating to the Carriage of Passengers and their Luggage by Sea, 1974 1976 Protocol	28 22	28/04/87 30/04/89	30/08/94(34) 30/08/94(36)	28/04/87(35) 30/04/89(37)	–
Convention on Limitation of Liability for Maritime Claims, 1976 1996 Protocol	37 4	01/12/86 –	01/07/97(38) –	01/12/86(39) –	–
Convention for the Suppression of Unlawful Acts Against the Safety of Maritime Navigation, 1988 1988 Protocol	70 63	01/03/92 01/03/92	01/03/92(40) 01/03/92(40)	– –	04/04/96(41) –
International Convention on Salvage, 1989	40	14/07/96	14/07/96(42)	14/07/96(43)	V
International Convention on Oil Pollution Preparedness, Response and Co-operation, 1990	66	13/05/95	30/06/98(44)	(45)	(46)
International Convention on Tonnage Measurement of Ships, 1969	134	18/07/82	18/07/82(47)	18/07/82(48)	19/11/99(49)
International Convention for Prevention of Collisions at Sea, 1972	141	15/07/77	07/01/86(50)	15/07/77(51)	22/03/99 (52)
'Brussels' Conventions (Source: CMI, 2001)	**Parties**	**Into force**	**China**	**HK**	**Macao**
International Convention for the Unification of Certain Rules of Law with Respect to Collision between Vessels, 1910	82	01/03/31	–(53)	(2), (53)	–
Convention for the Unification of Certain Rules of Law Relating to Assistance and Salvage at Sea, 1910	83	01/03/31	–(53)	(2), (53)	–
International Convention for the Unification of Certain Rules Relating to the Limitation of the Liability of Owners of Sea-going Vessels, 1924	9	02/06/31	–	–	–
International Convention for the Unification of Certain Rules of Law Relating to Bills of Lading (Hague Rules), 1924	80	02/06/31	–(53)	(2), (53)	–
Protocol to Amend the International Convention for the Unification of Certain Rules Relating to Bills of Lading (SDR Protocol), 1968	18	14/02/84	–(53)	(2), (53)	–

'Brussels' Conventions (Source: CMI, 2001)	Parties	Into force	China	HK	Macao
International Convention for the Unification of Certain Rules Relating to Maritime Liens and Mortgages, 1926	24	02/06/31	–	–	–
International Convention for the Unification of Certain Rules Concerning the Immunity of State Ownerships, 1926/1934	30	08/01/37	–	–	–
International Convention for the Unification of Certain Rules Relating to Civil Jurisdiction in Matters of Collision, 1952	62	14/09/55	–(53)	(2), (54)	–
International Convention for the Unification of Certain Rules Relating to Penal Jurisdiction in Matters of Collision and Other Incidents of Navigation, 1952	70	20/11/55	–(53)	(2), (53)	–
International Convention for the Unification of Certain Rules Relating to Arrest of Sea-going Ships, 1952	70	24/02/56	–(53)	(2), (53)	–
International Convention Relating to the Limitation of the Liability of Owners of Sea-going Ships, 1957 Protocol 1979	39 7	31/05/68 06/10/84	–(53) –	(2), (53) (2)	V V
International Convention Relating to Stowaways, 1957	10	–	–	–	–
International Convention for the Unification of Certain Rules Relating to Carriage of Passengers by Sea, 1961	11	04/06/65	–	–	–
International Convention Relating to the Liability of Operators of Nuclear Ships, 1962	7	–	–	–	–
International Convention for the Unification of Certain Rules Relating to Carriage of Passengers' Luggage by Sea, 1967	2	–	–	–	–
International Convention Relating to the Registration of Rights in Respect of Vessels under Construction, 1967	5	–	–	–	–

'Brussels' Conventions (Source: CMI, 2001)	Parties	Into force	China	HK	Macao
International Convention for the Unification of Certain Rules Relating to Maritime Liens and Mortgages, 1967	5	–	–	–	–
Conventions adopted by ILO (Source: ILO, 2001)	**Parties**	**Into force**	**China**	**HK**	**Macao**
7 Minimum Age (Sea) Convention, 1920	53	27/09/21	02/12/36	–	24/10/60
8 Unemployment Indemnity (Shipwreck) Convention, 1920	58	16/03/23	–	12/03/26	19/05/81
9 Placing of Seamen Convention, 1920	38	23/11/21	–	–	–
16 Medical Examination (Sea) Convention, 1921	79	20/11/22	02/12/36	08/03/26	–
22 Seamen's Articles of Agreement Convention, 1926	56	04/04/28	02/12/36	23/05/83	14/06/29
23 Repatriation of Seamen Convention, 1926	44	16/04/28	02/12/36	03/06/85	23/05/83
27 Marking of Weight on Heavy Packages (Transported by Vessels) Convention, 1929	64	09/03/32	24/06/31	–	01/03/32
28 Protection Against Accidents (Dockers) Convention, 1932	4	01/04/32	–	–	–
32 Protection Against Accidents (Dockers) Convention, 1932	44	31/10/34	30/11/35	10/01/35	–
53 Officer's Competency Certificates Convention, 1936	32	29/03/39	–	29/10/38	–
54 Holidays with Pay (Sea) Convention, 1936	6	–	–	–	–
55 Shipowners' Liability (Sick and Injured Seamen) Convention, 1936	16	29/10/39	–	–	–
56 Sickness Insurance (Sea) Convention, 1936	18	09/12/49	–	30/09/44	–
57 Hours of Work and Manning (Sea) Convention, 1936	4	–	–	–	–
58 Minimum Age (Sea) Convention (Revised), 1936	52	11/04/39	–	–	–

Conventions adopted by ILO (Source: ILO, 2001)	Parties	Into force	China	HK	Macao
68 Food and Catering (Ships' Crews) Convention, 1946	23	24/03/57	–	06/08/53	13/06/52
69 Certification of Ships' Cooks Convention, 1946	35	22/04/53	–	29/07/49	13/06/52
70 Social Security (Seafarers) Convention, 1946	7	–	–	20/05/53	–
71 Seafarers' Pensions Convention, 1946	13	10/10/62	–	–	–
72 Paid Vacations (Seafarers) Convention, 1946	5	–	–	–	–
73 Medical Examination (Seafarers) Convention, 1946	41	17/08/55	–	–	13/06/52
74 Certification of Able Seamen Convention, 1946	26	14/07/51	–	13/05/52	13/06/52
75 Accommodation of Crews Convention, 1946	5	–	–	–	–
76 Wages, Hours of Work and Manning (Sea) Convention, 1946	1	–	–	–	–
91 Paid Vacations (Seafarers) Convention (Revised), 1949	23	14/09/67	–	–	29/07/52
92 Accommodation of Crews Convention (Revised), 1949	41	29/01/53	–	06/08/53	29/07/52
93 Wages, Hours of Work and Manning (Sea) Convention (Revised), 1949	6	–	–	–	–
108 Seafarers' Identity Documents Convention, 1958	57	19/02/61	–	18/02/64	03/08/67
109 Wages, Hours of Work and Manning (Sea) Convention (Revised), 1958	15	–	–	–	09/01/81
112 Minimum Age (Fishermen) Convention, 1959	30	07/11/61	–	–	–
113 Medical Examination (Fishermen) Convention, 1959	28	07/11/61	–	–	–
114 Fishermen's Articles of Agreement Convention, 1959	21	07/11/61	–	20/12/74	–
125 Fishermen's Competency Certificates Convention, 1966	10	15/07/69	–	–	–
126 Accommodation of Crews (Fishermen) Convention, 1966	21	06/11/68	–	13/08/85	–

Conventions adopted by ILO (Source: ILO, 2001)	Parties	Into force	China	HK	Macao
133 Accommodation of Crews (Supplementary Provisions) Convention, 1970	25	27/08/91	–	26/03/81	–
134 Prevention of Accidents (Seafarers) Convention, 1970	27	17/02/73	–	–	–
145 Continuity of Employment (Seafarers) Convention, 1976	17	03/05/79	–	–	23/05/83
146 Seafarers' Annual Leave with Pay Convention, 1976	12	13/06/79	–	–	25/06/84
147 Merchant Shipping (Minimum Standards) Convention, 1976 [and Protocol, 1996]	35	28/11/81	–	28/11/80	02/05/85
152 Occupational Safety and Health (Dock Work) Convention, 1979	18	05/12/81	–	–	–
153 Hours of Work and Rest Periods (Road Transport) Convention, 1979	7	10/02/83	–	–	–
163 Seafarers' Welfare Convention, 1987	10	03/10/90	–	–	–
164 Health Protection and Medical Care (Seafarers) Convention, 1987	8	11/01/91	–	–	–
165 Social Security (Seafarers) Convention, 1987	2	02/07/92	–	–	–
166 Repatriation of Seafarers Convention, 1987	6	03/07/91	–	–	–
178 Inspection of Seafarers' Working and Living Conditions Convention, 1996	0	–	–	–	–
179 Recruitment and Placement of Seafarers Convention, 1996	0	–	–	–	–
180 Seafarers' Hours of Work and the Manning of Ships Convention, 1996	0	–	–	–	–

Notes:

(1) Hong Kong and Macao are Associate Members of the IMO.

(2) 'V': ratified date unknown.

(3) Applies to the Hong Kong Special Administrative Region with effect from 1 July 1997.

(4) Ratification by the United Kingdom was declared to be effective in respect of Hong Kong with effect from 25 May 1980.

(5) Applies to Macao with effect from 24 August 1999.

(6) Applies to the Hong Kong Special Administrative Region with effect from 1 July 1997. Applies to the Macao Special Administrative Region with effect from 20 December 1999.

(7) Ratification by the United Kingdom was declared to be effective in respect of Hong Kong with effect from 25 November 1981.

(8) Applies to Macao with effect from 24 August 1999, and ceased to apply to Macao with effect from 20 December 1999.

(9) Applies to the Hong Kong Special Administrative Region with effect from 1 July 1997.

(10) Ratification by the United Kingdom was declared to be effective in respect to Hong Kong as from 30 May 1997 and ceased to apply to Hong Kong with effect from 1 July 1997.

(11) Applies to the Hong Kong Special Administrative Region with effect from 1 July 1997.

(12) Ratification by the United Kingdom was declared to be effective also in respect of Hong Kong as from 3 November 1984 and ceased to apply to Hong Kong with effect from 1 July 1997.

(13) The instrument of approval of the People's Republic of China contained the following declaration (in the English language): 'The delimitation of search and rescue regions, as stipulated in the Annex to the Convention 2.1.7, is not related to and shall not prejudice the delimitation of any boundary between States, either is not related to and shall not prejudice the delimitation of any exclusive economic zone and continental shelf between States.'

(14) The signature on behalf of the United Kingdom is in respect also of Hong Kong and ceased to apply to Hong Kong with effect from 1 July 1997.

(15) Applies to the Hong Kong Special Administrative Region with effect from 1 July 1997.

(16) The United Kingdom declared that the Convention 'shall apply to the registers of British ships registered in ports of register in the United Kingdom, in Hong Kong and in Bermuda'. Ceased to apply to Hong Kong with effect from 1 July 1997.

(17) Applies to the Hong Kong Special Administrative Region with effect from 1 July 1997.

(18) Ceased to apply to Hong Kong with effect from 1 July 1997.

(19) Applies to the Hong Kong Special Administrative Region with effect from 1 July 1997. Applies to the Macao Special Administrative Region with effect from 20 December 1999. The instrument of accession of the People's Republic of China contained a declaration in accordance with Article 14 of the Convention that it 'is not bound by Annexes III, IV and V of the Convention'.

(20) Ratification by the United Kingdom was declared to be effective in respect of: Hong Kong from 11 April 1985 – in respect of Annexes I and II of the Convention only; Hong Kong from 7 March 1995 – in respect of Annex III of the Convention; Hong Kong from 27 March 1996 – in respect of Annex V of the Convention. Ceased to apply to Hong Kong with effect from 1 July 1997.

(21) Applies to Macao with effect from 24 August 1999 and ceased to apply to Macao with effect from 20 December 1999.

(22) Applies to the Hong Kong Special Administrative Region with effect from 1 July 1997. Applies to the Macao Special Administrative Region with effect from 20 December 1999.

(23) The United Kingdom declared ratification to be effective also in respect of Hong Kong, the effective date is 17 November 1975, and it ceased to apply to Hong Kong with effect from 1 July 1997.

(24) Applies to Macao with effect from 12 May 1999.

(25) Applies to the Hong Kong Special Administrative Region with effect from 1 July 1997.

(26) Applies to the Hong Kong Special Administrative Region with effect from 1 July 1997. At the time of depositing its instrument of accession, the Representative of the People's Republic of China declared that 'the signature to the Convention by Taiwan authorities is illegal and null and void'.

(27) With a notification under Article V(9)(c) of the Convention, as amended by the Protocol, see section v. Applies to the Hong Kong Special Administrative Region with effect from 1 July 1997.

(28) The United Kingdom declared ratification to be effective also in respect of Hong Kong. Ceased to apply to Hong Kong with effect from 1 July 1997.

(29) China declared that the Protocol will also be applicable to the Hong Kong Special Administrative Region.

(30) Applies only to the Hong Kong Special Administrative Region.

(31) The United Kingdom declared ratification to be effective also in respect of Hong Kong and ceased to apply to Hong Kong with effect from 1 July 1997.

(32) China declared that the Protocol will be applicable to the Hong Kong Special Administrative Region only.

(33) When the UK declared ratification to be effective in respect of its colonies, it did not mention Hong Kong.

(34) Applies to the Hong Kong Special Administrative Region with effect from 1 July 1997.

(35) The United Kingdom declared ratification to be effective also in respect of Hong Kong and ceased to apply to Hong Kong with effect from 1 July 1997.

(36) Applies to the Hong Kong Special Administrative Region with effect from 1 July 1997.

(37) With a notification that '... in accordance with Article 9.3 of the Convention, as amended by Article II(3) of the Protocol, the manner of calculation employed by the United Kingdom pursuant to Article 9.1 of the Convention, as amended, shall be the method of valuation applied by the International Monetary Fund'.

The United Kingdom declared ratification to be effective also in respect of Hong Kong and ceased to apply to Hong Kong with effect from 1 July 1997.

(38) By notification dated 5 June 1997 from the People's Republic of China with respect to the Hong Kong Special Administrative Region, it reserves the right in accordance with Article 18(1) to exclude the application of Article 2(1)(d). Applies only to the Hong Kong Special Administrative Region. The manner of calculation employed with respect to Article 8(1) of the Convention concerning the unit of account shall be the method of valuation applied by the International Monetary Fund.

(39) The United Kingdom declared its ratification to be effective also in respect of Hong Kong and ceased to apply to Hong Kong with effect from 1 July 1997.

(40) The following statement was made at the time of signature of the Convention:

> The People's Republic of China shall not be bound by paragraph 1 of Article 16 of the said Convention.

This statement was reaffirmed in the instrument of ratification of the People's Republic of China.

(41) The instrument of accession of the Portuguese Republic contained the following declaration:

> In face of its internal law Portugal considers that the handing over of the suspect mentioned in Article 8 of the Convention can only be based on strong suspicions that he committed any of the crimes mentioned in Article 3, and will always depend on a court decision. Furthermore it will not be admitted in the event that the crime ascribed entails the death sentence.

(42) Applies to the Hong Kong Special Administrative Region with effect from 1 July 1997.

The instrument of accession of the People's Republic of China contained the following statement: 'that in accordance with the provisions of Article 30, paragraph 1 of the

International Convention on Salvage 1989, the government of the People's Republic of China reserves the right not to apply the provisions of Article 30, paragraph 1(a), (b) and (d) of the said Convention.' By notification dated 5 June 1997 the government of the People's Republic of China made the following declaration:

It reserves the right for the Hong Kong Special Administrative Region, in accordance with paragraph 1(a), (b) and (d) of Article 30, not to apply the provisions of the Convention when:

(a) the salvage operation takes place in inland waters and all ships involved are of inland navigation; or

(b) the salvage operations take place in inland waters and no ship is involved; or

(c) the property involved is maritime cultural property of prehistoric, archaeological or historic interest and situated on the sea-bed.

(43) The United Kingdom declared its ratification to be effective in respect of Hong Kong and ceased to apply to Hong Kong with effect from 1 July 1997.

(44) Applies to the Hong Kong and Macao Special Administrative Regions with effect from 1 May 2001.

(45) Applies to the Hong Kong Special Administrative Regions with effect from 1 May 2001.

(46) Applies to the Macao Special Administrative Regions with effect from 1 May 2001.

(47) The instrument of accession of the People's Republic of China contains the following declaration:

The government of the People's Republic of China wishes to declare illegal and null and void the signing of the Convention by the Authorities in Taiwan in the name of China.

Applies to the Hong Kong Special Administrative Region with effect from 1 July 1997.

(48) The Convention has been extended to Hong Kong, and the date of entry into force was set at 18 July 1982. This convention ceased to apply to Hong Kong with effect from 1 July 1997.

(49) The Convention has been extended to Macao, and the date of entry into force was set at 19 November 1999. Ceased to apply to Macao with effect from 20 December 1999.

(50) Applies to the Hong Kong Special Administrative Region with effect from 1 July 1997. Applies to the Macao Special Administrative Region with effect from 20 December 1999.

(51) The United Kingdom declared acceptance to be effective also in respect of Hong Kong from 15 July 1977. Ceased to apply to Hong Kong with effect from 1 July 1997.

(52) Applies to Macao with effect from 22 March 1999. Ceased to apply to Macao with effect from 20 December 1999.

(53) By a letter dated 4 June 1997, the Embassy of the People's Republic of China in the Kingdom of Belgium informed the Minister of Foreign Affairs of Belgium that the Convention will continue to apply to the Hong Kong Special Administrative Region with effect from 1 July 1997. It stated that the responsibility for the international rights and obligations arising from the application of the above Convention will be assumed by the government of the People's Republic of China.

(54) In addition to Note (1), China made the following reservations:

(a) The government of the People's Republic of China reserves, for the Hong Special Administrative Region, the right not to observe the provisions of Article 1 of the Convention in the case of any ship if the State whose flag the ship was flying has as regards that ship or any class of ships to which that ship belongs consented to the institution of criminal or disciplinary proceedings before the judicial or administrative authorities of the Hong Kong Special Administrative Region.

(b) In accordance with Article 4 of the Convention, the government of the People's Republic of China reserves, for the Hong Kong Special Administrative Region, the right to take proceedings in respect of offences committed within waters under the jurisdiction of the Hong Kong Special Administrative Region.

Table 3 Comparison on arrest of ships in China with other regimes[93]

	Provisions on arrest	China[(a)]	English[(b)]	1952 Conv[(c)]	1999 Conv[(d)]
1	loss or damage: collision, oil pollution	yes	yes	yes	yes
2	loss of life and personal injury	yes	yes	yes	yes
3	salvage and towage	yes	yes	yes	yes
4	environmental damage	yes	no	no	yes
5	wreck removal	yes	no	no	yes
6	use or hire of ship, eg, c/p	yes	yes[(e)]	yes	yes
7	carriage of goods or passengers	yes	yes	yes	yes
8	loss of or damage to goods and luggage	yes	no	no	yes
9	general average	yes	yes	yes	yes
10	provisions and services	yes	no	no	yes
11	port and pilotage dues	yes	yes	yes	yes
12	construction and repair	yes	yes	yes	yes
13	crew wages	yes	yes	yes	yes
14	disbursements	yes	yes	yes	yes
15	insurance premiums or Club calls	yes	no	no	yes
16	commission and brokerage	yes	no	no	yes
17	ownership and possession	yes	yes	yes	yes
18	mortgage or hypothecation	yes	yes	yes	yes
19	contract for sale of ship	yes	no	no	yes
20	maritime lien	yes	yes	yes	no
21	bottomry	no	yes	yes	no
22	arrest for security	yes	yes	yes	yes
23	arrest for establishment of jurisdiction	yes	yes[(f)]	yes	yes
24	arrest for arbitration claim	yes	yes	yes	yes
25	arrest for enforced judgments or awards	no	no[(g)]	no	no
26	bareboat/demise chartered ship arrest	yes	yes	yes	yes
27	time/voyage chartered ship arrest	no	no[(h)]	yes	no
28	claim against managers or operators	yes	no	no	yes
29	sister-ship arrest	yes	yes[(i)]	yes	yes
30	arrest of cargo	yes	yes	no	no
31	arrest of charterer's bunker	yes	no	no	no
32	caveat against arrest and release	no	yes	no	no

93 Li, KX, 'Maritime jurisdiction and arrest of ships under China's maritime procedure law (1999)' (2001) 32(4) Journal of Maritime Law and Commerce 655–72.

33	re-arrest and multiple arrest for the same claim	yes	no	no	yes
34	limit of security to ship's value	yes	yes[j]	yes	yes
35	counter-security	yes	no	no	yes
36	claim for wrongful arrest	yes	no	no	yes

Sources:

(a) The China Civil Procedure Law 1991; the China Maritime Procedure Law 1999.

(b) The Supreme Court Act 1981; the Civil Procedure Rules; the Admiralty Court Practice Direction.

(c) The Arrest Convention 1952.

(d) The Arrest Convention 1999.

(e) *The Span Terza* [1984] 1 Lloyd's Rep 119.

(f) *The Maciej Rataj* [1995] 1 Lloyd's Rep 302; *The Anna H* [1995] 1 Lloyd's Rep 11.

(g) *The Bumbesti* [1999] 2 Lloyd's Rep 481; *The Despina GK* [1982] 2 Lloyd's Rep 555.

(h) Not to be confused with arrest of sister-ships owned by charterers, which are allowable: *The Sextum* [1982] 2 Lloyd's Rep 532; *The Span Terza* [1984] 1 Lloyd's Rep 119. Charterers include slot charterers: *Tychy* [1999] 2 Lloyd's Rep 11.

(i) *The Evpo Agnic* [1988] 2 Lloyd's Rep 411; *The Nazym Khikmet* [1996] 2 Lloyd's Rep 362.

(j) *The Moscanthy* [1971] 1 Lloyd's Rep 37; *The Tribels* [1985] 1 Lloyd's Rep 128.

Note: This table reflects only the general principle under relevant regimes, where exceptions may exist.

PART 2

THE MARITIME CODE OF THE PRC 1993

(Adopted at the 28th Meeting of the Standing Committee of the 7th National People's Congress on 7 November 1992, promulgated by Order No 64 of the President of the People's Republic of China on 7 November 1992, and effective as of 1 July 1993)

Table of Contents

Chapter 1 General provisions

Article 1

This Code is enacted for the purpose of regulating the relations arising from maritime transport and those pertaining to ships, securing and protecting the legitimate rights and interests of the parties concerned, and promoting the development of maritime transport, economy and trade.

Article 2

'Maritime transport' as referred to in this Code means the carriage of goods and passengers by sea, including sea-river and river-sea direct transport.

The provisions concerning contracts of carriage of goods by sea contained in Chapter 4 shall not be applicable to the maritime transport of goods between the ports of the People's Republic of China.

Article 3

'Ship' as referred to in this Code means a sea-going ship or other mobile unit, but does not include a ship or craft to be used for military or public service purposes, nor a small ship of less than 20 tons gross tonnage.

The term 'ship' as referred to in the preceding paragraph shall also include ship's apparel.

Article 4

Maritime transport and towage services between the ports of the People's Republic of China shall be undertaken only by ships flying the national flag of the People's Republic of China, except as otherwise provided for by laws or administrative rules and regulations.

No foreign ships may engage in the maritime transport or towage services between the ports of the People's Republic of China unless permitted by the competent authorities of transport and communications under the State Council.

Article 5

Ships are entitled to sail under the national flag of the People's Republic of China after being registered, as required by law, and granted the nationality of the People's Republic of China.

Illegally flying the national flag of the People's Republic of China by any ship is prohibited and relevant parties may be fined by the authorities concerned.

Article 6

All matters pertaining to maritime transport shall be administered by the competent authorities of transport and communications under the State Council. The specific measures governing such administration shall be worked out by such authorities and implemented after being submitted to and approved by the State Council.

Chapter 2 Ships

Section 1 Ownership of ships

Article 7

Ownership of a ship shall mean the shipowner's rights to lawfully possess, utilize, profit from and dispose of the ship.

Article 8

With respect to a State-owned ship operated by an enterprise owned by the whole people having the status of a legal person granted by the State, the provisions of the Code regarding the shipowner shall apply to that enterprise.

Article 9

The acquisition, transfer or extinction of the ownership of a ship shall be registered with the ship registration authorities; no acquisition, transfer or extinction of the ship's ownership shall be valid against a third party unless registered.

The transfer of the ownership of a ship shall be made by a contract in writing.

Article 10

Where a ship is jointly owned by two or more legal persons or individuals, the joint ownership thereof shall be registered with the ship registration authorities. The joint ownership of the ship shall not be valid against a third party unless registered.

Section 2 Mortgage of ships

Article 11

The right of mortgage with respect to a ship is the right of preferred compensation enjoyed by the mortgagee of that ship from the proceeds of an auction sale made in accordance with law where and when the mortgagor fails to pay his debt to the mortgagee secured by the mortgage of that ship.

Article 12

The owner of a ship or anyone authorised by him may effect a mortgage of the ship.

The mortgage of a ship shall be effected by a contract in writing.

Article 13

The mortgage of a ship shall be registered with the ship registration authorities jointly by the mortgagee and the mortgagor. No mortgage is valid against a third party unless it is registered.

The main items required for the registration of the mortgage of a ship shall be:

(1) name or designation and address of the mortgagee and the name or designation and address of the mortgagor of the ship;

(2) name and nationality of the mortgaged ship, and the authorities that issued the certificate of ownership and the certificate number thereof;

(3) amount of debt secured, the interest rate and the period for the repayment of the debt.

Information about the registration of mortgages of ships shall be available to the public on enquiry.

Article 14

A mortgage may be effected on a ship under construction.

In registering the mortgage of a ship under construction, the building contract of the ship shall also be submitted to the ship registration authorities.

Article 15

A mortgaged ship shall be insured by the mortgagor unless the contract provides otherwise. In the case where the ship is not insured, the mortgagee has the right to place the ship under insurance coverage and the mortgagor shall pay for the premium thereof.

Article 16

The effecting of a mortgage by the joint owners of a ship shall, unless otherwise agreed upon among the joint owners, be subject to the agreement of those joint owners who have more than two-thirds of the shares thereof.

The mortgage effected by the joint owners of a ship shall not be affected by virtue of the division of the ownership.

Article 17

Once a mortgage is effected on a ship, the ownership of the mortgaged ship shall not be transferred without the consent of the mortgagee.

Article 18

Where the mortgagee has transferred all or part of his right to the debt secured by the mortgaged ship to another person, the mortgage shall be transferred accordingly.

Article 19

Two or more mortgages may be effected on the same ship. The ranking of the mortgages shall be determined according to the dates of their respective registrations.

Where two or more mortgages are effected, the mortgagees shall be paid out of the proceeds of the auction sale of the ship in the order of registration of their respective mortgages. Mortgages registered on the same date shall rank equally for payment.

Article 20

Mortgages shall be extinguished when the mortgaged ship is lost. With respect to the compensation paid from the insurance coverage on account of the loss of the ship, the mortgagee shall be entitled to enjoy priority in compensation over other creditors.

Section 3 Maritime liens

Article 21

A maritime lien is the right of a claimant, subject to the provisions of Article 22, to take priority in compensation over shipowners, demise charterers or ship operators with respect to the ship which gave rise to the said claim.

Article 22

The following maritime claims shall be entitled to maritime liens:

(1) claims for wages, other remuneration, crew repatriation and social insurance costs due to the Master, crew members and other members of the complement in accordance with the relevant labour laws, administrative rules and regulations or labour contracts;

(2) claims in respect of loss of life or personal injury sustained in the operation of the ship;

(3) claims for ship's tonnage dues, pilotage dues, harbour dues and other port charges;

(4) claims for salvage reward;

(5) claims for loss of or damage to property resulting from tortious acts in the course of the operation of the ship.

Claims for oil pollution damage caused by a ship carrying more than 2,000 tons of oil in bulk as cargo that has a valid certificate attesting that the ship has oil pollution liability insurance coverage or other appropriate financial security are not within the scope of sub-paragraph (5) of the preceding paragraph.

Article 23

The maritime claims set out in paragraph 1 of Article 22 shall be satisfied in the order listed. However, any maritime claim set out in sub-paragraph (4) arising later than those under sub-paragraph (1)–(3) shall have priority over those under sub-paragraph (1)–(3).

Where there is more than one maritime claim under sub-paragraphs (1), (2), (3) or (5) of paragraph 1 of Article 22, they shall be satisfied at the same time regardless of their respective occurrences; where they cannot be paid in full, they shall be paid in proportion. Should there be more than one maritime claim under sub-paragraph (4), those arising later shall be satisfied first.

Article 24

The costs and expenses of enforcing maritime liens, preserving and selling the ship, distributing the proceeds of sale, and other expenses incurred for the common interests of the claimants, shall be deducted and paid first from the proceeds of the auction sale of the ship.

Article 25

A maritime lien shall have priority over a possessory lien, and a possessory lien shall have priority over a ship mortgage.

A possessory lien referred to in the preceding paragraph means the right of a ship builder or repairer to secure the cost of building or repairing the ship by means of detaining the ship in his possession when the other party to the contract fails in the performance thereof. A possessory lien shall be extinguished when the ship builder or repairer no longer possesses the ship he has built or repaired.

Article 26

Maritime liens shall not be extinguished by virtue of the transfer of the ownership of the ship, except those that have not been enforced within 60 days of a public notice of the transfer of the ownership of the ship made by a court at the request of the transferee when the transfer was effected.

Article 27

Where maritime claims provided for in Article 22 are transferred, the maritime liens attached thereto shall be transferred accordingly.

Article 28

A maritime lien shall be enforced by a court by arresting the ship that gave rise to the maritime lien.

Article 29

A maritime lien shall, except as provided for in Article 26, be extinguished in the following circumstances:

(1) the maritime claim attached secured by a maritime lien has not been enforced within one year of the existence of such a maritime lien;

(2) the ship in question has been the subject of a forced sale by the court;

(3) the ship has been lost.

The period of one year specified in sub-paragraph (1) of the preceding paragraph shall not be suspended or interrupted.

Article 30

The provisions of this section shall not affect the implementation of the limitation of liability for maritime claims provided for in Chapter 11.

Chapter 3 Master and crew

Section 1 Basic principles

Article 31

The term 'crew' means the entire complement of the ship, including the Master.

Article 32

The Master, deck officers, chief engineer, engineers, electrical engineer and radio operator must be in possession of appropriate certificates of competency.

Article 33

Chinese crew engaged in international voyages must possess the Seaman's Book and other relevant certificates issued by the harbour superintendency authorities of the People's Republic of China.

Article 34

In the absence of specific stipulations in this Code as regards the employment of the crew and labour-related rights and obligations, the provisions of the relevant laws and administrative rules and regulations shall apply.

Section 2 The Master

Article 35

The Master shall be responsible for the management and navigation of the ship.

Orders given by the Master within the scope of his functions and powers must be carried out by other members of the crew, the passengers and all persons on board.

The Master shall take necessary measures to protect the ship and persons, documents, postal items, goods and other property carried on board.

Article 36

To ensure the safety of the ship and all persons on board, the Master shall be entitled to confine, or take other necessary measures against those who have committed crimes or violated laws or regulations on board, and to guard against concealment, destruction or forging of evidence.

The Master, having taken actions as referred to in the preceding paragraph, shall make a written report of the case, which shall bear the signatures of the Master and of two or more others on board, and which shall be handed over, together with the offender, to the authorities concerned for disposition.

Article 37

The Master shall make entries in the log book of any occurrence on board of birth or death and shall issue a certificate to that effect in the presence of two witnesses. A death certificate shall be attached to it with a list of personal belongings of the deceased, and attestation shall be given by the Master to the will, if any, of the deceased. Both the death certificate and the will shall be taken into safe-keeping by the Master and handed over to the family members of the deceased or the organisations concerned.

Article 38

Where a casualty has occurred to a ship and the life and property on board have thus been threatened, the Master shall, with crew members and other persons on board under his command, make best efforts to save the ship. Should the foundering and loss of the ship have become inevitable, the Master may decide to abandon the ship. However, such abandonment shall be reported to the shipowner for approval except in case of emergency.

Upon abandoning of the ship, the Master must take all measures first to evacuate the passengers safely from the ship in an orderly way, then make arrangements for crew members to evacuate, while the Master shall be the last to evacuate.

Before leaving the ship, the Master shall direct the crew members to do their utmost to rescue the deck log book, the engine log book, the oil record book, the radio log book, the charts, documents and papers used in the current voyage, as well as valuables, postal items and cash money.

Article 39

The presence of a pilot on board shall not discharge the duty of the Master of management and navigation of the ship.

Article 40

Should the Master die or become unable to perform his duties for any reason, the deck officer with the highest rank shall act as the Master; before the ship sails from its next port of call, the shipowner shall appoint a new Master to take command.

Chapter 4 Contracts of carriage of goods by sea

Section 1 Basic principles

Article 41

A contract of carriage of goods by sea is a contract under which the carrier, against payment of freight, undertakes to carry by sea goods contracted for shipment by the shipper from one port to another.

Article 42

For the purposes of this Chapter:

(1) 'carrier' means any person by whom or in whose name a contract of carriage of goods by sea has been concluded with a shipper;

(2) 'actual carrier' means any person to whom the performance of the carriage of goods, or of part of the carriage, has been entrusted by the carrier, and includes any other person to whom such performance has been entrusted under a sub-contract;

(3) 'shipper' means:

   (a) any person by whom or in whose name or on whose behalf a contract of carriage of goods by sea has been concluded with a carrier;

   (b) any person by whom or in whose name or on whose behalf the goods have been delivered to the carrier involved in the contract of carriage of goods by sea;

(4) 'consignee' means the person who is entitled to take delivery of the goods;

(5) 'goods' includes live animals and containers, pallets or similar articles of transport supplied by the shipper for consolidating the goods.

Article 43

The carrier or the shipper may demand confirmation of a contract of carriage of goods by sea in writing. A voyage charter shall be effected in writing. Telegrams, telexes and telefaxes have the effect of written documents.

Article 44

Any stipulation in a contract of carriage of goods by sea or a bill of lading or other similar documents evidencing such a contract that derogates from the provisions of this Chapter shall be null and void. However, such nullity and voidness shall not affect the validity of other provisions of the contract or the bill of lading or other similar documents. A clause assigning the benefit of insurance of the goods in favour of the carrier or any similar clause shall be null and void.

Article 45

The provisions of Article 44 shall not prejudice any increase in the duties and obligations of the carrier besides those set out in this Chapter.

Section 2 Carrier's responsibilities

Article 46

The responsibilities of the carrier with regard to goods carried in containers cover the entire period during which the carrier is in charge of the goods, starting from the time the carrier has taken over the goods at the port of loading until the goods have been delivered at the port of discharge. The responsibility of the carrier with respect to non-containerised goods covers the period during which the carrier is in charge of the goods, starting from the time of loading of the goods onto the ship until the time the goods are discharged therefrom. During the period the carrier is in charge of the goods, the carrier shall be liable for the loss of or damage to the goods, except as otherwise provided for in this section.

The provisions of the preceding paragraph shall not prevent the carrier from entering into any agreement concerning carrier's responsibilities with regard to non-containerised goods prior to loading onto and after discharging from the ship.

Article 47

The carrier shall, before and at the beginning of the voyage, exercise due diligence to make the ship seaworthy, to properly man, equip and supply the ship and to make the holds, refrigerating and cool chambers and all other parts of the ship in which goods are carried, fit and safe for their reception, carriage and preservation.

Article 48

The carrier shall properly and carefully load, handle, stow, carry, keep, care for and discharge the goods carried.

Article 49

The carrier shall carry the goods to the port of discharge on the agreed or customary or geographically direct route.

Any deviation in saving or attempting to save life or property at sea or any reasonable deviation shall not be deemed to be an act deviating from the provisions of the preceding paragraph.

Article 50

Delay in delivery occurs when the goods have not been delivered at the designated port of discharge within the time expressly agreed upon.

The carrier shall be liable for loss of or damage to the goods caused by delay in delivery due to the fault of the carrier, except that arising or resulting from causes for which the carrier is not liable as provided for in the relevant Articles of this Chapter.

The carrier shall be liable for economic losses caused by delay in delivery of the goods due to the fault of the carrier, even if no loss of or damage to the goods had actually occurred, unless such economic losses had occurred from causes for which the carrier is not liable as provided for in the relevant Articles of this Chapter.

The person entitled to make a claim for the loss of goods may treat the goods as lost when the carrier has not delivered the goods within 60 days from the expiry of the time for delivery specified in paragraph 1 of this Article.

Article 51

The carrier shall not be liable for loss of or damage to the goods sustained during the period of the carrier's responsibility arising or resulting from any of the following causes:

(1) fault of the Master, crew members, pilot or servant of the carrier in the navigation or management of the ship;

(2) fire, unless caused by the actual fault of the carrier;

(3) *force majeure* and perils, dangers and accidents of the sea or other navigable waters;

(4) war or armed conflict;

(5) act of the government or competent authorities, quarantine restrictions or seizure under legal process;

(6) strikes, stoppages or restraint of labour;

(7) saving or attempting to save life or property at sea;

(8) act of the shipper or owner of the goods or their agents;

(9) nature or inherent vice of the goods;

(10) inadequacy of packing or insufficiency or illegibility of marks;

(11) latent defect of the ship not discoverable by due diligence;

(12) any other cause arising without the fault of the carrier or his servant or agent.

A carrier who is entitled to exoneration from the liability for compensation as provided for in the preceding paragraph shall, with the exception of the cause given in sub-paragraph (2), bear the burden of proof.

Article 52

The carrier shall not be liable for loss of or damage to the live animals arising or resulting from the special risks inherent in the carriage thereof. However, the carrier shall be bound to prove that he has fulfilled the special requirements of the shipper with regard to the carriage of the live animals and that under the circumstances of the sea carriage, the loss or damage has occurred due to the special risks inherent therein.

Article 53

Where the carrier intends to ship goods on deck, he shall do so in agreement with the shipper or in compliance with the custom of the trade or the relevant laws or administrative rules and regulations.

When the goods have been shipped on deck in accordance with the provisions of the preceding paragraph, the carrier shall not be liable for the loss of or damage to the goods caused by the special risks involved in such carriage.

If the carrier, in breach of the provisions of the first paragraph of this Article, has shipped the goods on deck and the goods have consequently suffered loss or damage, the carrier shall be liable thereof.

Article 54

Where loss, damage or delay in delivery has occurred from causes from which the carrier or his servant or agent is not entitled to exoneration from liability, together with another cause, the carrier shall be liable only to the extent that the loss, damage or delay in delivery is attributable to the causes from which the carrier is not entitled to exoneration from liability; however, the carrier shall bear the burden of proof with respect to the loss, damage or delay in delivery resulting from the other causes.

Article 55

The amount of indemnity for loss of the goods shall be calculated on the basis of the actual value of the goods so lost, while that for damage to the goods shall be calculated on the basis of the difference between the values of the goods before and after the damage, or on the basis of the expenses for the repair.

The actual value shall be the value of the goods at the time of shipment plus insurance and freight.

From the actual value referred to in the preceding paragraph, deduction shall be made, at the time of compensation, of the expenses that had been reduced or avoided as a result of the loss or damage occurred.

Article 56

The carrier's liability for the loss of or damage to the goods shall be limited to an amount equivalent to 666.67 Units of Account per package or other shipping unit, or two Units of Account per kilogram of the gross weight of the goods lost or damaged, whichever is the higher, except where the nature and value of the goods had been declared by the shipper before shipment and inserted in the bill of lading, or where a higher amount than the amount of limitation of liability set out in this Article had been agreed upon between the carrier and the shipper.

Where a container, pallet or similar article of transport is used to consolidate goods, the number of packages or other shipping units enumerated in the bill of lading as packed in such articles of transport shall be deemed to be the number of packages or shipping units. If not so enumerated, one article of transport shall be deemed to be one package or one shipping unit.

Where an article of transport is not owned or furnished by the carrier, such an article of transport shall be deemed to be one package or one shipping unit.

Article 57

The liability of the carrier for economic losses resulting from delay in delivery of the goods shall be limited to an amount equivalent to the freight payable for the goods so delayed. Where the loss of or damage to the goods has occurred concurrently with the delay in delivery thereof, the limitation of liability of the carrier shall be that as provided for in paragraph 1 of Article 56.

Article 58

The defences and limitation of liability provided for in this Chapter shall apply to any legal action brought against the carrier with regard to loss of or damage to or delay in delivery of goods covered by a contract of carriage of goods by sea, whether the claimant is a party to the contract or whether the action is founded in contract or in tort.

The provisions of the preceding paragraph shall apply if the action referred to in the preceding paragraph is brought against the carrier's servant or agent, and the carrier's servant or agent proves that his action was within the scope of his employment or agency.

Article 59

The carrier shall not be entitled to the benefit of the limitation of liability provided for in Article 56 or 57 if it is proved that the loss, damage or delay in delivery of the goods resulted from an act or omission of the carrier done with the intent to cause such loss, damage or delay or recklessly and with knowledge that such loss, damage or delay would probably result.

The servant or agent of the carrier shall not be entitled to the benefit of limitation of liability provided for in Article 56 or 57, if it is proved that the loss, damage or delay in delivery resulted from an act or omission of the servant or agent of the carrier done with the intent to cause such loss, damage or delay or recklessly and with knowledge that such loss, damage or delay would probably result.

Article 60

Where performance of the carriage or part thereof has been entrusted to an actual carrier, the carrier shall nevertheless remain responsible for the entire carriage according to the provisions of this Chapter. The carrier shall be responsible, in relation to the carriage performed by the actual carrier, for the act or omission of the actual carrier and of his servant or agent acting within the scope of his employment or agency.

Notwithstanding the provisions of the preceding paragraph, where a contract of carriage by sea provides explicitly that a specified part of the carriage covered by the said contract is to be performed by a named actual carrier other than the carrier, the contract may nevertheless provide that the carrier shall not be liable for the loss, damage or delay in delivery arising from an occurrence which takes place while the goods are in the charge of the actual carrier during such part of the carriage.

Article 61

The provisions with respect to the responsibility of the carrier contained in this Chapter shall be applicable to the actual carrier. Where an action is brought against the servant or agent of the actual carrier, the provisions contained in paragraph 2 of Article 58 and paragraph 2 of Article 59 shall apply.

Article 62

Any special agreement under which the carrier assumes obligations not provided for in this Chapter or waives rights conferred by this Chapter shall be binding upon the actual carrier when the actual carrier has agreed in writing to the contents thereof. The provisions of such a special agreement shall be binding upon the carrier whether the actual carrier has agreed to the contents or not.

Article 63

Where both the carrier and the actual carrier are liable, they shall be jointly and severally liable within the scope of such liability.

Article 64

If claims for compensation have been separately made against the carrier, the actual carrier and their servants or agents with regard to the loss of or damage to the goods, the aggregate amount of compensation shall not be in excess of the limitation provided for in Article 56.

Article 65

The provisions of Articles 60–64 shall not affect any right of recourse as between the carrier and the actual carrier.

Section 3 Shipper's responsibilities

Article 66

The shipper shall have the goods properly packed and shall guarantee the accuracy of the description, marks, number of packages or pieces, weight and quantity of the goods at the time of shipment and must indemnify the carrier against any loss resulting from inadequacy of packing or inaccuracies in the above-mentioned information.

The carrier's right to indemnification as provided for in the preceding paragraph shall not affect the obligation of the carrier under the contract of carriage of goods towards those other than the shipper.

Article 67

The shipper shall perform all necessary procedures at the port, customs, quarantine, inspection or other competent authorities with respect to the shipment of the goods and shall furnish the carrier with all relevant documents concerning the procedures the shipper has gone through. The shipper shall be liable for any damage to the interest of the carrier resulting from the inadequacy or inaccuracy or delay in delivery of such documents.

Article 68

At the time of shipment of dangerous goods, the shipper shall, in compliance with the regulations governing the carriage of such goods, ensure they are properly packed, distinctly marked and labelled and notify the carrier in writing of their proper description, nature and the precautions to be taken. Where the shipper fails to notify the carrier or notifies him inaccurately, the carrier may have such goods landed, destroyed or rendered innocuous when and where circumstances so require, without compensation. The shipper shall be liable to the carrier for any loss, damage or expense resulting from such shipment.

Notwithstanding the carrier's knowledge of the nature of the dangerous goods and his consent to their carriage, he may still have such goods landed, destroyed or rendered innocuous, without compensation, when they become an actual danger to the ship, the crew and other persons on board or to other goods. However, the provisions of this paragraph shall not prejudice the contribution in general average, if any.

Article 69

The shipper shall pay the freight to the carrier as agreed.

The shipper and the carrier may agree that the freight shall be paid by the consignee. However, such an agreement shall be noted in the transport documents.

Article 70

The shipper shall not be liable for loss sustained by the carrier or the actual carrier, or for damage sustained by the ship, unless such loss or damage was caused by the fault of the shipper, his servant or agent.

The servant or agent of the shipper shall not be liable for loss sustained by the carrier or the actual carrier or for damage sustained by the ship, unless the loss or damage was caused by the fault of the servant or agent of the shipper.

Section 4 Transport documents

Article 71

A bill of lading is a document which serves as evidence of the contract of carriage of goods by sea and the taking over or loading of the goods by the carrier, and based on which the carrier undertakes to deliver the goods against surrendering the same. A provision in the document stating that the goods are to be delivered to the order of a named person, or to order, or to bearer, constitutes such an undertaking.

Article 72

When the goods have been taken over by the carrier or have been loaded on board, the carrier shall, on demand of the shipper, issue to the shipper a bill of lading.

The bill of lading may be signed by a person authorised by the carrier. A bill of lading signed by the Master of the ship carrying the goods is deemed to have been signed on behalf of the carrier.

Article 73

A bill of lading shall contain the following particulars:

(1) description of the goods, mark, number of packages or pieces, weight or quantity, and a statement, if applicable, as to the dangerous nature of the goods;

(2) name and principal place of business of the carrier;

(3) name of the ship;

(4) name of the shipper;

(5) name of the consignee;

(6) port of loading and the date on which the goods were taken over by the carrier at the port of loading;

(7) port of discharge;

(8) place where the goods were taken over and the place where the goods are to be delivered in case of a multimodal transport bill of lading;

(9) date and place of issue of the bill of lading and the number of originals issued;

(10) payment of freight;

(11) signature of the carrier or of a person acting on his behalf.

In a bill of lading, the lack of one or more particulars referred to in the preceding paragraph does not affect the function of the bill of lading as such, provided that it nevertheless meets the requirements set forth in Article 71.

Article 74

If the carrier has issued, on demand of the shipper, a received-for-shipment bill of lading or other similar document before the goods are loaded on board, the shipper may surrender the same to the carrier in exchange for a shipped bill of lading when the goods have been loaded on board. The carrier may also note on a received-for-shipment bill of lading or other similar document the name of the carrying ship and the date of loading, and, when so noted, the received-for-shipment bill of lading or other similar document shall be deemed to constitute a shipped bill of lading.

Article 75

If the bill of lading contains particulars concerning the description, marks, number of packages or pieces, weight or quantity of the goods with respect to which the carrier or the other person issuing the bill of lading on his behalf knows or has reasonable grounds to suspect that such particulars do not accurately represent the goods actually received, or, where a shipped bill of lading is issued, loaded, or if he has had no reasonable means of checking, the carrier or such other person may make a note in the bill of lading specifying those inaccuracies, the grounds for suspicion or the lack of reasonable means of checking.

Article 76

If the carrier or the other person issuing a bill of lading on his behalf made no note in the bill of lading regarding the apparent order and condition of the goods, the goods shall be deemed to be in good order and condition.

Article 77

Except for a note made in accordance with the provisions of Article 75, the bill of lading issued by a carrier or other person acting on his behalf is *prima facie* evidence of the taking over or loading by the carrier of the goods as described therein. Proof to the contrary by the carrier shall not be admissible if the bill of lading has been transferred to a third party, including a consignee, who has acted in good faith in reliance on the description of the goods contained therein.

Article 78

The relationship between the carrier and the holder of the bill of lading with respect to their rights and obligations shall be determined in accordance with the bill of lading.

Neither the consignee nor the holder of the bill of lading shall be liable for the demurrage, dead freight and all other expenses in respect of loading occurred at the loading port unless the bill of lading clearly states that the aforesaid demurrage, dead freight and all other expenses shall be borne by the consignee and the holder of the bill of lading.

Article 79

The negotiability of a bill of lading shall be governed by the following provisions:

(1) a straight bill of lading is not negotiable;

(2) an order bill of lading may be negotiated with endorsement to order or endorsement in blank;

(3) a bearer bill of lading is negotiable without endorsement.

Article 80

Where a carrier has issued a document other than a bill of lading as evidence of the receipt of the goods to be carried, such a document is *prima facie* evidence of the conclusion of the contract of carriage of goods by sea and the taking over by the carrier of the goods as described therein.

Such documents that are issued by the carrier shall not be negotiable.

Section 5 Delivery of goods

Article 81

Unless notice of loss or damage is given in writing by the consignee to the carrier at the time of delivery of the goods by the carrier to the consignee, such delivery shall be deemed to be *prima facie* evidence of the delivery of the goods by the carrier as described in the transport documents and of the apparent good order and condition of such goods.

Where the loss of or damage to the goods is not apparent, the provisions of the preceding paragraph shall apply if the consignee has not given notice in writing within seven consecutive days after the day of the delivery of the goods, or, in the case of containerised goods, within 15 consecutive days after the day of the delivery thereof.

Notice in writing regarding loss or damage need not be given if the state of the goods has, at the time of delivery, been the subject of a joint survey or inspection by the carrier and the consignee.

Article 82

The carrier shall not be held liable if no notice on economic losses resulting from delay in delivery of the goods has been received from the consignee within 60 consecutive days from the day on which the goods were delivered by the carrier to the consignee.

Article 83

The consignee may, before taking delivery of the goods at the port of destination, and the carrier may, before delivering the goods at the port of destination, request that an inspection agency inspects the goods. The party requesting such inspection shall bear the cost thereof but is entitled to recover the same from the party causing the damage.

Article 84

The carrier and the consignee shall mutually provide reasonable facilities for the survey and inspection stipulated in Articles 81 and 83.

Article 85

Where the goods have been delivered by the actual carrier, notice in writing given by the consignee to the actual carrier under Article 81 shall have the same effect as that given to the carrier, and that given to the carrier shall have the same effect as that given to the actual carrier.

Article 86

If the goods were not taken delivery of at the port of discharge or if the consignee has delayed or refused the taking delivery of the goods, the Master may discharge the goods into warehouses or other appropriate places, and any expenses or risks arising there from shall be borne by the consignee.

Article 87

If freight, contribution in general average, demurrage to be paid to the carrier and other necessary charges paid by the carrier on behalf of the owner of the goods as well as other charges to be paid to the carrier have not been paid in full, nor has appropriate security been given, the carrier may have a lien, to a reasonable extent, on the goods.

Article 88

If goods under lien in accordance with the provisions of Article 87 have not been taken delivery of within 60 days from the day of the ship's arrival at the port of discharge, the carrier may apply to the court for an order for sale of the goods by auction; where the goods are perishable or the expenses for keeping such goods would exceed their value, the carrier may apply for an earlier sale by auction.

The proceeds from the auction sale shall be used to pay the expenses for the storage and auction sale of the goods, the freight and other related charges to be paid to the carrier. If the proceeds fall short of such expenses, the carrier is entitled to claim the difference from the shipper, whereas any amount in surplus shall be refunded to the shipper. If there is no way to make the refund and such surplus amount has not been claimed at the end of one full year after the auction sale, it shall go to the State Treasury.

Section 6 Cancellation of contract

Article 89

A shipper may request the cancellation of a contract of carriage of goods by sea before the ship sails from the port of loading. However, except as otherwise provided for in the contract, the shipper shall in this case pay half of the agreed amount of freight; if the goods have already been loaded on board, the shipper shall bear the expenses for the loading and discharge and other related charges.

Article 90

Either a carrier or a shipper may request the cancellation of the contract and neither shall be liable to the other if, due to *force majeure* or other causes not attributable to the fault of the carrier or the shipper; the contract could not be performed prior to the ship's sailing from its port of loading. If the freight has already been paid, it shall be refunded to the shipper, and, if the goods have already been loaded on board, the loading/discharge expenses shall be borne by the shipper. If a bill of lading has already been issued, it shall be returned by the shipper to the carrier.

Article 91

If, due to *force majeure* or any other causes not attributable to the fault of the carrier or the shipper, the ship could not discharge its goods at the port of destination as provided for in the contract of carriage, unless the contract provides otherwise, the Master shall be entitled to discharge the goods at a safe port or place near the port of destination and the contract of carriage shall be deemed to have been fulfilled.

In deciding on the discharge of the goods, the Master shall inform the shipper or the consignee and shall take the interests of the shipper or the consignee into consideration.

Section 7 Special provisions regarding voyage charter-party

Article 92

A voyage charter-party is a charter-party under which the shipowner charters out and the charterer charters in the whole or part of the ship's space for the carriage by sea of the intended goods from one port to another and the charterer pays the agreed amount of freight.

Article 93

A voyage charter-party shall contain, *inter alia*, the name of the shipowner, the name of the charterer, the name and nationality of the ship, its bale or grain capacity, description of the goods to be loaded, port of loading, port of destination, laydays, time for loading and discharge, payment of freight, demurrage, dispatch and other relevant matters.

Article 94

The provisions of Articles 47 and 49 shall apply to the shipowner under a voyage charter-party.

The other provisions in this Chapter regarding the rights and obligations of the parties to a contract shall apply to the shipowner and the charterer under a voyage charter-party only in the absence of relevant provisions or in the absence of provisions differing therefrom in the voyage charter.

Article 95

Where the holder of a bill of lading is not the charterer in the case of a bill of lading issued under a voyage charter-party, the rights and obligations of the carrier and the holder of the bill of lading shall be governed by the clauses of the bill of lading. However, if the clauses of the voyage charter-party are incorporated into the bill of lading, the relevant clauses of the voyage charter-party shall apply.

Article 96

The shipowner shall provide the intended ship. The intended ship may be substituted with the consent of the charterer. However, if the ship substituted does not meet the requirements of the charter-party, the charterer may reject the ship or cancel the charter. Should any damage or loss occur to the charterer as a result of the shipowner's failure to provide the intended ship due to his fault, the shipowner shall be liable for compensation.

Article 97

If the shipowner has failed to provide the ship within the laydays fixed in the charter, the charterer is entitled to cancel the charter-party. However, if the shipowner had notified the charterer of the delay of the ship and the expected date of its arrival at the port of loading, the charterer shall notify the shipowner of his decision whether the charter-party is cancelled or not within 48 hours after the receipt of the shipowner's notification.

Where the charterer has suffered losses as a result of delay in providing the ship due to the fault of the shipowner, the shipowner shall be liable to pay compensation.

Article 98

Under a voyage charter-party, the time for loading and discharge and the method of calculation thereof, as well as the rate of demurrage that would occur after the expiration of the laytime and the rate of dispatch money to be paid as a result of the completion of loading or discharge ahead of schedule, shall be fixed by the shipowner and the charterer by mutual agreement.

Article 99

The charterer may sub-let the ship he chartered, but the rights and obligations under the head charter shall not be affected.

Article 100

The charterer shall provide the intended goods, but he may replace the goods with the consent of the shipowner. However, if the goods replaced are detrimental to the interests of the shipowner, the shipowner shall be entitled to reject such goods and cancel the charter.

Where the shipowner has suffered losses as a result of the failure of the charterer to provide the intended goods, the charterer shall be liable to pay compensation.

Article 101

The shipowner shall discharge the goods at the port of discharge specified in the charter-party. Where the charter-party contains a clause allowing the choice of the port of discharge by the charterer, the Master may choose one from among the agreed selected ports to discharge the goods, if the charterer did not, as agreed in the charter-party, instruct in a timely manner as to the port chosen for discharging the goods. Where the charterer did not instruct in a timely manner as to the chosen port of discharge, as agreed in the charter-party, and the shipowner suffered loss thereby, the charterer shall be liable to pay compensation; where the charterer has suffered loss as a result of the shipowner's arbitrary choice of a port to discharge the goods, in disregard of the provisions in the relevant charter-party, the shipowner shall be liable to pay compensation.

Section 8 Special provisions regarding multimodal transport contracts

Article 102

A multimodal transport contract as referred to in this Code means a contract under which a multimodal transport operator undertakes to transport goods, against the payment of freight for the entire transport, from the place where the goods were received in his charge to the destination and to deliver them to the consignee by two or more different modes of transport, one of which is to be sea carriage.

A multimodal transport operator as referred to in the preceding paragraph means the person who has entered into a multimodal transport contract with the shipper either by himself or by another person acting on his behalf.

Article 103

The responsibility of a multimodal transport operator with respect to the goods under multimodal transport contract covers the period from the time he takes the goods in his charge to the time of their delivery.

Article 104

A multimodal transport operator shall be responsible for the performance of the multimodal transport contract or the procurement of the performance thereof, and shall be responsible for the entire transport.

The multimodal transport operator may enter into separate contracts with the carriers of the different modes defining their responsibilities with regard to the different sections of the transport under the multimodal transport contract. However, such separate contracts shall not affect the responsibility of the multimodal transport operator with respect to the entire transport.

Article 105

If loss of or damage to goods has occurred in a specified section of the transport, the provisions of the relevant laws and regulations governing that specific section of the multimodal transport shall be applicable to matters concerning the liability of the multimodal transport operator and the limitation thereof.

Article 106

If the section of transport in which the loss of or damage to the goods occurred could not be ascertained, the multimodal transport operator shall be liable for compensation in accordance with the stipulations regarding the carrier's liability and the limitation thereof as set out in this Chapter.

Chapter 5 Contracts of carriage of passengers by sea

Article 107

A contract of carriage of passengers by sea is a contract whereby a carrier undertakes to carry passengers and their luggage by sea from one port to another by ships suitable for that purpose against payment of fare by the passengers.

Article 108

For the purposes of this Chapter:

(1) 'carrier' means a person by whom or in whose name a contract of carriage of passengers by sea has been entered into with the passengers;

(2) 'actual carrier' means a person by whom the whole or part of the carriage of passengers has been performed as entrusted by the carrier, including those engaged in such carriage under a sub-contract;

(3) 'passenger' means a person carried under a contract of carriage of passengers by sea. A person who, with the consent of the carrier, is supervising the carriage of goods aboard a ship covered by a contract of carriage of goods is regarded as a passenger;

(4) 'luggage' means any article or vehicle shipped by the carrier under the contract of carriage of passengers by sea, with the exception of live animals;

(5) 'cabin luggage' means the luggage which the passenger has in his cabin or is otherwise in his possession, custody or control.

Article 109

The provisions regarding the responsibilities of the carrier contained in this Chapter shall be applicable to the actual carrier, and the provisions regarding the responsibilities of the servant or agent of the carrier contained in this Chapter shall be applicable to the servant or agent of the actual carrier.

Article 110

The ticket serves as evidence that a contract of carriage of passengers by sea has been entered into.

Article 111

The period of carriage for the carriage of passengers by sea commences at the time of embarkation of the passengers and terminates at the time of their disembarkation, including any period during which the passengers are transported by water from land to the ship or vice versa, if such cost of transport is included in the fare. However, the period of carriage does not include time when the passengers are at a marine terminal or station or on a quay or in or on any other port installations.

The period of carriage for the cabin luggage of the passengers shall be the same as that stipulated in the preceding paragraph. The period of carriage for luggage other than the cabin luggage commences at the time when the carrier or his servant or agent receives it into his charge and terminates at the time when the carrier or his servant or agent redelivers it to the passengers.

Article 112

A passenger travelling without a ticket or taking a higher class berth than booked or going beyond the distance paid for shall pay for the fare or the excess fare as required by relevant regulations, and the carrier may, according to the relevant regulations, charge an additional fare. Should any passenger refuse to pay, the Master is entitled to order him to disembark at a suitable place and the carrier has a right of recourse against him.

Article 113

No passenger may take on board or pack in their luggage contraband goods or any article of an inflammable, explosive, poisonous, corrosive or radioactive nature or other dangerous goods that would endanger the safety of life and property on board.

The carrier may have the contraband or dangerous goods which have been brought on board by the passenger or packed in his luggage in breach of the provisions of the preceding paragraph discharged, destroyed or rendered innocuous at any time and at any place or handed over to the appropriate authorities, without being liable for compensation.

The passenger shall be liable to pay compensation if any loss or damage occurs as a result of his breach of the provisions of paragraph 1 of this Article.

Article 114

During the period of carriage of the passengers and their luggage as provided for in Article 111, the carrier shall be liable for death of or personal injury to passengers or the loss of or damage to their luggage resulting from accidents caused by the fault or neglect of the carrier or his servant or agent committed within the scope of his employment or agency.

The claimant shall bear the burden of proof regarding the fault or neglect of the carrier or his servant or agent, with the exception, however, of the circumstances specified in paragraphs 3 and 4 of this Article.

If the death of or personal injury to the passengers or loss of or damage to the passengers' cabin luggage occurred as a result of shipwreck, collision, stranding, explosion, fire or the defect of the ship, it shall be presumed that the carrier or his servant or agent has committed a fault, unless proof to the contrary has been given by the carrier or his servant or agent.

As to any loss of or damage to luggage other than the passengers' cabin luggage, unless the carrier or his servant or agent proves to the contrary, it shall be presumed that the carrier or his servant or agent has committed a fault, no matter how the loss or damage was caused.

Article 115

If it is proved by the carrier that the death of or personal injury to the passenger or the loss of or damage to his luggage was caused by the fault of the passenger himself or the faults of the carrier and the passenger combined, the carrier's liability may be exonerated or appropriately mitigated.

If it is proved by the carrier that the death of or personal injury to the passenger or the loss of or damage to the passenger's luggage was intentionally caused by the passenger himself, or the death or personal injury was due to his health condition, the carrier shall not be liable thereof.

Article 116

The carrier shall not be liable for any loss of or damage to monies, gold, silver, jewellery, negotiable securities or other valuables of the passengers.

If the passenger has entrusted the above-mentioned valuables to the safe-keeping of the carrier under an agreement for that purpose, the carrier shall be liable for compensation in accordance with the provisions of Article 117. Where the limitation of liability agreed upon between the carrier and the passenger in writing is higher than that set out in Article 117, the carrier shall pay compensation in accordance with that higher amount.

Article 117

Except the circumstances specified in paragraph 4 of this Article, the limitation of liability of the carrier under each contract of carriage of passengers by sea shall be governed by the following:

(1) for death of or personal injury to a passenger: not exceeding 46,666 Units of Account per passenger;

(2) for loss of or damage to a passenger's cabin luggage: not exceeding 833 Units of Account per passenger;

(3) for loss of or damage to a passenger's vehicle including the luggage carried therein: not exceeding 3,333 Units of Account per vehicle;

(4) for loss of or damage to luggage other than that described in sub-paragraphs (2) and (3) above: not exceeding 1,200 Units of Account per passenger.

A carrier and a passenger may agree with respect to the deductibles applicable to compensation for loss of or damage to the passenger's vehicle and luggage other than vehicles. However, the deductible with respect to the loss of or damage to passengers' vehicles shall not exceed 117 Units of Account per vehicle, while the deductible for the loss of or damage to luggage other than a vehicle shall not exceed 13 Units of Account per piece of luggage per passenger. In calculating the amount of compensation for the loss of or damage to a passenger's vehicle or the luggage other than the vehicle, deduction shall be made of the agreed deductibles the carrier is entitled to.

A higher limitation of liability than that set out in sub-paragraph (1) above may be agreed upon between the carrier and the passenger in writing.

The limitation of liability of the carrier with respect to the carriage of passengers by sea between the ports of the People's Republic of China shall be fixed by the competent authorities of transport and communications under the State Council and implemented after its being submitted to and approved by the State Council.

Article 118

If it is proved that death of or personal injury to the passenger or loss of or damage to the passenger's luggage resulted from an act or omission of the carrier done with the intent to cause such loss or damage or recklessly and with knowledge that such death or personal injury or such loss or damage would probably result, the carrier may not invoke the provisions regarding the limitation of liability contained in Articles 116 and 117.

If it is proved that death of or personal injury to a passenger or loss of or damage to a passenger's luggage resulted from an act or omission of the servant or agent of the carrier done with the intent to cause such loss or damage or recklessly and with knowledge that such death or personal injury or such loss or damage would probably result, the servant or agent of the carrier may not invoke the provisions regarding the limitation of liability contained in Articles 116 and 117.

Article 119

In case of apparent damage to luggage, the passenger shall notify the carrier or his servant or agent in writing according to the following:

(1) notice with respect to cabin luggage shall be made before or at the time of his disembarkation;

(2) notice regarding luggage other than cabin luggage shall be made before or at the time of redelivery thereof.

If the damage to the luggage is not apparent and it is difficult for the passenger to discover such damage at the time of his disembarkation or of the redelivery of the luggage, or if the luggage has been lost, the passenger shall notify the carrier or his servant or agent in writing within 15 days from the day of disembarkation of the passenger or when the redelivery of the luggage should have taken place.

If the passenger fails to send in notice in writing in a timely manner in accordance with the provisions of sub-paragraphs (1) and (2) of this Article, it shall be presumed that the luggage has been received undamaged, unless the contrary is proved.

Where luggage has been jointly surveyed or inspected by the passenger and the carrier at the time of redelivery thereof, the above-mentioned notice need not be given.

Article 120

With regard to claims against a carrier's servant or agent, such servant or agent shall be entitled to invoke the provisions regarding defences and limitation of liability contained in Articles 115, 116 and 117 if such servant or agent proves that his act or omission was within the scope of his employment or agency.

Article 121

Where the performance of the carriage of passengers or part thereof has been entrusted by the carrier to an actual carrier, the carrier shall, as stipulated in this Chapter, remain liable for the entire carriage. Where the carriage is performed by the actual carrier, the carrier shall be liable for the act or omission of the actual carrier or the act or omission of his servant or agent within the scope of his employment or agency.

Article 122

Any special agreement under which the carrier assumes obligations not provided for in this Chapter or waives the rights conferred by this Chapter shall be binding upon the actual carrier where the actual carrier has expressly agreed in writing to the contents thereof. Such a special agreement shall be binding upon the carrier whether the actual carrier has agreed to its contents or not.

Article 123

Where both the carrier and the actual carrier are liable to pay compensation, they shall be liable jointly and severally within the scope of such liability.

Article 124

Where separate claims have been brought against the carrier, the actual carrier and their servants or agents with respect to the death of or personal injury to the passengers or the loss of or damage to their luggage, the aggregate amount of compensation shall not be in excess of the limitation prescribed in Article 117.

Article 125

The provisions of Articles 121–24 shall not affect any right of recourse between the carrier and the actual carrier.

Article 126

Any of the following clauses contained in a contract of carriage of passengers by sea shall be null and void:

(1) any clause that relieves the carrier of his statutory responsibility in respect of the passenger;

(2) any clause that reduces the limitation of liability of the carrier as contained in this Chapter;

(3) any clause that contains provisions contrary to those of this Chapter concerning burden of proof;

(4) any clause that restricts the right of the passenger to claim.

The nullity and voidness of the clauses set out in the preceding paragraph shall not prejudice the validity of the other clauses of the contract.

Chapter 6 Charter-parties

Section 1 Basic principles

Article 127

The provisions concerning the rights and obligations of the shipowner and the charterer in this Chapter shall apply only when there are no stipulations or no different stipulations in this regard in the charter-party.

Article 128

Charter-parties including time charter-parties and demise charter-parties shall be concluded in writing.

Section 2 Time charter-party

Article 129

A time charter-party is a contract under which the shipowner provides a designated manned ship to the charterer, and the charterer employs the ship during the contractual period for the agreed service against payment of hire.

Article 130

A time charter-party contains at least the name of the shipowner, the name of the charterer; the name, nationality, class, tonnage, capacity, speed and fuel consumption of the ship; the trading area; the agreed service, the contractual period, the time, place and conditions of delivery and redelivery of the ship; the hire and the way of its payment and other relevant matters.

Article 131

The shipowner shall deliver the ship within the time agreed upon in the charter-party.

Where a shipowner acts contrary to the preceding paragraph, the charterer is entitled to cancel the charter-party. However, if the shipowner has notified the charterer of the anticipated delay in delivery and has given an estimated time of arrival of the ship at the port of delivery, the charterer shall notify the shipowner, within 48 hours of the receipt of such notice from the shipowner, of his decision whether to cancel the charter-party or not.

The shipowner shall be liable for the charterer's loss resulting from the delay in delivery of the ship due to the shipowner's fault.

Article 132

At the time of delivery, the shipowner shall exercise due diligence to make the ship seaworthy. The ship delivered shall be fit for the intended service.

Where the shipowner acts against the provisions in the preceding paragraph, the charterer shall be entitled to cancel the charter-party and claim any losses resulting therefrom.

Article 133

During the charter period, if the ship is found to be unseaworthy, or its conditions are found not to comply with the charter-party, the shipowner shall take all reasonable measures to make the ship seaworthy or otherwise comply.

Where the ship has not been operated normally for 24 consecutive hours due to failure to maintain the seaworthiness or the other conditions as agreed upon, the charterer shall not pay the hire for the operating time so lost, unless such failure was caused by the charterer.

Article 134

The charterer is deemed to guarantee that the ship shall be employed in the agreed maritime transport between the safe ports or places within the trading area agreed upon.

If the charterer acts against the provisions of the preceding paragraph, the shipowner is entitled to cancel the charter-party and claim any losses resulting therefrom.

Article 135

A charterer shall guarantee that the ship shall be employed to carry the agreed lawful merchandise.

Where the ship is to be employed by the charterer to carry live animals or dangerous goods, prior consent of the shipowner is required.

The charterer shall be liable for any loss of the shipowner resulting from the charterer's violation of the provisions of paragraph 1 or paragraph 2 of this Article.

Article 136

A charterer shall be entitled to give the Master instructions with respect to the operation of the ship. However, such instructions shall not be inconsistent with the stipulations of the time charter-party.

Article 137

A charterer may sub-let the ship under charter-party, but he shall notify the shipowner of the sub-let immediately. The rights and obligations agreed upon in the head charter-party shall not be affected by a sub-charter-party.

Article 138

Where ownership of the ship under charter-party has been transferred by the shipowner, the rights and obligations agreed upon under the original charter-party shall not be affected. However, the shipowner shall inform the charterer thereof in a timely manner. After such transfer, the transferee and the charterer shall continue to perform the original charter.

Article 139

Should the ship be engaged in salvage operations during the charter-party period, the charterer shall be entitled to half of the amount of the payment for salvage operations after deducting therefrom the salvage expenses, compensation for damage, the portion due to crew members and other relevant costs.

Article 140

The charterer shall pay the hire as agreed upon in the charter-party. Where the charterer fails to pay the hire as agreed upon, the shipowner shall be entitled to cancel the charter-party and claim any losses resulting therefrom.

Article 141

If the charterer fails to pay the hire or other sums of money as agreed upon in the charter-party, the shipowner shall have a lien on the charterer's goods, other property on board and earnings from any sub-charter.

Article 142

When the charterer redelivers the ship to the shipowner, the ship shall be in the same good order and condition as it was at the time of delivery, fair wear and tear excepted.

Where, upon redelivery, the ship is not in the same good order and condition as it was at the time of delivery, the charterer shall be responsible for rehabilitation or to pay compensation.

Article 143

If, on the basis of a reasonable calculation, a ship may be able to complete its last voyage at around the time of redelivery specified in the charter-party and probably thereafter, the charterer is entitled to continue to use the ship in order to complete that voyage even if its time of redelivery will be overdue. During the extended period, the charterer shall pay the hire at the rate fixed by the charter-party, and, if the current market rate of hire is higher than that specified in the charter-party, the charterer shall pay the hire at the current market rate.

Section 3 Demise charter-party

Article 144

A demise charter-party is a charter-party under which the shipowner provides the charterer with an unmanned ship which the charterer shall possess, employ and operate within an agreed period and for which the charterer shall pay the shipowner the hire.

Article 145

A demise charter-party shall contain at least the name of the shipowner and the name of the charterer; the name, nationality, class, tonnage and capacity of the ship; the trading area; the employment of the ship and the charter period; the time, place and condition of delivery and redelivery; the survey, maintenance and repair of the ship; the hire and its payment; the insurance of the ship; the time and condition for the termination of the charter-party and other relevant matters.

Article 146

The shipowner shall deliver the ship and its certificates to the charterer at the port or place and time as stipulated in the charter-party. At the time of delivery, the shipowner shall exercise due diligence to make the ship seaworthy.

The ship delivered shall be fit for the agreed service.

Where the shipowner fails to comply with the preceding paragraph, the charterer shall be entitled to cancel the charter-party and claim any losses resulting therefrom.

Article 147

The charterer shall be responsible for the maintenance and repair of the ship during the demise charter period.

Article 148

During the demise charter period, the ship shall be insured, at the value agreed upon in the charter-party and as agreed by the shipowner, by the charterer at his expense.

Article 149

During the demise charter period, should the charterer's possession, employment or operation of the ship have affected the interests of the shipowner or caused any losses thereto, the charterer shall be liable to eliminate the harmful effect or to pay compensation for the losses.

Should the ship be arrested due to any disputes over its ownership or debts owed by the shipowner, the shipowner is deemed to have guaranteed that the interest of the charterer is not affected. The shipowner shall be liable to pay compensation for any losses suffered by the charterer thereby.

Article 150

During the demise charter period, the charterer shall not assign the rights and obligations stipulated in the charter-party or sub-let the ship under demise charter-party without the shipowner's consent in writing.

Article 151

The shipowner shall not establish any mortgage of the ship during the demise charter period without the prior consent in writing by the charterer.

Where the shipowner fails to comply with the preceding paragraph and thereby causes losses to the charterer, the shipowner shall be liable to pay compensation.

Article 152

The charterer shall pay the hire as stipulated in the charter-party. In default of payment by the charterer for seven consecutive days or more after the time as agreed in the charter-party for such payment, the shipowner is entitled to cancel the charter-party, without prejudice to any claim for the loss arising from the charterer's default.

Should the ship be lost or missing, payment of hire shall cease from the day when the ship was lost or last heard of. Any hire paid in advance shall be refunded in proportion.

Article 153

The provisions of Article 134, paragraph 1 of Article 135, Article 142 and Article 143 shall be applicable to demise charter-parties.

Article 154

The ownership of a ship under demise charter-party containing a lease-purchase clause shall be transferred to the charterer when the charterer has paid off the lease-purchase price to the shipowner as stipulated in the charter-party.

Chapter 7 Contracts of sea towage

Article 155

A contract of sea towage is a contract whereby a tugowner undertakes to tow an object by sea with a tug from one place to another and the tow-party pays the towage.

The provisions of this Chapter are not applicable to towage service rendered to ships within the port area.

Article 156

A contract of sea towage shall be made in writing. Its contents shall include at least the name and address of the tugowner; the name and address of the tow-party; the name and main particulars of the tug and the name and main particulars of the object to be towed; the horse power of the tug; place of commencement of the towage and the destination; the date of commencement of the towage; towage price and the way of payment thereof; as well as other relevant matters.

Article 157

The tugowner shall, before and at the beginning of the towage, exercise due diligence to make the tug seaworthy and towworthy and to properly man the tug and equip it with gears and tow lines and to provide all other necessary supplies and appliances for the intended voyage.

The tow-party shall, before and at the beginning of the towage, make all necessary preparations and exercise due diligence to make the object to be towed towworthy and shall give a true account of the object to be towed and provide the certificate of towworthiness and other documents issued by the relevant survey and inspection organisations.

Article 158

If, before the commencement of the towage service, due to *force majeure* or other causes not attributable to the fault of either party, the towage contract cannot be performed, either party may cancel the contract and neither shall be liable to the other. In such event, the towage price that had already been paid shall be returned to the tow-party by the tugowner, unless otherwise agreed upon in the towage contract.

Article 159

If, after the commencement of the towage service, due to *force majeure* or other causes not attributable to the fault of either party, the towage contract cannot be performed, either party may cancel the towage contract and neither shall be liable to the other.

Article 160

Where the object towed could not reach its destination due to *force majeure* or other causes not attributable to the fault of either party, unless the towage contract provides otherwise, the tugowner may deliver the object towed to the tow-party or its agent at a place near the destination or at a safe port or an anchorage chosen by the Master of the tug, and the contract of towage shall be deemed to have been fulfilled.

Article 161

Where the tow-party fails to pay the towage price or other reasonable expenses as agreed, the tugowner shall have a lien on the object towed.

Article 162

If, in the course of the sea towage, damage suffered by the tugowner or the tow-party was caused by the fault of one of the parties, the party at fault shall be liable to pay compensation. If the damage was caused by the fault of both parties, both parties shall be liable to pay compensation in proportion to the extent of their respective faults.

Notwithstanding the provisions of the preceding paragraph, the tugowner shall not be liable if he proves that the damage suffered by the tow-party is due to one of the following causes:

(1) fault of the Master or other crew members of the tug or the pilot or other servants or agents of the tugowner in the navigation and management of the tug;

(2) fault of the tug in saving or attempting to save life or property at sea.

The provisions of this Article shall only apply if and when there are no provisions or no different provisions in this regard in the sea towage contract.

Article 163

If death of or personal injury to a third party or damage to property thereof has occurred during sea towage due to the fault of the tugowner or the tow-party, the tugowner and the tow-party shall be liable jointly and severally to that third party. Except as otherwise provided for in the towage contract, the party that has jointly and severally paid compensation in an amount exceeding the proportion for which it is liable shall have the right of recourse against the other party.

Article 164

Where a tugowner tows a barge owned or operated by him to transport goods by sea from one port to another, it shall be deemed to be an act of carriage of goods by sea.

Chapter 8 Collision of ships

Article 165

Collision of ships means an accident arising from the touching of ships at sea or in other navigable waters adjacent thereto.

Ships referred to in the preceding paragraph shall include those non-military or public service ships or craft that collide with the ships mentioned in Article 3.

Article 166

After a collision, the Master of each of the ships in collision is bound, so far as he can without serious danger to his ship and persons on board, to render assistance to the other ship and persons on board.

The Masters of collided ships are likewise bound, so far as possible, to make known to the other ship the name of his ship, its port of registry, port of departure and port of destination.

Article 167

Neither of the parties shall be liable to the other if the collision is caused by *force majeure* or other causes not attributable to the fault of either party or if the cause thereof is left in doubt.

Article 168

If the collision is caused by the fault of one of the ships, the one at fault shall be liable thereof.

Article 169

If the colliding ships are all at fault, each ship shall be liable in proportion to the extent of its fault; if the respective faults are equal in proportion or, if it is impossible to determine the extent of the proportion of the respective faults, the liability of the colliding ships shall be apportioned equally.

The ships at fault shall be liable for the damage to the ship, the goods and other property on board pursuant to the proportions prescribed in the preceding paragraph. Where damage is caused to the property of a third party, the liability of any of the colliding ships to pay compensation shall not exceed that proportion.

If the ships at fault have caused loss of life or personal injury to a third party, they shall be jointly and severally liable therefor. If a ship has paid an amount of compensation in excess of the proportion prescribed in paragraph 1 of this Article, it shall have the right of recourse against the other ship(s) at fault.

Article 170

Where a ship has caused damage to another ship and persons, goods or other property on board that ship, either by the execution or non-execution of a manoeuvre or by the non-observance of navigation regulations, even if no collision has actually occurred, the provisions of this Chapter shall apply.

Chapter 9 Salvage at sea

Article 171

The provisions of this Chapter shall apply to salvage operations rendered at sea or any other navigable waters adjacent thereto to ships and other property in distress.

Article 172

For the purposes of this Chapter:

(1) 'ship' means any ship referred to in Article 3 and any other non-military, public service ship or craft that has been involved in a salvage operation therewith;

(2) 'property' means any property not permanently and intentionally attached to the shoreline and includes freight at risk;

(3) 'payment' means any reward, remuneration or compensation for salvage operations to be paid by the salved party to the salvor pursuant to the provisions of this Chapter.

Article 173

The provisions of this Chapter shall not apply to fixed or floating platforms or mobile offshore drilling units when such platforms or units are on location engaged in the exploration, exploitation or production of sea-bed mineral resources.

Article 174

Every Master is bound, so far as he can without serious danger to his ship and persons on board, to render assistance to any person in danger of being lost at sea.

Article 175

A contract for salvage operations at sea is concluded when an agreement has been reached between the salvor and the salved party regarding the salvage operations to be undertaken.

The Master of a ship in distress shall have the authority to conclude a contract for salvage operations on behalf of the shipowner. The Master of the ship in distress or its owner shall have the authority to conclude a contract for salvage operations on behalf of the owner of property on board.

Article 176

The salvage contract may be modified by a judgment of a court which has entertained the suit brought by either party, or modified by an award of the arbitration organisation to which the dispute has been submitted for arbitration upon the agreement of the parties, under any of the following circumstances:

(1) the contract has been entered into under undue influence or the influence of danger and its terms are obviously inequitable;

(2) the payment under the contract is in an excessive degree too large or too small for the services actually rendered.

Article 177

During a salvage operation, the salvor shall owe a duty to the salved party to:

(1) carry out the salvage operation with due care;

(2) exercise due care to prevent or minimise pollution damage to the environment;

(3) seek the assistance of other salvors where reasonably necessary;

(4) accept the reasonable request of the salved party to seek the participation in the salvage operation of other salvors. However, if the request is not well founded, the amount of payment due to the original salvor shall not be affected.

Article 178

During a salvage operation, the party salved is under an obligation to the salvor to:

(1) co-operate fully with the salvor;

(2) exercise due care to prevent or minimise the pollution damage to the environment;

(3) promptly accept the request of the salvor to take delivery of the ship or property salved when such ship or property has been brought to a place of safety.

(1) the salvage operation is carried out as a duty to normally perform a towage contract or other service contract, with the exception, however, of providing special services beyond the performance of this duty;
(2) the salvage operation is carried out in spite of the express and reasonable prohibition on the part of the Master of the ship in distress, the owner of the ship in question and the owner of the other property.

Article 187

Where the salvage operations have become necessary or more difficult due to the fault of the salvor or where the salvor has committed fraud or otherwise conducted himself dishonestly, the salvor shall be deprived of the whole or part of the payment payable to him.

Article 188

After the completion of the salvage operation, the party salved shall, at the request of the salvor, provide satisfactory security for salvage reward and other charges.

Without prejudice to the provisions of the preceding paragraph, the owner of the ship salved shall, before the release of the goods, use his best endeavours to cause the owners of property salved to provide satisfactory security for the share of the payment that they ought to bear.

Without the consent of the salvor, the ship or other property salved shall not be removed from the port or place at which they first arrived after the completion of the salvage operation, until satisfactory security has been provided with respect to the ship or other property salved, as demanded by the salvor.

Article 189

A court or arbitration organisation handling the salvor's claim for payment may, in light of the specific circumstances and under fair and just terms, decide or make an award ordering the party salved to pay on account an appropriate amount to the salvor.

On the basis of a payment on account made by the party salved in accordance with the provisions of the preceding paragraph, the security provided under Article 188 shall be reduced accordingly.

Article 190

If the party whose property is salved has neither made the payment nor provided satisfactory security for the ship and other property salved after 90 days of the salvage, the salvor may apply to the court for an order of forced sale by auction. With respect to the ship or the property salved that cannot be kept or cannot be properly kept, or where the storage charge to be incurred may exceed its value, the salvor may apply for an earlier forced sale by auction.

The proceeds of sale shall, after deduction of the expenses incurred for the storage and sale, be used for the payment in accordance with the provisions of this Code. The remainder, if any, shall be returned to the party salved, and, if there is no way to return the remainder or if the remainder has not been claimed after one year of the forced sale, it shall go to the State Treasury. In case of any deficiency, the salvor has the right of recourse against the party salved.

Article 191

The provisions of this Chapter shall apply to the salvor's right to the payment for the salvage operations carried out between the ships of the same owner.

Article 192

With respect to salvage operations performed or controlled by the relevant competent authorities of the State, the salvors shall be entitled to avail themselves of the rights and remedies provided for in this Chapter in respect of salvage operations.

Chapter 10 General average

Article 193

General average means extraordinary sacrifice or expenditure intentionally and reasonably made or incurred for the common safety for the purpose of preserving from peril the ship, goods or other property involved in a common maritime adventure.

Loss or damage sustained by the ship or goods through delay, whether on the voyage or subsequently, such as demurrage and loss of market as well as other indirect losses, shall not be admitted as general average.

Article 194

When a ship, after having been damaged in consequence of accident, sacrifice or other extraordinary circumstances, has entered a port or place of refuge or returned to its port or place of loading to effect repairs which are necessary for the safe prosecution of the voyage, then port charges paid, wages and maintenance of the crew incurred and fuel and stores consumed during the extra period of detention in such port or place, as well as loss or damage and charges arising from the discharge, storage, reloading and handling of the goods, fuel, stores and other property on board in order to have the repairs done shall be allowed as general average.

Article 195

Any extra expense incurred in place of another expense which would have been allowed as general average shall be deemed to be general average and so allowed, but the amount of such expense incurred shall not be in excess of the general average expense avoided.

Article 196

The burden of proof shall be upon the party claiming in general average to show that the loss or expense claimed is properly allowable as general average.

Article 197

Rights to contribution in general average shall not be affected, though the event which gave rise to the sacrifice or expenditure may have been due to the fault of one of the parties to the adventure. However, this shall not prejudice any remedies or defences which may be open against or to that party in respect of such fault.

Article 198

The amounts of sacrifice of the ship, goods and freight shall be respectively determined as follows:

(1) The amount of sacrifice of the ship shall be calculated on the basis of the repair cost of the ship actually paid, from which any reasonable deduction in respect of 'new for old' being made. Where the ship has not been repaired after the sacrifice, the amount of sacrifice thereof shall be calculated on the basis of the reasonable reduced value of ship after the general average sacrifice. Such amount shall not exceed the estimated cost of repair.

Where the ship is an actual total loss or where the cost of repair would exceed the value of the ship after the repair, the amount of sacrifice of the ship shall be calculated on the basis of the estimated sound value of the ship, less the estimated cost of repair not allowable as general average, as well as the value of the ship after the damage.

(2) The amount of sacrifice of the goods already lost shall be calculated on the basis of the value of the goods at the time of shipment plus insurance and freight, from which the freight that need not be paid due to the sacrifice made being deducted. For damaged goods that had already been sold before an agreement was reached on the extent of the damage sustained, the amount of sacrifice thereof shall be calculated on the basis of the difference between the value of the goods at the time of shipment plus insurance and freight, and the net proceeds of the goods so sold.

(3) The amount of sacrifice of freight shall be calculated on the basis of the amount of loss of freight on account of the sacrifice of the goods, from which the operating expenses that ought to be paid in order to earn such freight but need not be paid because of the sacrifice shall be deducted.

Article 199

Contribution in general average shall be made in proportion to the contributory values of the respective beneficiaries.

The contributory value in general average by the ship, goods and freight shall be determined as follows:

(1) The contributory value of the ship shall be calculated on the basis of the sound value of the ship at the place where the voyage ends, from which any damage that does not come under general average sacrifice being deducted; or on the basis of the actual value of the ship at the place where the voyage ends plus the amount of general average sacrifice.

(2) The contributory value of the goods shall be calculated on the basis of the value of the goods at the time of shipment plus insurance and freight, from which damage that does not come under the general average sacrifice and the carrier's freight at risk shall be deducted. Where goods had been sold before the ship's arrival at the port of destination, their value for contribution shall be the net proceeds plus the amount of general average sacrifice.

Passenger's luggage and personal belongings shall not be included in the value for contribution.

(3) The contributory value of freight shall be calculated on the basis of the amount of freight at the risk of the carrier and which the carrier is entitled to collect at the end of the voyage, less any expense incurred for the prosecution of the voyage after the general average, in order to earn the freight, plus the amount of general average sacrifice.

Article 200

Goods undeclared or wrongfully declared shall be liable for the contribution to general average, but special sacrifice sustained by such goods shall not be allowed as general average.

Where the value of goods has been improperly declared at a value below their actual value, the contribution to general average shall be made on the basis of their actual value and, where a general average sacrifice has occurred, the amount of sacrifice shall be calculated on the basis of the declared value.

Article 201

Interest shall be allowed on general average sacrifice and general average expenses paid on account. A commission shall be allowed for the general average expenses paid on account, except those for the wages and maintenance of the crew and fuel and store consumed.

Article 202

Contributing parties shall provide security for general average contribution at the request of parties that have an interest therein.

Where security has been provided in the form of cash deposits, such deposits shall be made in a bank by an average adjuster in the name of a trustee.

The provision, use and refund of the deposits shall be without prejudice to the ultimate liability of the contributing parties.

Article 203

The adjustment of general average shall be governed by the average adjustment rules agreed upon in the relevant contract. In the absence of such an agreement in the contract, the relevant provisions contained in this Chapter shall apply.

Chapter 11 Limitation of liability for maritime claims

Article 204

Shipowners and salvors may limit their liability in accordance with the provisions of this Chapter for claims set out in Article 207.

Shipowners referred to in the preceding paragraph include the charterer and the operator of a ship.

Article 205

If the claims set out in Article 207 are not made against shipowners or salvors themselves but against persons for whose act, neglect or default the shipowners or salvors are responsible, such persons may limit their liability in accordance with the provisions of this Chapter.

Article 206

Where an assured may limit his liability in accordance with the provisions of this Chapter, an insurer liable for the maritime claims shall be entitled to the limitation of liability under this Chapter to the same extent as the assured.

Article 207

Except as provided otherwise in Articles 208 and 209, with respect to the following maritime claims, a person liable may limit his liability in accordance with the provisions of this Chapter, whatever the basis of liability may be:

(1) claims in respect of loss of life or personal injury or loss of or damage to property including damage to harbour works, basins and waterways and aids to navigation occurring on board or in direct connection with the operation of the ship or with salvage operations, as well as consequential damages resulting therefrom;

(2) claims in respect of loss resulting from delay in delivery in the carriage of goods by sea or from delay in the arrival of passengers or their luggage;

(3) claims in respect of other loss resulting from infringement of rights other than contractual rights occurring in direct connection with the operation of the ship or salvage operations;

(4) claims of a person other than the person liable in respect of measures taken to avert or minimise loss for which the person liable may limit his liability in accordance with the provisions of this Chapter, and further loss caused by such measures.

All the claims set out in the preceding paragraph may be entitled to limitation of liability regardless of the way they are brought. However, with respect to the remuneration set out in sub-paragraph (4) for which a person liable pays as agreed in the contract, in relation to the obligation for payment, the person liable may not invoke the provisions on limitation of liability of this Article.

Article 208

The provisions of this Chapter shall not be applicable to the following claims:

(1) claims for salvage payment or contribution in general average;

(2) claims for oil pollution damage under the International Convention on Civil Liability for Oil Pollution Damage to which the People's Republic of China is a party;

(3) claims for nuclear damage under the International Convention on Limitation of Liability for Nuclear Damage to which the People's Republic of China is a party;

(4) claims against the shipowner of a nuclear ship for nuclear damage;

(5) claims by servants of the shipowner or salvor, if under the law governing the contract of employment, the shipowner or salvor is not entitled to limit his liability or if he is by law only permitted to limit his liability to an amount greater than that provided for in this Chapter.

Article 209

A person liable shall not be entitled to limit his liability in accordance with the provisions of this Chapter, if it is proved that the loss resulted from his act or omission done with the intent to cause such loss or recklessly and with knowledge that such loss would probably result.

Article 210

The limitation of liability for maritime claims, except as otherwise provided for in Article 211, shall be calculated as follows:

(1) In respect of claims for loss of life or personal injury:

(a) 333,000 Units of Account for a ship with a gross tonnage ranging from 300 to 500 tons;

(b) for a ship with a gross tonnage in excess of 500 tons, the limitation under (a) above shall be applicable to the first 500 tons and the following amounts in addition to that set out under (a) shall be applicable to the gross tonnage in excess of 500 tons:

for each ton from 501 to 3,000 tons: 500 Units of Account;

for each ton from 3,001 to 30,000 tons: 333 Units of Account;

for each ton from 30,001 to 70,000 tons: 250 Units of Account;

for each ton in excess of 70,000 tons: 167 Units of Account.

(2) In respect of claims other than that for loss of life or personal injury:

(a) 167,000 Units of Account for a ship with a gross tonnage ranging from 300 to 500 tons;

(b) for a ship with a gross tonnage in excess of 500 tons, the limitation under (a) above shall be applicable to the first 500 tons, and the following amounts in addition to that under (a) shall be applicable to the part in excess of 500 tons:

for each ton from 501 to 30,000 tons: 167 Units of Account;

for each ton from 30,001 to 70,000 tons: 125 Units of Account;

for each ton in excess of 70,000 tons: 83 Units of Account.

(3) Where the amount calculated in accordance with sub-paragraph (1) above is insufficient for payment of claims for loss of life or personal injury set

out therein in full, the amount calculated in accordance with sub-paragraph (2) shall be available for payment of the unpaid balance of claims under sub-paragraph (1), and such unpaid balance shall rank rateably with claims set out under sub-paragraph (2).

(4) However, without prejudice to the right of claims for loss of life or personal injury under sub-paragraph (3), claims in respect of damage to harbour works, basins and waterways and aids to navigation shall have priority over other claims under sub-paragraph (2).

(5) The limitation of liability for any salvor not operating from any ship or for any salvor operating solely on the ship to, or in respect of which, he is rendering salvage services, shall be calculated according to a gross tonnage of 1,500 tons.

The limitation of liability for ships with a gross tonnage not exceeding 300 tons and those engaging in transport services between the ports of the People's Republic of China as well as those for other coastal works shall be agreed by the competent authorities of transport and communications under the State Council and implemented after its being submitted to and approved by the State Council.

Article 211

In respect of claims for loss of life or personal injury to passengers carried by sea, the limitation of liability of the shipowner thereof shall be an amount of 46,666 Units of Account multiplied by the number of passengers which the ship is authorised to carry according to the ship's relevant certificate, but the maximum amount of compensation shall not exceed 25,000,000 Units of Account.

The limitation of liability for claims for loss of life or personal injury to passengers carried by sea between the ports of the People's Republic of China shall be agreed by the competent authorities of transport and communications under the State Council and implemented after its being submitted to and approved by the State Council.

Article 212

Limitation of liability under Articles 210 and 211 shall apply to the aggregate of all claims that may arise on any given occasion against shipowners and salvors themselves, and any person for whose act, neglect or fault the shipowners and the salvors are responsible.

Article 213

Any person liable claiming limitation of liability under this Code may constitute a limitation fund with a court having jurisdiction. The fund shall be constituted in the sum of such an amount set out respectively in Articles 210 and 211, together with interest thereon from the date of the occurrence giving rise to the liability until the date of the constitution of the fund.

Article 214

Where a limitation fund has been constituted by a person liable, any person having made a claim against the person liable may not exercise any right against any assets of the person liable. Where any ship or other property belonging to the person constituting the fund has been arrested or attached, or, where a security has been provided by such person, the court shall order without delay the release of the ship arrested or the property attached or the return of the security provided.

Article 215

Where a person entitled to limitation of liability under the provisions of this Chapter has a counter-claim against the claimant arising out of the same occurrence, their respective claims shall be set off against each other and the provisions of this Chapter shall only apply to the balance, if any.

Chapter 12 Contracts of marine insurance

Section 1 Basic principles

Article 216

A contract of marine insurance is a contract whereby the insurer undertakes, as agreed, to indemnify loss to the subject matter insured and liability of the insured caused by perils covered by the insurance against the payment of an insurance premium by the insured.

The covered perils referred to in the preceding paragraph mean any maritime perils agreed upon between the insurer and the insured, including perils occurring in inland rivers or on land which is related to a maritime adventure.

Article 217

A contract of marine insurance shall at least include the following items:

(1) name of the insurer;

(2) name of the insured;

(3) subject matter insured;

(4) insured value;

(5) insured amount;

(6) perils insured against and perils excepted;

(7) duration of insurance coverage;

(8) insurance premium.

Article 218

The following items may be the subject matter of marine insurance:

(1) ship;

(2) cargo;

(3) income from the operation of the ship including freight, charter hire and passenger's fare;

(4) expected profit on cargo;
(5) crew's wages and other remuneration;
(6) liabilities to a third person;
(7) other property which may sustain loss from a maritime peril and the liability and expenses arising therefrom.

The insurer may reinsure the insurance of the subject matter enumerated in the preceding paragraph. Unless otherwise agreed in the contract, the original insured shall not be entitled to the benefit of the reinsurance.

Article 219

The insurable value of the subject matter insured shall be agreed upon between the insurer and the insured.

Where no insurable value has been agreed upon between the insurer and the insured, the insurable value shall be calculated as follows:

(1) the insurable value of the ship shall be the value of the ship at the time when the insurance liability commences, being the total value of the ship's hull, machinery, equipment, fuel, stores, gear, provisions and fresh water on board as well as the insurance premium;
(2) the insurable value of the cargo shall be the aggregate of the invoice value of the cargo or the actual value of the non-trade commodity at the place of shipment, plus freight and insurance premium when the insurance liability commences;
(3) the insurable value of the freight shall be the aggregate of the total amount of freight payable to the carrier and the insurance premium when the insurance liability commences;
(4) the insurable value of other subject matter insured shall be the aggregate of the actual value of the subject matter insured and the insurance premium when the insurance liability commences.

Article 220

The insured amount shall be agreed upon between the insurer and the insured.

The insured amount shall not exceed the insured value. Where the insured amount exceeds the insured value, the portion in excess shall be null and void.

Section 2 Conclusion, termination and assignment of contract

Article 221

A contract of marine insurance comes into being after the insured puts forth a proposal for insurance and the insurer agrees to accept the proposal and the insurer and the insured agree on the terms and conditions of the insurance. The insurer shall issue to the insured an insurance policy or other certificate of insurance in a timely manner, and the contents of the contract shall be contained therein.

Article 222

Before a contract is concluded, an insured shall truthfully inform the insurer of material circumstances which the insured has knowledge of or ought to have knowledge of in the ordinary course of business and which may influence the insurer in fixing the premium or determining whether he agrees to insure.

The insured need not inform the insurer of the facts which the insurer has knowledge of or ought to have knowledge of in the ordinary course of business.

Article 223

Upon failure of the insured to truthfully inform the insurer of the material circumstances referred to in paragraph 1 of Article 222 due to his intentional act, the insurer has the right to terminate the contract without refunding the premium. The insurer shall not be liable for any loss arising from the perils insured against before the contract is terminated.

If, not due to the insured's intentional act, the insured did not truthfully inform the insurer of the material circumstances set out in paragraph 1 of Article 222, the insurer has the right to terminate the contract or to demand a corresponding increase in the premium. Where the contract is terminated by the insurer, the insurer shall be liable for the loss arising from the perils insured against which occurred prior to the termination of the contract, except where the material circumstances uninformed of, or wrongly informed of, have an impact on the occurrence of such perils.

Article 224

Where the insured was aware or ought to have been aware that the subject matter insured had suffered a loss due to the occurrence of a peril insured against when the contract was concluded, the insurer shall not be liable for indemnification but shall have the right to the premium. Where the insurer was aware or ought to have been aware that the occurrence of a loss to the subject matter insured due to a peril insured against was impossible, the insured shall have the right to recover the premium paid.

Article 225

Where the insured concludes insurance with two or more insurers for the same subject matter insured and against the same risk, and the insured amount of the said subject matter insured thereby exceeds the insured value, then, unless otherwise agreed in the contract, the insured may demand indemnification from any of the insurers and the aggregate amount to be indemnified shall not exceed the loss value of the subject matter insured. The liability of each insurer shall be in proportion to that which the amount he insured bears to the total of the amounts insured by all insurers. Any insurer, who has paid an indemnification in an amount greater than that he should be liable for, shall have the right of recourse against those who have not paid their indemnification in the amounts for which they are liable.

Article 226

Prior to the commencement of the insurance liability, the insured may demand the termination of the insurance contract but shall pay the handling fees to the insurer, and the insurer shall refund the premium.

Article 227

Unless otherwise agreed in the contract, neither the insurer nor the insured may terminate the contract after the commencement of the insurance liability.

Where the insurance contract provides that the contract may be terminated after the commencement of the liability, and the insured demands the termination of the contract, the insurer shall have the right to the premium payable from the day of the commencement of the insurance liability to the day of termination of the contract and shall refund the remaining portion. If it is the insurer who demands the termination of the contract, the unexpired premium from the day of the termination of the contract to the day of the expiration of the period of insurance shall be refunded to the insured.

Article 228

Notwithstanding the stipulations in Article 227, the insured may not demand termination of the contract for cargo insurance and voyage insurance on a ship after the commencement of the insurance liability.

Article 229

A contract of marine insurance for the carriage of goods by sea may be assigned by the insured by endorsement or otherwise, and the rights and obligations under the contract are assigned accordingly. The insured and the assignee shall be jointly and severally liable for the payment of the premium if such premium remains unpaid up to the time of the assignment of the contract.

Article 230

The consent of the insurer shall be obtained where the insurance contract is assigned in consequence of the transfer of the ownership of the ship insured. In the absence of such consent, the contract shall be terminated from the time of the transfer of the ownership of the ship. Where the transfer takes place during the voyage, the contract shall be terminated when the voyage ends.

Upon termination of the contract, the insurer shall refund the unexpired premium to the insured calculated from the day of the termination of the contract to the day of its expiration.

Article 231

The insured may conclude an open cover with the insurer for goods to be shipped or received in batches within a given period. The open cover shall be evidenced by an open policy to be issued by the insurer.

Article 232

The insurer shall, at the request of the insured, issued insurance certificates separately for cargo shipped in batches according to the open cover.

Where the contents of insurance certificates issued by the insurer separately differ from those of an open policy, the insurance certificates issued separately shall prevail.

Article 232

The insurer shall, at the request of the insured, issue insurance certificates separately for cargo shipped in batches according to the open cover.

Where the contents of insurance certificates issued by an insurer separately differ from those of the open policy, the insurance certificates issued separately shall prevail.

Article 233

The insured shall notify the insurer immediately on learning that the cargo insured under an open cover has been shipped or has arrived. The items to be notified of shall include the name of the carrying ship, the voyage, the value of the cargo and the insured amount.

Section 3 Obligations of the insured

Article 234

Unless otherwise agreed in the insurance contract, the insured shall pay the premium immediately upon conclusion of the contract. The insurer may refuse to issue the insurance policy or other insurance certificate before the premium is paid by the insured.

Article 235

The insured shall notify the insurer in writing immediately where the insured has not complied with the warranties under the contract. The insurer may, upon receipt of the notice, terminate the contract or demand an amendment to the terms and conditions of the insurance coverage or an increase in the premium.

Article 236

Upon the occurrence of a peril insured against, the insured shall notify the insurer immediately and shall take necessary and reasonable measures to avoid or minimise the loss. Where special instructions for the adoption of reasonable measures to avoid or minimise the loss are received from the insurer, the insured shall act according to such instructions.

The insurer shall not be liable for extended loss caused by the insured's breach of the provisions of the preceding paragraph.

Section 4 Liability of the insurer

Article 237

An insurer shall indemnify the insured promptly after any loss from a peril insured against has occurred.

Article 238

An insurer's indemnification for the loss from the peril insured against shall be limited to the insured amount. Where the insured amount is lower than the insured value, the insurer shall indemnify in the proportion that the insured amount bears to the insured value.

Article 239

An insurer shall be liable for loss of the subject matter insured arising from several perils insured against during the period of the insurance even though the aggregate of the amounts of loss exceeds the insured amount. However, the insurer shall only be liable for the total loss where the total loss occurs after the partial loss which has not been repaired.

Article 240

An insurer shall pay, in addition to the indemnification to be paid with regard to the subject matter insured, necessary and reasonable expenses incurred by an insured for avoiding or minimising the loss recoverable under the contract, reasonable expenses for survey and assessment of the value for the purpose of ascertaining the nature and extent of the peril insured against and expenses incurred for acting on the special instructions of the insurer.

Payment by the insurer of the expenses referred to in the preceding paragraph shall be limited to that equivalent to the insured amount.

Where the insured amount is lower than the insured value, the insurer shall be liable for the expenses referred to in this Article in the proportion that the insured amount bears to the insured value, unless the contract provides otherwise.

Article 241

Where the insured amount is lower than the value for contribution under the general average, the insurer shall be liable for the general average contribution in the proportion that the insured amount bears to the value for contribution.

Article 242

An insurer shall not be liable for any loss caused by the intentional act of the insured.

Article 243

Unless otherwise agreed in the insurance contract, an insurer shall not be liable for loss of or damage to insured cargo arising from any of the following causes:

(1) delay in the voyage or in the delivery of cargo or change of market price;

(2) fair wear and tear, inherent vice or nature of the cargo;

(3) improper packing.

Article 244

Unless otherwise agreed in the insurance contract, an insurer shall not be liable for the loss of or damage to the insured ship arising from any of the following causes:

(1) unseaworthiness of the ship at the time of the commencement of the voyage, except where, under a time policy, the insured has no knowledge thereof;

(2) wear and tear or corrosion of the ship.

The provisions of this Article apply *mutatis mutandis* to the insurance of freight.

Section 5 Loss of or damage to the subject matter insured and abandonment

Article 245

Where, after the occurrence of a peril insured against, the subject matter insured is lost or is so seriously damaged that it is completely deprived of its original structure and usage or the insured is deprived of the possession thereof, it shall constitute an actual total loss.

Article 246

Where a ship's total loss is considered to be unavoidable after the occurrence of a peril insured against or the expenses necessary for avoiding the occurrence of an actual total loss would exceed the insured value, it shall constitute a constructive total loss.

Where an actual total loss is considered to be unavoidable after cargo has suffered a peril insured against, or the expenses to be incurred for avoiding the total actual loss plus that for forwarding the cargo to its destination would exceed its insured value, it shall constitute a constructive total loss.

Article 247

Any loss other than an actual total loss or a constructive total loss is a partial loss.

Article 248

Where a ship fails to arrive at its destination within a reasonable time from the place where it was last heard of, unless the contract provides otherwise, if it remains unheard of upon the expiry of two months, it shall be considered missing. Such missing shall be deemed to be an actual total loss.

Article 249

Where the subject matter insured has become a constructive total loss and the insured demands indemnification from the insurer on the basis of a total loss, the subject matter insured shall be abandoned to the insurer. The insurer may accept the abandonment or choose not to, but shall inform the insured of his decision whether to accept the abandonment within a reasonable time.

The abandonment shall not be subject to any conditions. Once the abandonment is accepted by the insurer, it shall not be withdrawn.

Article 250

Where the insurer has accepted the abandonment, all rights and obligations relating to the property abandoned are transferred to the insurer.

Section 6 Payment of indemnity

Article 251

After the occurrence of a peril insured against and before the payment of indemnity, the insurer may demand that the insured submit evidence and materials related to the ascertainment of the nature of the peril and the extent of the loss.

Article 252

Where loss of or damage to the subject matter insured within the insurance coverage is caused by a third person, the right of the insured to demand compensation from the third person shall be subrogated to the insurer from the time the indemnity is paid.

The insured shall furnish the insurer with necessary documents and information that should come to his knowledge and shall endeavour to assist the insurer in pursuing recovery from the third person.

Article 253

Where the insured waives his right of claim against the third person without the consent of the insurer or the insurer is unable to exercise the right of recourse due to the fault of the insured, the insurer may make a corresponding reduction from the amount of indemnity.

Article 254

In effecting payment of indemnity to the insured, the insurer may make a corresponding reduction therefrom of the amount already paid by a third person to the insured.

Where the compensation obtained by the insurer from the third person exceeds the amount of indemnity paid by the insurer, the part in excess shall be returned to the insured.

Article 255

After the occurrence of a peril insured against, the insurer is entitled to waive his right to the subject matter insured and pay the insured the amount in full to relieve himself of the obligations under the contract.

In exercising the right mentioned in the preceding paragraph, the insurer shall notify the insured thereof within seven days from the day of the receipt of the notice from the insured regarding the indemnity. The insurer shall remain liable for the necessary and reasonable expenses paid by the insured for avoiding or minimising the loss prior to his receipt of the said notice.

Article 256

Except as stipulated in Article 255, where a total loss occurs to the subject matter insured and the full insured amount is paid, the insurer shall acquire the full right to the subject matter insured. In the case of under-insurance, the insurer shall acquire the right to the subject matter insured in the proportion that the insured amount bears to the insured value.

Chapter 13 Limitation of time

Article 257

The limitation period for claims against the carrier with regard to the carriage of goods by sea is one year, counting from the day on which the goods were delivered or should have been delivered by the carrier. Within the limitation period or after the expiration thereof, if the person allegedly liable has brought a claim for recourse against a third person, that claim is time-barred at the expiration of 90 days, counting from the day on which the person claiming for the recourse settled the claim, or was served with a copy of the process by the court handling the claim against him.

The limitation period for claims against the carrier with regard to a voyage charter-party is two years, counting from the day on which the claimant knew or should have known that his right had been infringed.

Article 258

The limitation period for claims against the carrier with regard to the carriage of passengers by sea is two years, counting respectively as follows:

(1) claims for personal injury: counting from the day on which the passenger disembarked or should have disembarked;

(2) claims for death of passengers that occurred during the period of carriage: counting from the day on which the passenger should have disembarked; whereas those for the death of passengers that occurred after the disembarkation but resulted from an injury that occurred during the period of carriage by sea, counting from the day of the death of the passenger concerned, provided that this period does not exceed three years from the time of disembarkation;

(3) claims for loss of or damage to the luggage: counting from the day of disembarkation or the day on which the passenger should have disembarked.

Article 259

The limitation period for claims with regard to charter-parties is two years, counting from the day on which the claimant knew or should have known that his right had been infringed.

Article 260

The limitation period for claims with regard to sea towage is one year, counting from the day on which the claimant knew or should have known that his rights had been infringed.

Article 261

The limitation period for claims with regard to collision of ships is two years, counting from the day on which the collision occurred. The limitation period for claims with regard to the right of recourse as provided for in paragraph 3 of Article 169 is one year, counting from the day on which the parties concerned jointly and severally paid the amount of compensation for the damage occurred.

Article 262

The limitation period for claims with regard to salvage at sea is two years, counting from the day on which the salvage operation was completed.

Article 263

The limitation period for claims with regard to contribution in general average is one year, counting from the day on which the adjustment was finished.

Article 264

The limitation period for claims with regard to contracts of marine insurance is two years, counting from the day on which the peril insured against occurred.

Article 265

The limitation period for claims with regard to compensation for oil pollution damage from ships is three years, counting from the day on which the pollution damage occurred. However, in no case shall the limitation period exceed six years, counting from the day on which the accident causing the pollution occurred.

Article 266

Within the last six months of a limitation period if *force majeure* or other causes prevent the claim from being made, the limitation period shall be suspended. The counting of the limitation period shall be resumed when the cause of suspension no longer exists.

Article 267

Limitation of time shall be discontinued as a result of the bringing of an action or the submission of the case for arbitration by the claimant or the admission of fulfilment of obligations by the defendant. However, the limitation of time shall not be discontinued if the claimant withdraws his action or his submission for arbitration, or his action has been rejected by a decision of the court.

Where the claimant makes a claim for the arrest of a ship, the limitation of time shall be discontinued from the day on which the claim is made.

The limitation period shall be counted anew from the time of discontinuance.

Chapter 14 Application of law in relation to foreign-related matters

Article 268

If any international treaty concluded or acceded to by the People's Republic of China contains provisions differing from those contained in this Code, the provisions of the relevant international treaty shall apply, unless the provisions are those on which the People's Republic of China has made reservations.

International practice may be applied to matters for which neither the relevant laws of the People's Republic of China nor any international treaty concluded or acceded to by the People's Republic of China contain any relevant provisions.

Article 269

The parties to a contract may choose the law applicable to such contract, unless the law provides otherwise. Where the parties to a contract have not made a choice, the law of the country having the closest connection with the contract shall apply.

Article 270

The law of the flag State of a ship shall apply to the acquisition, transfer and extinction of the ownership of the ship.

Article 271

The law of the flag State of a ship shall apply to the mortgage of the ship.

The law of the original country of registry of a ship shall apply to the mortgage of the ship if its mortgage is effected before or during its demise charter period.

Article 272

The law of the place where the court hearing the case is located shall apply to matters pertaining to maritime liens.

Article 273

The law of the place where an infringing act is committed shall apply to claims for damages arising from collision of ships.

The law of the place where the court hearing the case is located shall apply to claims for damages arising from collision of ships on the high seas.

If colliding ships belong to the same country, no matter where the collision occurs, the law of the flag State shall apply to claims against one another for damages arising from such collision.

Article 274

The law where adjustment of general average is made shall apply to the adjustment of general average.

Article 275

The law of the place where the court hearing the case is located shall apply to the limitation of liability for maritime claims.

Article 276

The application of foreign laws or international practices pursuant to the provisions of this Chapter shall not jeopardise the public interests of the People's Republic of China.

Chapter 15 Supplementary provisions

Article 277

The Unit of Account referred to in this Code is the Special Drawing Right as defined by the International Monetary Fund; the amount of the Chinese currency (RMB) in terms of the Special Drawing Right shall be that computed on the basis of the method of conversion established by the authorities in charge of foreign exchange control of this country on the date of the judgment by the court or the date of the award by the arbitration organisation or the date mutually agreed upon by the parties.

Article 278

This Code shall come into force as of 1 July 1993.

PART 3

THE MARITIME PROCEDURE LAW OF THE PRC 1999

(Adopted on 25 December 1999 by the 13th Session of the Standing Committee of the 9th National People's Congress. Promulgated on 25 December 1999 by Order No 28 of the President of the People's Republic of China)

Table of Contents

Chapter 1 General principles

Article 1

This law is enacted for the purpose of safeguarding the procedural rights of parties in maritime proceedings and ensuring that the People's Courts ascertain the facts, establish liability, apply laws properly and hear maritime cases promptly.

Article 2

The Civil Procedure Law of the People's Republic of China and this law shall apply in maritime proceedings conducted within the territory of the People's Republic of China. This law shall prevail wherever its provisions are applicable.

Article 3

Where an international treaty concluded or acceded to by the People's Republic of China contains provisions that differ from those of the Civil Procedure Law of the People's Republic of China and this law, those of the international treaty shall prevail, except where the People's Republic of China has made reservations.

Article 4

The Maritime Courts shall entertain actions brought up by relevant parties in respect of maritime torts, maritime contracts and other maritime disputes provided for by law.

Article 5

The Maritime Courts, their local High People's Courts and the Supreme People's Court shall apply this law in maritime proceedings.

Chapter 2 Jurisdiction

Article 6

The following provisions, as well as those of the Civil Procedure Law of the People's Republic of China on territorial jurisdiction, shall apply to maritime proceedings:

(1) jurisdiction over cases arising from maritime torts may be exercised by the Maritime Court of the place where the ship was registered, as well as by the courts specified in Articles 29–31 of the Civil Procedure Law;
(2) jurisdiction over cases arising from maritime contracts may be exercised by the Maritime Court of the place where a transshipment was carried out, as well as by the courts specified in Article 28 of the Civil Procedure;
(3) jurisdiction over cases relating to charter-parties of sea-going ships shall be exercised by the Maritime Courts of the places where a ship was delivered to, or redelivered to, or registered at, or where the defendant is domiciled;
(4) jurisdiction over cases arising from marine insurance contracts shall be exercised by the Maritime Courts of the place where the insured object was located, or where the accident occurred, or where the defendant is domiciled;
(5) jurisdiction over cases arising from seafarers' employment contracts shall be exercised by the Maritime Courts of the place where the claimant is domiciled, or where the contract was concluded, or where the seafarer embarked or disembarked, or where the defendant is domiciled;
(6) jurisdiction over cases arising from maritime security shall be exercised by the Maritime Court in the place where the collateral is provided, or where the defendant is domiciled; jurisdiction over cases arising from ship mortgages may also be exercised by the Maritime Court of the place where the ship is registered; and

(7) jurisdiction over cases arising from the ownership, possession, usage, and maritime lien of a sea-going ship shall be exercised by the Maritime Court of the place where the ship is located, or registered, or where the defendant is domiciled.

Article 7

The following maritime cases shall be subject to the exclusive jurisdiction of the Maritime Courts stipulated herein:

(1) jurisdiction over cases arising from port operations shall be exercised by the Maritime Court of the place where the port is located;

(2) jurisdiction over cases relating to discharge, leaking, or dumping of oil products or other harmful substances from a ship, and cases relating to marine pollution and damage caused by marine activities or operations or caused by the demolition and repair of a ship shall be exercised by the Maritime Court of the place where the pollution occurred, or where the damage was caused, or where preventative measures were taken; and

(3) jurisdiction over cases arising from marine exploration and exploitation contracts within the territorial sea of the People's Republic of China and other sea areas over which the People's Republic of China has jurisdictional authority shall be exercised by the Maritime Court of the place where the contract was performed.

Article 8

Where all parties to a maritime case are aliens, stateless persons or foreign enterprises or organisations, but have agreed in writing to the jurisdiction of the Maritime Courts of the People's Republic of China, such courts thereby have jurisdiction over the case, even if the place that the case is associated with is not within the territory of the People's Republic of China.

Article 9

Applications for determining unclaimed property at sea shall be submitted to the Maritime Court of the place where the property is located. Applications for declarations of deaths of persons as a result of maritime accidents shall be submitted to the Maritime Court of the place where the competent authority in charge of handling the maritime accident is located, or to the Maritime Court that has entertained cases in relation to the accident.

Article 10

Any dispute in respect of jurisdiction between a Maritime Court and a local People's Court shall be resolved by consultation between the two courts; in the absence of which the matter shall be submitted to their common superior People's Court for a designation of jurisdiction.

Article 11

Applications for execution of maritime arbitration awards, or for recognition and execution of foreign judgments or rulings, or foreign maritime arbitration awards shall be submitted to the Maritime Court of the location where the

(11) pilotage;
(12) materials supplied or service rendered to the ship for its operation, management, preservation or maintenance;
(13) construction, reconstruction, repair, converting or equipping of the ship;
(14) port, canal, dock, harbour and other waterway dues and charges;
(15) wages and other sums due to the crew including costs of repatriation and social insurance contributions payable on their behalf;
(16) disbursements incurred on behalf of the ship or its owners;
(17) insurance premiums (including mutual insurance calls) in respect of the ship, payable by or on behalf of the shipowner or demise charterer;
(18) any commissions, brokerages or agency fees payable in respect of the ship by or on behalf of the shipowner or demise charterer;
(19) any dispute as to ownership or possession of the ship;
(20) any dispute between joint-owners of the ship as to the employment or earnings of the ship;
(21) a mortgage or a charge of the same nature on the ship; or
(22) any dispute arising out of a contract for the sale of the ship.

Article 22

A ship may be arrested only in respect of maritime claims specified in Article 21 except for enforcement of a judgment, arbitration award and other enforceable legal documents.

Article 23

The Maritime Courts may arrest the ship in any of the following circumstances:

(1) the owner of the ship is liable for the claim, and is still the owner of the ship when the arrest is effected;
(2) the demise charterer of the ship is liable for the claim, and is the demise charterer or owner of the ship when the arrest is effected;
(3) the claim is based upon a mortgage or a charge of the same nature on the ship;
(4) the claim relates to the ownership or possession of the ship; or
(5) the claim is secured by a maritime lien.

The Maritime Courts may arrest other ships at the time of the arrest, owned by an owner, demise charterer, time charterer, or voyage charterer, who is liable for the maritime claim; except claims in respect of ownership or possession of the ship.

Military and public service ships cannot be arrested.

Article 24

A claimant cannot apply for an arrest of a ship that has already been arrested for the same maritime claim except where:

(1) the respondent has not provided sufficient security; or

(2) the guarantor is likely to be unable to fully or partially perform his obligations under the security; or

(3) the claimant consented on reasonable grounds to release the arrested ship or return the security already provided; or where reasonable measures cannot be taken by the claimant to prevent the release of the arrested ship or the return of security already provided.

Article 25

A claimant may apply for an arrest of the ship concerned notwithstanding that fact that the name of the respondent cannot be immediately ascertained.

Article 26

The Maritime Courts may notify relevant organisations requesting assistance in execution of an order to arrest or release a ship. The notice shall state the scope and substance of the assistance with regard to the execution. The organisations concerned have an obligation to assist the execution. The Maritime Courts may, where it is necessary, send officers on board the ship to supervise the arrest.

Article 27

A ship under maritime preservation may, with the consent of the claimant, be allowed to resume operations subject to restrictions on disposing of the ship or creating a new mortgage on the ship.

Article 28

The time limit for arrest of a ship under maritime preservation is 30 days.

Where proceedings or arbitration are commenced within 30 days of the arrest or the arrest is effected in the course of proceedings or arbitration, the arrest shall not be subject to the time limit stipulated in the preceding paragraph.

Article 29

Where the respondent has not, within the time limit, provided security and the ship is not suitable to remain under arrest, the claimant may, after commencing proceedings or applying for arbitration, apply to the Maritime Courts for sale by auction of the ship.

Article 30

Upon receipt of an application for sale by auction of a ship, the Maritime Courts shall examine the case and make a ruling approving or disapproving the auction of the ship.

Within five days upon receipt of the ruling, any party objecting to the ruling may request a review, upon receipt of which the Maritime Courts shall render a decision on the review within five days. The execution of the ruling shall be suspended during the period of the review.

Article 31

Where the claimant applies to terminate the auction once it has been commenced, the Maritime Court has the power to decide whether or not the application is admissible. Where the Maritime Court rules that the auction be terminated, the expenses incurred in the preparation of the auction shall be borne by the claimant.

Article 32

The Maritime Courts, after ruling for the auction of the ship, shall issue a public notice in newspapers or through other news media, or through overseas newspapers or other news media where a foreign flag ship is to be auctioned.

The public notice shall include the following:

(1) the name and nationality of the ship to be auctioned;

(2) reasons and grounds for the auction;

(3) composition of the Auction Committee;

(4) time and venue of the auction;

(5) time and venue for inspection;

(6) formality of bidding;

(7) formality of credit registration; and

(8) other matters deemed to be necessary for the notice.

The time limit of the public notice shall be no less than 30 days.

Article 33

Maritime Courts shall notify the registration authorities and holders of maritime liens, mortgagees and owners who are known to the court not less than 30 days prior to the auction.

The notice shall contain the name of the ship to be auctioned, the time and the venue of the auction, the reasons and grounds for the auction, as well as the formality of credit registration, etc.

The notice shall be in writing or some other form whereby receipt of the notice can be confirmed.

Article 34

The auction shall be carried out by an Auction Committee, which shall consist of four or five persons including Court Execution Officers, and also auctioneers and inspectors appointed by the Maritime Court.

The Auction Committee is in charge of appraising and evaluating the ship, organising and conducting the auction, signing the confirmation of auction with the bidder, and handling the transfer of the ship.

The Auction Committee answers to and is under the supervision of the Maritime Court.

Article 35

Bidders shall register their bids with the Auction Committee within the time limit. At registration, bidders, or their legal representatives, shall submit for verification their identity certificates and powers of representative together with payment of a specified amount of bidding deposit.

Article 36

Prior to the auction, the Auction Committee shall make the ship available for inspection and provide other necessary documents and information about the ship.

Article 37

The successful bidder (buyer) shall immediately make a payment of not less than 20% of the price after signing the confirmation of auction, and the remaining amount must be paid in full within seven days of the date of confirmation, unless the Auction Committee has agreed otherwise with the buyer.

Article 38

Upon payment of the full amount of the price, the original owner shall transfer the ship in its existing condition to the buyer at the place where the ship is berthed within a specified time limit. The Auction Committee shall arrange and supervise the transfer, and sign a confirmation of transfer of the ship with the buyer.

Upon the completion of transfer, the Maritime Court shall issue an order releasing the ship from arrest.

Article 39

Maritime Courts, after the transfer, shall issue a public notice, through newspapers or other news media, announcing that the ship has been auctioned and transferred to the buyer.

Article 40

Upon acceptance of the ship, the buyer shall, with the confirmation of transfer and other relevant documents, have the ship registered. The original owner of the ship shall deregister his ownership. However, the transfer of ownership shall not be affected by such deregistration.

Article 41

Where there is a deliberate collusion between the bidders, the auction is void. Bidders who participate in a malicious collaboration shall be liable for the costs of the auction and any losses occurred, and Maritime Courts may impose upon them a fine ranging from 10% to 30% of the highest bid in amount.

Article 42

The relevant provisions of the Auction Law of the People's Republic of China, as well as the provisions of this Section, shall apply to auction of ships.

Article 43

The relevant provisions of this Section apply *mutatis mutandis* to the auction of ships in execution of a judgment.

Section 3 Attachment and auction of goods carried on board

Article 44

A claimant may apply for attachment of goods carried on board a ship to ensure his maritime claims can be fulfilled.

Goods to be attached must be owned by the respondent.

Article 45

The value of goods to be attached shall be in the range of the claim amount.

Article 46

The time limit for attachment of goods in preservation of a maritime claim is 15 days.

Where proceedings or an arbitration are commenced within 15 days of the attachment, or the attachment is effected in the course of proceedings or an arbitration, the attachment shall not be subject to the time limit stipulated in the preceding paragraph.

Article 47

Where the respondent fails to provide security within the time limit and due to the nature of the goods it is not appropriate to continue the attachment, the claimant may, after commencing proceedings or applying for arbitration, apply to Maritime Courts for an order of auction of the goods.

The claimant may apply for an earlier auction where it is impossible or difficult for the goods to be kept, or storage fees are likely to surpass the value of the goods.

Article 48

Within seven days of receipt of an application for the auction of the goods, the Maritime Courts shall examine the case and grant a ruling approving or disapproving the application for an auction.

Within five days of receipt of a ruling, a party objecting to the ruling may once and for all apply for a review, upon receipt of which, Maritime Courts shall within five days render a decision of the review. The execution of the ruling shall be suspended during the review.

Article 49

The auction of goods shall be carried out by an Auction Body consisting of a Court Execution Officer and other professional auctioneers, or a delegated organisation.

The relevant provisions in Section 2 of this Chapter in respect of the auction of ships may apply *mutatis mutandis* to auction of goods where it is appropriate.

Article 50

The provisions of this Section shall apply to maritime preservation on bunkers and supplies carried on board a ship.

Chapter 4 Maritime injunctions

Article 51

A maritime injunction is a coercive measure granted by Maritime Courts, upon the request of a claimant, by means of an order requiring a respondent to do or refrain from doing something, so as to prevent the legitimate rights and interest of the claimant being infringed.

Article 52

An application for a maritime injunction prior to proceedings shall be submitted to the Maritime Court of the place where the dispute arose.

Article 53

A maritime injunction shall not be prejudiced by a jurisdiction or arbitration agreement between the parties in relation to the maritime claim.

Article 54

An application for a maritime injunction shall be submitted in writing to the Maritime Court, stating the grounds for the application together with relevant evidence.

Article 55

Upon receipt of the application, the Maritime Court may order the claimant to provide security. If there is failure to comply with such an order, the application shall be rejected.

Article 56

The following conditions shall be satisfied before a maritime injunction can be granted:

(1) the applicant has a specific maritime claim;

(2) remedies are necessary for the violation of law or breach of a contract on the part of respondents; and

(3) if a maritime injunction is not granted as a matter of urgency, further damage is inevitable.

Article 57

Upon receipt of the application, the Maritime Court shall grant a ruling within 48 hours. A maritime injunction so granted shall be enforced forthwith. The application shall be rejected where the conditions of granting a maritime injunction are not satisfied.

Article 58

Upon receipt of the ruling, parties objecting to the ruling may once and for all apply for a review, upon receipt of which the Maritime Court shall render a decision within five days of the review. The execution of the ruling shall not be affected by the review.

An interested party may raise an objection to the ruling of the maritime injunction. The Maritime Court shall annul the maritime injunction if the objection is found to be justified.

Article 59

Maritime Courts may in accordance with the gravity of the situation impose a fine or detention on a respondent who refuses to comply with the maritime injunction; where the act constitutes an offence, criminal liability may be imposed.

A fine can be imposed from RMB 1,000 up to RMB 30,000 for an individual, from RMB 30,000 up to RMB 100,000 for an organisation.

Detention can be ordered for up to 15 days.

Article 60

The claimant shall be liable for any loss sustained by the respondent due to a wrongful application for a maritime injunction.

Article 61

After the execution of a maritime injunction, any party may, if proceedings or arbitration have not been commenced, commence proceedings in respect of maritime claims in either the Maritime Court where the maritime injunction was granted or the Maritime Court that has jurisdiction over the case, unless a jurisdiction or arbitration agreement between the parties provides otherwise.

Chapter 5 Preservation of maritime evidence

Article 62

Preservation of maritime evidence is a coercive measure taken by Maritime Courts upon request of a claimant to take, preserve or seal up evidence related to a maritime claim.

Article 63

The application for preservation of maritime evidence prior to commencing proceedings shall be submitted by a party to the Maritime Court at the place where the evidence to be preserved is located.

Article 64

Preservation of maritime evidence shall not be prejudiced by a jurisdiction or arbitration agreement between the parties in respect of the maritime claim.

Article 65

The application shall be submitted to the Maritime Court in writing stating the evidence to be preserved, the relationship between the evidence and the maritime claim, and the grounds.

Article 66

Upon receipt of an application for preservation of maritime evidence, the Maritime Court may order the claimant to provide security. The application shall be rejected if the applicant fails to comply with the order.

Article 67

The following conditions shall be satisfied before the preservation of maritime evidence can be ordered:

(1) the applicant is a party to a maritime claim;

(2) the evidence to be preserved is substantial to the maritime claim;

(3) the evidence is traceable to the respondent; and

(4) without preservation being granted as a matter of urgency, the evidence will be lost or inevitably become inaccessible.

Article 68

Maritime Courts shall grant a ruling within 48 hours upon receipt of an application. The ruling for preservation of maritime evidence shall be enforced forthwith. The application shall be rejected if it does not conform to the requirements for a preservation order.

Article 69

Within five days upon receipt of the ruling, any party objecting to the ruling may once and for all apply for a review. The Maritime Court shall within five days of receipt of the application render a decision on the review. The execution of the ruling shall be suspended during the period of review. However, the preserved evidence shall be returned to the respondent if his application is found to be justifiable.

An interested party may raise an objection to the preservation of maritime evidence. The Maritime Court shall return the relevant evidence to the interested party if the objection is found to be justified.

Article 70

Maritime Courts may make preservation by means of sealing the evidence, or producing a duplicate or copy, or taking photographs and video records, or producing extracts and notes where it is appropriate, and may seize the original evidence where it is necessary.

Article 71

The claimants shall indemnify any damage sustained by the respondent or any interested party for a wrongful application of preservation.

Article 72

After the preservation of maritime evidence, parties may, if proceedings or arbitration have not been commenced, commence proceedings in respect of the maritime claim before either the Maritime Court where the evidence was preserved or the Maritime Court which has jurisdiction over the case, unless a jurisdiction or arbitration agreement between the parties provides otherwise.

Chapter 6 Maritime security

Article 73

Maritime security means any security relating to maritime preservation, maritime injunctions and preservation of maritime evidence as stipulated in this law.

Maritime security may be provided in the form of cash, guarantee, mortgage or pledge.

Article 74

Security provided by claimants shall be submitted to Maritime Courts; security provided by respondents may be presented either to Maritime Courts or to the claimant.

Article 75

The form and amount of security provided by the claimant shall be determined by the Maritime Court, whilst that provided by the respondent may be agreed by the parties; in absence of such an agreement, the form and amount shall be determined by the Maritime Court.

Article 76

The amount of security requested by the claimant in preservation of a maritime claim shall be in the range of the value of his claim, and shall not exceed the value of the property under preservation.

The amount of security provided by the claimant shall be in line with the loss likely to be sustained by the respondent due to the claimant's wrongful application, and shall be determined by the Maritime Court.

Article 77

After provision of security, the provider may, based on reasonable grounds, apply to the Maritime Court to reduce, modify or cancel the security.

Article 78

The claimant shall be liable for any loss sustained by the respondent due to demand for an excessive amount of security.

Article 79

The provision of this Chapter may apply *mutatis mutandis* to the provision of security in the constitution of a limitation fund and preliminary execution.

Chapter 7 Service

Article 80

Service of legal documents in maritime proceedings shall comply with the relevant provisions of the Civil Procedure Law of the People's Republic of China, and, where appropriate, legal documents may also be served:

(1) upon the agent *ad litem* entrusted by the person upon whom documents are to be served; or

(2) upon the representative or branch office established in the People's Republic of China by the person upon whom documents are to be served or upon his agent; or

(3) by other suitable means such that the receipt of the documents can be confirmed.

Documents of arrest of a ship may also be served upon the Master of the ship concerned.

Article 81

Where a person under the obligation to accept legal documents refuses to accept or acknowledge receipt, the server shall record the fact on the receipt, signed and 'chopped' by the server and any witnesses, in which case service shall be deemed to be completed.

Chapter 8 Trial procedures

Section 1 Collision cases

Article 82

Both the claimant and the defendant shall complete a maritime accident investigation form in good faith at the time of bringing an action or defending the case.

Article 83

The Maritime Courts, when serving the Statement of Claim or Statement of Defence on the parties, shall not enclose relevant evidential material.

Article 84

The parties shall submit all relevant evidence prior to the court hearing. Parties shall provide the Maritime Court with a statement after completion of submission before they are allowed to cross-examine evidential materials concerning the ships' collision.

Article 85

Parties are estopped from reversing a statement previously made in the maritime accident investigation form and evidence provided, unless producing new evidence which was, on reasonable grounds, unavailable at the time of proof.

Article 86

Ship inspection and valuation shall be undertaken by professional institutions or individuals approved by the Authorities. Maritime Courts shall not admit as evidence any survey or valuation report issued by others.

Article 87

Collision cases shall be concluded within one year after the filing of such cases for trial. Any extension beyond the one year limit in special circumstances shall be approved by the President of the Court.

Section 2 General average cases

Article 88

Parties may agree to submit a general average dispute to average adjusters for adjustment or commence proceedings directly before the Maritime Court. The Maritime Court may appoint average adjusters for adjustment of the general average dispute.

Article 89

Where there is no objection from either party, the general average statement issued by the average adjusters can be admissible as the basis of contribution of general average; in the absence of such an agreement, Maritime Courts shall decide on the admissibility of the statement.

Article 90

A party may bring an action against the liable party for non-general average claims arising from the same maritime accident without being prejudiced by the general average proceedings.

Article 91

An action brought by a party against the liable party for both general average contribution and non-general average claims arising from the same maritime accident can be consolidated by the Maritime Court that hears both actions.

Article 92

General average cases shall be concluded within one year after the filing of such cases for trial. Any extension beyond the one year limit in special circumstances shall be approved by the President of the Court.

Section 3 Subrogation in marine insurance

Article 93

Where a third party is liable for an insured accident and the insurer has indemnified the assured, the insurer obtains by subrogation the rights against the third party for indemnity insofar as the assured has been indemnified.

Article 94

When exercising the right of subrogation, the insurer may bring an action in his own name against a liable third party if the assured has not commenced proceedings.

Article 95

When exercising the right of subrogation, the insurer may apply to the court for alteration of the name of the litigating party where the assured has already commenced proceedings against the liable third party.

Where the loss caused by the third party is not fully covered by insurance, the insurer and assured may act as joint-claimants against the third party.

Article 96

When commencing or joining proceedings pursuant to Article 94 or 95 the insurer shall submit to the Maritime Court evidence of payment of the insurance indemnity and other documents necessary for proceedings.

Article 97

Victims of oil pollution damage caused by a ship may bring action directly against the insurer or financial guarantor for the ship's oil pollution liability, as well as against the owner of the ship causing the damage.

An insurer or financial guarantor being sued directly is entitled to request the owner of the ship to join the proceedings.

Section 4 Summary, supervision and public notice

Article 98

Maritime Courts may apply the summary procedure provided in the Civil Procedure Law of the People's Republic of China when hearing small and simple cases in which facts and merits are clear.

Article 99

Where a creditor is requesting payment of a pecuniary debt or delivery of securities from a debtor in relation to a maritime matter, the creditor may apply to the Maritime Court which has jurisdiction to issue an Order of Payment in accordance with the Civil Procedure Law of the People's Republic of China.

Where a debtor is an alien, or a Stateless person, or a foreign enterprise, or an organisation having a domicile, a representative or a branch in the territory of the People's Republic of China that can be served with an Order of Payment, the creditor may apply to the Maritime Court which has jurisdiction to issue an Order of Payment.

Article 100

A holder of a bill of lading or a similar document for taking delivery of goods, which is out of his control or lost, may apply to the Maritime Court in the place where the goods are located for a public assertion of his claim.

Chapter 9 Constitution of limitation funds

Article 101

Following a maritime accident, the owner, charterer, operator, salvor or insurer of the ship may apply to the Maritime Court to constitute a limitation fund for maritime claims.

Where oil pollution damage is caused by a ship, the owner and the insurer or other financial guarantor of the ship, in order to be entitled to limit their liability under relevant law, shall apply to the Maritime Court to constitute a limitation fund for oil pollution claims.

Application for constitution of limitation funds may be submitted prior to or during proceedings, but not later than the delivery of the first instance judgment.

Article 102

Applications for constitution of a limitation fund prior to proceedings shall be submitted to the Maritime Court of the place where the accident occurred, or where the contract was performed, or where the ship was arrested.

Article 103

Constitution of limitation funds shall not be prejudiced by a jurisdiction or arbitration agreement between the parties.

Article 104

Applications for constitution of limitation funds shall be submitted in writing to Maritime Courts stating the amount of the limitation fund and the grounds thereof, as well as the names, addresses and means of communication of all interested parties known to the applicant and with the attachment of relevant evidence.

Article 105

Within seven days upon receipt of an application for the constitution of a limitation fund, the Maritime Court shall notify all known interested parties, and at the same time issue a public notice through newspapers or some other news media, which shall include the following:

(1) the name of the applicant;

(2) the facts and grounds of the application;

(3) claims creating the imitation fund;

(4) procedure of registering other claims; and

(5) other matters deemed to be necessary for the notice.

Article 106

Any objection to the application of constitution of limitation funds from an interested party shall be submitted in writing to the Maritime Court within seven days of receipt of the notification or 30 days after the public notice where notification has not been received.

Within 15 days of receipt of a written objection, the Maritime Court shall examine the case and grant a ruling to reject the application for constitution of the limitation fund if the objection is found to be justifiable, or to allow the constitution of the limitation fund if the objection is found to be unjustified.

Within seven days upon receipt of the ruling, any party objecting to the ruling may appeal. The People's Court of Second Instance shall render a ruling within 15 days upon receipt of the appeal.

Article 107

Where no objection has been made by interested parties within the time limit, the Maritime Court shall allow the limitation fund to be constituted.

Article 108

After a ruling for the constitution of a limitation fund comes into effect, the applicant shall constitute the limitation fund in the Maritime Court.

The limitation fund can be constituted by means of a cash deposit or provision of security which is acceptable by Maritime Courts.

The amount of a limitation fund shall be the amount of the claim plus interest calculated from the date of the accident to the date the limitation fund is constituted. The amount of security to be issued shall cover the amount of the limitation fund plus interest during the period of the constitution of the limitation fund.

The date of the constitution of a limitation fund is the date that the sum is transferred into the account designated by the Maritime Court, or the date of receipt of the security by the Maritime Court.

Article 109

After the constitution of the limitation fund, parties shall commence proceedings concerning the maritime dispute before the Maritime Court of the place where the limitation fund has been constituted, unless a jurisdiction or arbitration agreement provides otherwise.

Article 110

The applicant shall be liable for any loss sustained by an interested party due to a wrongful application for the constitution of a limitation fund.

Chapter 10 Registration and payment of claims

Article 111

After a public notice of an order for auctioning a ship by the Maritime Court, creditors shall register their claims to the ship within the period of notice. In the event of failure to comply, any claims shall be deemed to have ceased.

Article 112

After public notice on the constitution of the limitation fund issued by the Maritime Court, creditors shall register their claims relating to the maritime accident within the period of notice; failure to comply shall result in a claim being deemed to have been abandoned.

Article 113

To register a claim, a creditor shall apply to the Maritime Court in writing with evidence for the claim.

Evidence for a claim includes an enforceable judgment, ruling, conciliation statement, arbitration award and notarised creditor's documents, as well as other evidence supporting the maritime claim.

Article 114

Maritime Courts shall examine a creditor's application, and allow the claims which are proved by evidence to be registered; or reject those which are not proved.

Article 115

Maritime Courts shall examine a judgment, ruling, conciliation statement, arbitration award and notarised creditor's documents submitted by creditors as evidence for claims, and confirm their evidential power where they are found genuine and lawful.

Article 116

Where providing other evidence for maritime claims, creditors shall, after registration of the claims, commence proceedings before the Maritime Court of registration to confirm their rights. Where an arbitration agreement exists, parties shall apply for arbitration in good time.

Judgments and rulings rendered by the Maritime Court confirming the rights are final and unappealable.

Article 117

After confirming the rights, the Maritime Court shall notify creditors and arrange a creditors meeting.

Article 118

Creditors may at the meeting negotiate on distribution of an auction fund or a limitation fund, and sign an agreement for distribution thereafter.

An agreement for distribution confirmed by an order of the Maritime Court is enforceable.

In absence of such an agreement, the Maritime Court will rule on the distribution of the fund according to the ranking of the claims in accordance with the Maritime Code of the People's Republic of China and other laws.

Article 119

Funds and interest shall be distributed together.

Before distribution, litigation costs payable by a liable party, expenses incurred in preservation and auction of the ship and distribution of the funds, as well as other expenses for the common interests of the creditors, shall be firstly reimbursed from the fund.

Chapter 11 Maritime liens

Article 120

Where ownership of a ship is transferred, the transferee may apply to the Maritime Court for public assertion of maritime liens, so that maritime liens attached to the ship can be extinguished.

Article 121

An application for a public assertion of maritime liens shall be submitted to the court of the place where the ship is to be delivered or where the transferee is domiciled.

Article 122

An application for a public assertion of maritime liens shall be submitted in writing stating the name of the ship, the facts and grounds for the public invitation, together with the contract of transfer and technical details of the ship.

Article 123

Within seven days upon receipt of the application, the court, after examination thereof, shall grant a ruling approving or disapproving the application.

A transferee objecting to the ruling may apply once and for all for a review.

Article 124

After an order for approval becomes effective, the Maritime Court shall issue a public notice in newspapers and other news media. Claimants of maritime liens shall assert their maritime liens within the period of notice.

The period of notice for maritime liens is 60 days.

Article 125

Maritime liens shall be registered before the Maritime Court during the period of notice. In the event of failure to comply with this, any maritime liens are deemed to have ceased.

Article 126

Where no maritime lien is asserted during the period of notice, the Maritime Court upon request shall award a judgment, through a public notice, declaring that the ship transferred is clear from maritime liens.

Chapter 12 Addendum

Article 127

This law will come into force as of 1 July 2000.

PART 4

THE ARBITRATION LAW OF THE PRC 1994

(Adopted at the 9th Session of the Standing Committee of the 8th National People's Congress on 31 August 1994)

Table of Contents

Chapter 1 General provisions

Article 1

This law is formulated for the purpose of ensuring fair and timely arbitration of economic disputes, reliable protection of the legitimate rights and interests of the parties concerned and a healthy development of the socialist market economy.

Article 2

Contractual disputes between citizens of equal status, legal persons and other economic organisations and disputes arising from property rights may be referred to arbitration.

Article 3

The following disputes cannot be referred to arbitration:

(1) disputes arising from marriage, adoption, guardianship, bringing up of children and inheritance; and

(2) disputes that are required by law to be settled by administrative organs.

Article 4

In settling disputes through arbitration, an agreement to engage in arbitration should first of all be reached by the parties concerned. Without such an agreement, the arbitration tribunal shall refuse to accept an application for arbitration by any one party only.

Article 5

Where the parties concerned have reached an agreement for arbitration, the People's Court shall not accept a case brought to the court by any one party only involved, except where the agreement for arbitration is invalid.

Article 6

The members of the arbitration tribunal shall be chosen by the parties concerned.

Arbitration shall not be subject to the jurisdiction of administrative departments at any level or region.

Article 7

Arbitration shall be based on true facts and applicable laws to produce a fair and reasonable settlement for the parties concerned.

Article 8

Arbitration shall be conducted independently according to law, without interference from administrative organs, social groups or individuals.

Article 9

An arbitration award is final. After the award is given, the arbitration tribunal or the People's Court shall not accept the re-opening of the case concerning the same dispute by any of the parties concerned.

Where an award is cancelled or declared void under a ruling by the People's Court, the parties concerned in the dispute may reach another agreement for arbitration and apply for arbitration, or bring a suit in the People's Court.

Chapter 2 Arbitration commissions and associations

Article 10

An arbitration commission may be set up in cities where the people's governments of provinces or municipalities are relocated. They can also be established in other big cities as necessary, but not at every administrative level.

Arbitration commissions may be set up by the relevant departments or chambers of commerce under the co-ordination of the people's governments of the cities prescribed in the preceding paragraph.

The establishment of an arbitration commission shall be registered with the judicial administrative departments of provinces, autonomous regions and municipalities.

Article 11

An arbitration commission shall meet the following requirements:

(1) it shall have its own name, address and statute;

(2) it shall have property necessary for performance of its functions;

(3) it shall have its own members; and

(4) it shall have appointed arbitrators.

The constitution of an arbitration commission shall be formulated according to this law.

Article 12

An arbitration commission shall be composed of a chairman, 2–4 vice chairmen and 7–11 members.

The chairman, vice chairmen and members of an arbitration commission shall be experts in law, economy or trade with practical work experience. Experts in law, economy and trade shall make up at least two-thirds of the composition of an arbitration commission.

Article 13

Members of an arbitration commission shall be appointed from among people of good moral conduct.

An arbitrator shall meet one of the following requirements:

(1) at least eight years of work experience in arbitration;

(2) at least eight years of experience as a lawyer;

(3) at least eight years of experience as a judge; or

(4) engagement in law research and teaching, with a senior academic post.

An arbitration commission shall prepare a list of arbitrators setting out their different specialities.

Article 14

An arbitration commission shall be independent of any administrative organ, and shall not be subordinate to any administrative organ.

Article 15

The China Arbitration Association is a legal entity with all the separate arbitration commissions as its members. The statutes of the China Arbitration Association shall be formulated by the national congress of the Association.

The China Arbitration Association is a self-disciplinary organisation for arbitration commissions, to supervise the latter and their members and arbitrators.

The China Arbitration Association shall formulate arbitration rules according to this law and the civil procedure law.

Chapter 3 Agreement for arbitration

Article 16

An agreement for arbitration shall include the arbitration clauses stipulated in the contract or another written agreement for arbitration reached before or after a dispute occurs.

An arbitration agreement shall contain the following:

(1) the agreement for arbitration;

(2) matters for arbitration; and

(3) the arbitration commission chosen.

Article 17

An agreement for arbitration shall be invalid in the following cases:

(1) where the matters agreed for arbitration exceed the scope of arbitration allowed by law;

(2) where agreements are concluded by legally incapable people, or people having limited legal capabilities; or

(3) where an agreement is entered into by a party under duress.

Article 18

Where an agreement for arbitration fails to specify, or specify clearly, matters concerning arbitration or the choice of arbitration commission, the parties concerned may conclude a supplementary agreement. If a supplementary agreement cannot be reached, the agreement for arbitration is invalid.

Article 19

The effect of an agreement for arbitration shall stand independently and shall not be affected by the alteration, dissolution, termination or invalidity of a contract.

An arbitration tribunal has the right to establish the validity of a contract.

Article 20

Where parties concerned have doubts on the validity of an agreement for arbitration, a request can be made to the arbitration commission for a decision, or to the People's Court for a ruling. If one party requests the arbitration commission for a decision that the other party requests from the People's Court, the People's Court shall make the ruling.

Any doubts regarding the effectiveness of the arbitration agreement must be raised before the first hearing at the arbitration tribunal.

Chapter 4 Arbitration procedure

Section 1 Application and acceptance

Article 21

The following requirements shall be met in applying for arbitration:

(1) there is an agreement for arbitration;

(2) there are specific requests for arbitration and facts and reasons; and

(3) the matters to be referred to arbitration fall into the limits of the authority of the arbitration commission.

Article 22

In applying for arbitration, the parties concerned shall submit the agreement and the application for arbitration and copies thereof.

Article 23

An application for arbitration shall specify the following matters:

(1) the name, sex, age, profession and address of the parties concerned and the names of the organisations they belong to; the name and address of legal persons or other organisations involved and the name and position of the legal representatives or principal leading members;

(2) the claimants' claim and the facts and evidence on which the claim is based; and

(3) evidence and sources of evidence and the names and addresses of the witnesses.

Article 24

An arbitration commission shall accept an application within five days of the application being received if it considers that the application conforms to the requirements, and shall notify the parties concerned. If it considers that the application does not conform to the requirements, it shall notify the parties concerned in writing and state the reasons.

Article 25

After an arbitration commission has accepted an arbitration application, it shall deliver the arbitration rules and the list of the panel of arbitrators to the claimant within the time limit prescribed in the arbitration rules, and send copies of the arbitration application, the arbitration rules and the list of the panel of arbitrators to the respondent.

After a respondent has received the copy of the application for arbitration, he may file a counter-claim with the arbitration commission. After the arbitration commission has received a counter-claim from the respondent, it shall deliver the counter-claim to the claimant within the time limit set in the arbitration rules. If a respondent fails to submit a counter-claim, it does not affect the arbitration proceedings.

Article 26

When parties concerned have reached an agreement for arbitration but one party brings a suit in the People's Court without notifying the court that there is an agreement for arbitration and, after the People's Court has accepted the case, and the other party submits the agreement for arbitration before the opening of the arbitration tribunal, the People's Court shall reject the suit, except where the agreement for arbitration is invalid. If the other party fails to raise objection to the acceptance of the case by the court before the first hearing, it shall be regarded as having forfeited the agreement for arbitration, and the People's Court shall continue the hearing.

Article 27

A claimant may give up or alter his claim. The respondent may acknowledge or refute the claim and has the right to raise a counter-claim.

Article 28

Where due to the acts of one party or other reasons, an arbitration award could not, or could not reasonably be executed, the parties affected may apply to place property under custody.

Where a claimant has applied for custody of property, the arbitration commission shall, according to the relevant provisions of the Civil Procedure Law, submit the application of the claimant to the People's Court.

Where there are errors in the application, the claimant shall compensate the respondent for any losses arising from the custody of the property.

Article 29

The parties concerned or their legal representatives may entrust lawyers or other representatives with the handling of matters relating to arbitration. Where lawyers or other representatives are entrusted with the handling of arbitration matters, the representatives shall produce a power of attorney to the arbitration commission.

Section 2 Composition of arbitration tribunal

Article 30

An arbitration tribunal may be composed of three arbitrators or one arbitrator. If there are three arbitrators, there shall be a chief arbitrator.

Article 31

Where the parties concerned agree that the arbitration tribunal is to be composed of three arbitrators, each of them shall choose one arbitrator or entrust the appointment to the chairman of the arbitration commission, with the third arbitrator jointly chosen by the parties concerned or appointed by the chairman of the arbitration commission jointly entrusted by the two parties. The third arbitrator shall be the chief arbitrator.

Where the parties concerned agree to have the arbitration tribunal composed of one arbitrator, the two parties shall jointly choose the arbitrator or entrust the choice of the arbitrator to the chairman of the arbitration commission.

Article 32

Where the parties concerned fail to decide on the composition of the arbitration tribunal or fail to choose arbitrators within the time limit prescribed in the arbitration rules, the chairman of the arbitration commission shall make the decision.

Article 33

After the formation of an arbitration tribunal, the arbitration commission shall notify the parties in writing of the composition of the arbitration tribunal matters.

Article 34

An arbitrator shall withdraw and the parties concerned have the right to request withdrawal, where:

(1) the arbitrator is a party involved in the case or a blood relative of one of the parties concerned or their representative;
(2) the arbitrator has vital personal interests in the case;
(3) the arbitrator has other relationships with the parties or their representatives involved in the case that might affect the fair ruling of the case; or
(4) the arbitrator meets parties concerned or their representatives in private or has accepted gifts or attended banquets hosted by the parties concerned or their representatives.

Article 35

In requesting the withdrawal of an arbitrator, the parties concerned shall state the reasons before the first hearing of the tribunal. If the reasons are known only after the first hearing, they may be stated before the end of the last hearing.

Article 36

The withdrawal of an arbitrator shall be decided upon by the chairman of the arbitration commission. Where the chairman of the arbitration commission serves as an arbitrator, the withdrawal shall be decided upon collectively by the arbitration commission.

Article 37

Where an arbitrator withdraws or is unable to perform his duty for other reasons, another arbitrator shall be chosen or appointed according to the relevant provisions of this law.

Where re-selection or re-appointment of an arbitrator is made as a result of withdrawal, the parties concerned may apply for the re-start of the arbitration proceedings for the final decision of the arbitration tribunal. The arbitration tribunal itself may consider re-starting the arbitration proceedings based on the same reasons.

Article 38

Where an arbitrator has committed any misconduct as listed in sub-paragraph (6) of Article 58 or sub-paragraph (4) of Article 34, he shall bear the legal responsibility according to other relevant laws. The arbitration commission may remove him from the arbitration panel.

Article 39

An arbitration tribunal may hold oral hearings. Where the parties concerned agree not to hold oral hearings, the arbitration tribunal may give an award based on the arbitration application, claims and counter-claims and other documents.

Article 40

The arbitration tribunal may not hear a case in open session. But when parties concerned agree to have the case heard in open session, the hearing may be held openly, except for cases that involve State secrets.

Article 41

The arbitration commission shall notify the parties concerned of the date of the hearing within the time limit prescribed in the arbitration rules. With justifiable reasons, a party concerned may request the postponement of the hearing within the time limit set in the arbitration rules. The question of whether or not the hearing should be postponed shall be decided by the arbitration tribunal.

Article 42

Where a claimant is absent from the hearing without justifiable reason after receiving written notice or withdraws from the hearing during its course without the prior permission of the arbitration tribunal, it may be regarded as a withdrawal of his claim.

Where a respondent is absent from the hearing without justifiable reason after receiving written notice or withdraws from the hearing during its course without the prior permission by the arbitration tribunal, the tribunal may give an award by default.

Article 43

The parties concerned shall provide evidence to support their respective claims.

Where an arbitration tribunal deems it necessary to collect evidence, it may collect it on its own initiative.

Article 44

Where a specialised issue needs to be appraised, the arbitration tribunal may submit it to an appraisal body agreed by the parties concerned or designated by the arbitration tribunal.

At the request of the parties concerned or of the arbitration tribunal, the appraisal department shall send appraisers to the hearing. Parties concerned may, with the permission of the arbitration tribunal, raise questions to the appraisers.

Article 45

Evidence shall be produced during the course of the hearing and the parties concerned may question or substantiate their evidence.

Article 46

Where evidence is at risk of being destroyed or going missing and would need to be recovered, the parties concerned may apply for the evidence to be placed in custody. When a party applies for custody of evidence, the arbitration commission shall submit the evidence of the party concerned to the People's Court at the place where the evidence is to be obtained.

Article 47

The parties concerned have the right to take part in the hearing. At the end of the hearing, the chief arbitrator or the sole arbitrator shall ask the parties concerned for the final statement.

Article 48

The arbitration tribunal shall record hearings in writing. Where the parties concerned or other people involved in the arbitration find something in their statements left out in the recording or misrecorded, they have the right to apply for correction. Where corrections are not made, the application shall be recorded.

The written records of the hearings shall be signed or affixed with seals by the arbitrators, minute keepers, the parties concerned and other people participating in the arbitration.

Article 49

After the parties have applied for arbitration, they may reach agreement on the dispute on their own initiative. Where a settlement has been reached, a request may be made to the arbitration tribunal for an award based on the conciliation agreement, or the application for arbitration may be withdrawn.

Article 50

Where the parties concerned have withdrawn from a settlement, they may apply for arbitration according to the arbitration agreement.

Article 51

The arbitration tribunal may conciliate a case before passing the award. Where the parties concerned accept the conciliation effort of their own accord, the arbitration tribunal may conduct the conciliation. Should the conciliation fail, the arbitration tribunal shall make a timely award.

Where an agreement is reached through conciliation, the arbitration tribunal shall compile the conciliation document or make an award based on the results of the agreement. A document of conciliation and an arbitral award are equally legally binding.

Article 52

A document of conciliation shall specify the arbitration claims and the result of the agreement between the parties concerned. The document of conciliation shall be signed by the arbitrator and affixed with the seal of the arbitration commission before being delivered to the parties concerned.

The document of conciliation becomes legally binding immediately upon receipt by the parties concerned.

If any party concerned has gone back on his word after receiving the document of conciliation, the arbitration tribunal shall make a timely award.

Article 53

An arbitral award shall be decided by the majority of the arbitrators and the views of the minority shall be written down in the record. Where a majority decision cannot be reached, the award shall be decided based on the opinion of the chief arbitrator.

Article 54

An arbitral award shall specify the arbitration claims, facts in disputes, reasons for the award, result of the award, arbitration expenses and date of the award given. Where the parties concerned object to the specification of the facts in dispute or reasons for the ruling, such specification or reasons may be omitted. The arbitral award shall be signed by arbitrators and affixed with the seals of the arbitration commission. An arbitrator holding different views may or may not sign the award.

Article 55

In arbitrating disputes, the arbitration tribunal may make an award on part of the information that has already been made clear.

Article 56

An arbitration tribunal should correct the errors involving context or computation, and add things that have been omitted, in the rulings in the arbitral award. The parties concerned may apply for correction with the arbitration tribunal within 30 days after the receipt of the award.

Article 57

The arbitral award takes legal effect upon issue.

Chapter 5 Application for cancelling arbitral ruling

Article 58

If the parties concerned have evidence to substantiate one of the following cases, they may apply for the cancellation of the arbitral award with the Intermediate People's Court at the place where the arbitration commission is situated:

(1) there is no agreement for arbitration;

(2) the matters ruled are outside the scope of the agreement for arbitration or the limits of authority of an arbitration commission;

(3) the composition of the arbitration tribunal or the arbitration proceedings violate the legal requirements;

(4) the evidence on which the ruling is based is forged;

(5) matters that have an impact on the impartiality of the ruling have been concealed by the opposite party; or

(6) arbitrators have accepted bribes, resorted to deception for personal gains or perverted the law in the ruling.

The People's Court shall form a collegial bench to verify the case. Where one of the aforementioned cases is found, the arbitral award shall be cancelled by the court.

Where the People's Court establishes that an arbitral award is against the public interest, the award shall be cancelled by the court.

Article 59

An application filed by the parties concerned for the cancellation of an arbitral award shall be made within six months of the date of receipt of the award.

Article 60

The People's Court shall rule on cancellation of the award or rejection of the application within two months after the application for cancellation of an award is received.

Article 61

After the People's Court has accepted an application for the cancellation of an arbitral award and deems it necessary for the arbitration tribunal to make a new award, it shall notify the arbitration tribunal for a new ruling to be made within a specified time and order the termination of the cancellation procedure. Where the arbitration tribunal refuses to make a new award, the People's Court shall rule that the cancellation procedure be restored.

Chapter 6 Enforcement

Article 62

The parties concerned shall execute the arbitral award. If one of the parties refuses to execute the award, the other party may apply for enforcement with the People's Court according to the relevant provisions of the Civil Procedure Law. The People's Court with which the application is filed shall enforce it.

Article 63

If the respondent has produced evidence to substantiate one of the cases provided for in the second paragraph of Article 217 of the Civil Procedure Law, the award shall not be enforced after verification by the collegiate bench of the People's Court.

Article 64

Where one party applies for enforcement while the other applies for a cancellation of an award, the People's Court shall order the termination of the performance of the award.

Where the People's Court has ordered the cancellation of an award, it shall also order the termination of performance of the award. Where an application for the cancellation of an award is rejected, the People's Court shall order the restoration of the performance of the award.

Chapter 7 Special provisions on arbitration involving foreign interests

Article 65

The provisions in this Chapter apply to arbitration of disputes arising from foreign economic co-operation and trade, transportation and maritime matters. Matters not covered by this Chapter shall be handled according to other relevant provisions of this law.

Article 66

Foreign arbitration commissions may be formed by the China International Chamber of Commerce.

A foreign arbitration commission shall be composed of a chairman, a number of vice chairmen and members.

The chairman, vice chairmen and members of a foreign arbitration commission shall be appointed by the China International Chamber of Commerce.

Article 67

Members of a foreign arbitration commission may appoint arbitrators from among foreign nationals with specialised knowledge in law, economy and trade, science and technology.

Article 68

Where the parties involved in a foreign arbitration case apply for the custody of evidence, the foreign arbitration commission shall submit the application to the intermediate People's Court at places where the evidence is produced.

Article 69

A foreign arbitration tribunal may record its hearings, or produce summary records. The records shall be signed or affixed with the seals of the parties concerned and other people participating in the arbitration.

Article 70

Where a claimant has produced evidence to substantiate one of the cases provided for in the first paragraph of Article 260 of the Civil Procedure Law, the People's Court shall form a collegiate bench to verify the facts and order the cancellation of the award.

Article 71

Where a respondent has produced evidence to substantiate one of the cases provided for in the first paragraph of Article 260 of the Civil Procedure Law, the People's Court shall form a collegiate bench to verify the facts and order the non-performance of the award.

Article 72

Where a party involved in a foreign arbitration case applies for the enforcement of an award that has taken legal effect, the party may apply directly to a foreign court of law with the jurisdiction for recognition and enforcement if the party that should implement the award, or its property, is not within the territory of the People's Republic of China.

Article 73

The rules for foreign arbitration shall be formulated by the China International Chamber of Commerce according to this law and the relevant provisions of the Civil Procedure Law.

Chapter 8 Supplementary provisions

Article 74

Where laws stipulate time limits for effecting arbitration, the limits shall apply. In absence of the aforementioned laws, the time limits for proceedings shall apply.

Article 75

Until the China Arbitration Association has formulated arbitration rules, arbitration commissions may formulate interim rules for arbitration according to this law and the relevant provisions of the Civil Procedure Law.

Article 76

Parties concerned shall pay arbitration fees according to the relevant regulations.

The schedule of arbitration fees shall be submitted to the relevant authorities for approval.

Article 77

Arbitration of labour disputes and disputes arising from farm work contracts inside the collective agricultural organisation shall be formulated separately.

Article 78

Where relevant arbitration regulations formulated before the enforcement of this law come into conflict with the provisions of this law, the provisions of this law shall prevail.

Article 79

Arbitration organisations set up in cities where the people's governments of the municipalities, provinces and autonomous regions are located and other cities which have districts shall be re-organised according to the relevant provisions of this law. Those not re-organised shall be terminated one year after the date of the implementation of this law.

Other arbitration organisations set up before the implementation of this law and not in conformity with the provisions of this law shall be terminated starting from the date of the implementation of this law.

Article 80

This law shall be implemented as from 1 September 1995.

PART 5

ARBITRATION RULES OF THE CHINA MARITIME ARBITRATION COMMISSION 2001

(Revised and adopted on 22 November 2000 by China Chamber of International Commerce. Effective as from 1 January 2001)

Table of Contents

Chapter 1 General provisions

Section 1 Jurisdiction

Article 1

These Rules are formulated in accordance with the Arbitration Law and the provisions of the relevant laws of the People's Republic of China (PRC).

Article 2

The China Maritime Arbitration Commission (formerly known as the Maritime Arbitration Commission of the China Council for the Promotion of International Trade, and hereinafter referred to as the 'Arbitration Commission') independently and impartially resolves, by means of arbitration, contractual or non-contractual maritime disputes arising from, or in the process of, transportation, production and navigation by or at sea, in coastal waters and navigable waters adjacent to the sea, in order to protect the legitimate rights and interests of the parties and promote the development of the domestic and international industry of maritime commerce and economy and trade.

The Arbitration Commission shall take cognisance of cases relating to the following maritime disputes:

(1) disputes arising from salvage and general average;

(2) disputes arising from collision between ships and/or other offshore mobile units, or from contact of ships or other offshore mobile units with any

structure or installation on the sea, navigable waters adjacent thereto and in the harbours, as well as with a submarine or underwater installation;

(3) disputes arising from the carriage of goods at sea or in coastal waters or in navigable waters adjacent to the sea under a bill of lading, waybill, voyage charter-party or contract of multimodal transport containing a mode of transport by sea or any other transport documents, as well as from carriage of passengers by sea or in waters referred to above;

(4) disputes arising from time and demise chartering of ships, or from leasing of other offshore mobile units and containers or other transport articles, and from management, operation, agency, towage, raising and demolition of ships or other offshore mobile units;

(5) disputes arising from ownership of ships or other offshore mobile units and maritime liens;

(6) disputes arising from insurance of ships at sea, coastal waters or navigable waters adjacent to the sea and of other offshore mobile units, or from insurance on carriage of goods, or from insurance on carriage of passengers, or from insurance on offshore exploitation of resources, and from their reinsurance, as well as from the ship's protection and indemnity;

(7) disputes arising from sale, construction and repair of ships or other offshore movable units and containers or other transport articles;

(8) disputes arising from mortgage or loan of ships or other offshore mobile units;

(9) disputes arising from contracts of freight forwarding, supply of ship's stores, seamen's labour service, fishery production or fishing and so on;

(10) disputes arising from exploitation and utilisation of marine resources, or pollution damage to marine environment;

(11) disputes arising from maritime security; or

(12) other maritime disputes or disputes relating to maritime occurrences submitted for arbitration by agreement between the parties.

Article 3

The Arbitration Commission takes cognisance of cases in accordance with an arbitration agreement between the parties concluded before or after the occurrence of the dispute to refer their dispute to the Arbitration Commission for arbitration and upon the written application by one of the parties.

An arbitration agreement means an arbitration clause stipulated by the parties in their contract or a written agreement concluded by the parties in some other form to submit their dispute for arbitration.

Article 4

The Arbitration Commission has the power to decide on the existence or validity of an arbitration agreement and its jurisdiction over an arbitration case. If a party challenges the validity of an arbitration agreement and requests the Arbitration Commission to make a decision thereupon while the other party applies to the People's Court for a ruling, the latter's ruling shall prevail. However, in the event of a challenge against the validity of an arbitration agreement, if the acceptance of the application by the Arbitration Commission precedes that of the People's Court and a decision is made thereupon, the decision of the Arbitration Commission shall prevail.

Article 5

An arbitration clause contained in a contract shall be regarded as existing independently and separately from the other clauses of the contract, and an arbitration agreement attached to a contract shall be treated as a part of the contract existing independently and separately from the other parts of the contract. The validity of an arbitration clause or an arbitration agreement shall not be affected by the modification, rescission, termination, invalidity, revocation or non-existence of the contract.

Article 6

Any objections to an arbitration agreement or the jurisdiction over an arbitration case shall be raised before the first hearing conducted by the arbitration tribunal. Where a case is examined on the basis of documents only, objections to the jurisdiction should be raised before submission of the first substantive defence. Objections raised later than the prescribed time shall be disregarded.

Objections raised to an arbitration agreement or jurisdiction over the arbitration case shall not affect the process of the arbitration proceedings.

Article 7

Where the parties agree to submit their dispute to the Arbitration Commission for arbitration, they shall be deemed to have agreed to conduct the arbitration under these Rules. Nevertheless, where the parties have otherwise agreed upon other arbitration procedures and the Arbitration Commission agrees thereto, the agreement of the parties shall prevail.

Section 2 Organisation

Article 8

The Arbitration Commission shall have one honorary chairman and several advisers.

Article 9

The Arbitration Commission is composed of one chairman, several vice chairmen and a number of Commission members. The chairman performs the functions and duties vested in him by these Rules and the vice chairmen may perform the chairman's functions and duties with the chairman's authorisation.

The Arbitration Commission shall have a secretariat to handle its day-to-day work under the leadership of the Secretary General of the Arbitration Commission.

Article 10

The Arbitration Commission shall maintain a Panel of Arbitrators. The arbitrators shall be selected and appointed by the Arbitration Commission from among Chinese and foreign persons with special knowledge and practical experience in the fields of navigation, carriage by sea, foreign trade, insurance and management of risks, law and other fields.

Article 11

The Arbitration Commission is located in Beijing. The Arbitration Commission may, according to a growing need for its arbitration service, set up sub-Commissions or offices in other places within China's territory.

The Arbitration Commission shall have offices for public relations, consultancy and liaison, under the unified leadership of the Arbitration Commission, engaged in publicity, investigation, research and consultancy in respect of maritime arbitration. These offices shall assist the Arbitration Commission in arranging oral hearings held in their locality, but they shall not take cognisance of any case, collect fees or charges, nor shall they examine or hear any case.

Chapter 2 Arbitration proceedings

Section 1 Application for arbitration, defence and counter-claim

Article 12

The arbitration proceedings shall commence from the date on which the Notice of Arbitration is sent out by the Arbitration Commission.

Article 13

The claimant, when submitting his application for arbitration, shall:

(1) Submit an application for arbitration which shall specify:

   (a) the name and address of the claimant and those of the respondent, including the zip code, telephone number, telex number, fax number and cable number or other electronic communication address, if any;

   (b) the arbitration agreement relied upon by the claimant;

   (c) the facts of the case and the main points of dispute;

   (d) the claimant's claim, along with the underlying facts and evidence.

   The application for arbitration shall be signed and/or stamped by the claimant and/or a representative authorised by the claimant.

(2) Append to the application for arbitration the relevant documentary evidence on which the claimant's claim is based.

(3) Pay an arbitration fee in advance to the Arbitration Commission according to its Arbitration Fee Schedule.

Article 14

Where after receipt of the application for arbitration and its attachments, the Secretariat of the Arbitration Commission finds upon examination that the claimant has not completed the formalities required for arbitration, the Secretariat shall request the claimant to complete them, and where the

Secretariat finds that the claimant has completed the formalities, the Secretariat shall immediately send to the respondent a Notice of Arbitration together with one copy each of the claimant's application for arbitration and its attachments together with the Arbitration Rules, the Panel of Arbitrators and the Arbitration Fee Schedule of the Arbitration Commission, and shall simultaneously send to the claimant one copy each of the Notice of Arbitration, the Arbitration Rules, the Panel of Arbitrators and the Arbitration Fee Schedule.

The Secretariat of the Arbitration Commission, when sending the Notice of Arbitration to the claimant and respondent, shall appoint one of its staff members to take charge of procedural administration of the case.

Article 15

The claimant and the respondent shall, within 20 days from the date of receipt of the Notice of Arbitration, appoint respectively an arbitrator from among the Arbitrators on the Panel of the Arbitration Commission or authorise the Chairman of the Arbitration Commission to make such appointment. Both parties shall within the prescribed time jointly appoint, or jointly entrust the chairman of the Arbitration Commission with appointing a third arbitrator as the presiding arbitrator.

Article 16

The respondent shall, within 45 days from the date of receipt of the Notice of Arbitration, submit his written defence and relevant documentary evidence to the Secretariat of the Arbitration Commission. After the specified time, the arbitration tribunal is entitled to decide whether to accept a defence.

Article 17

The respondent shall, within 45 days from the date of receipt of the Notice of Arbitration, lodge with the Secretariat of the Arbitration Commission a counter-claim in writing, if any. The arbitration tribunal may, on request, extend that time limit if it considers that there is a justified reason.

When lodging a counter-claim, the respondent shall state in his written counter-claim his specific claim, reasons for his claim, the underlying facts and evidence for his claim and attach to his written counter-claim the relevant documentary evidence.

When lodging a counter-claim, the respondent shall pay an arbitration fee in advance according to the Arbitration Fee Schedule of the Arbitration Commission.

Article 18

The claimant may make a request to amend his claim whilst the respondent may make a request to amend his counter-claim. However, the arbitration tribunal may refuse such a request for amendment if it considers that it is too late to raise the amendment as it may affect the normal process of the arbitration proceedings.

Article 19

The parties shall submit, in quintuplicate, application for arbitration, written defence, statement of counter-claim, relevant documentary evidence and other documents. If the number of the parties exceeds two, additional copies shall be submitted accordingly; if the arbitration tribunal is composed of only one member, two sets of copies may be omitted.

Article 20

Neither the failure by the respondent to file his defence in writing nor the failure of the claimant to submit his written defence against a respondent's counter-claim shall affect the process of the arbitration proceedings.

Article 21

The parties may authorise arbitration agents to deal with the matters relating to arbitration; the authorised representative must produce a power of attorney to the Arbitration Commission.

Chinese and foreign citizens can be authorised to act as arbitration agents.

Article 22

Where a party applies for preservation of property, the Arbitration Commission shall submit the party's application to the Maritime Court of the place of the respondent's domicile or of the place of the property subject to preservation. Where a party applies for preservation of a maritime claim before the commencement of arbitration proceedings, he shall, according to the provisions of Chapter 3 of the Maritime Procedure Law of the People's Republic of China, submit the application direct to the Maritime Court of the place of the property subject to preservation.

Where a party applies for preservation of maritime evidence, the Arbitration Commission shall submit the party's application to the Maritime Court of the place where the evidence to be preserved is located. Where a party applies for preservation of maritime evidence before the commencement of arbitration proceedings, he shall, according to the provisions of Chapter 5 of the Maritime Procedure Law of the People's Republic of China, submit his application direct to the Maritime Court of the place where the evidence to be preserved is located.

Where a party applies for a maritime injunction, the Arbitration Commission shall submit the party's application to the Maritime Court of the place where the maritime dispute arises. Where a party applies for a maritime injunction before the commencement of the arbitration proceedings, he shall, according to the provisions of Chapter 4 of the Maritime Procedure Law of the People's Republic of China, submit his application direct to the Maritime Court of the place where the maritime dispute arises.

Article 23

Where a party applies for constitution of a limitation fund for maritime claims, the Arbitration Commission shall submit the party's application to the Maritime Court of the place of accident, the place of performance of the contract or the place of the ship arrest. Where a party applies for constitution of a limitation fund for maritime claims before the commencement of the arbitration proceedings, he shall, according to the provisions of Chapter 4 of the Maritime Procedure Law of the People's Republic of China, submit his application direct to the Maritime Court of the place of the accident, the place of performance of the contract or the place of the ship arrest.

Section 2 Formation of arbitration tribunal

Article 24

Each of the parties shall appoint one arbitrator from among the arbitrators on the Panel of the Arbitration Commission or entrust the chairman of the Arbitration Commission with the making of such appointment. The third arbitrator shall be jointly appointed by the parties or appointed by the chairman of the Arbitration Commission upon the parties' joint authorisation.

Where a claimant or respondent fails to appoint or fails to entrust the chairman of the Arbitration Commission with the appointment of an arbitrator respectively within 20 days from the day of receipt of the Notice of Arbitration, the chairman of the Arbitration Commission shall make such appointment.

Where the parties fail to jointly appoint or jointly entrust the chairman of the Arbitration Commission with the appointment of the third arbitrator within 20 days from the date on which the respondent receives the Notice of Arbitration, the third arbitrator shall be appointed by the chairman of the Arbitration Commission. The third arbitrator shall act as the presiding arbitrator.

The presiding arbitrator and the two arbitrators as appointed above shall jointly form an arbitration tribunal to hear the case.

Article 25

Both parties may jointly appoint or jointly authorise the chairman of the Arbitration Commission to appoint from the arbitrators on the Panel an arbitrator as the sole arbitrator to form an arbitration tribunal to hear the case alone.

If both parties have agreed on the appointment of a sole arbitrator to hear their case alone but have failed to agree on the choice of such a sole arbitrator within 20 days from the day of receipt by the respondent of the Notice of Arbitration, the chairman of the Arbitration Commission shall make such appointment.

Article 26

Where there are two or more claimants and/or respondents in an arbitration case, the claimant and/or the respondent each shall, through consultation, appoint or entrust the chairman of the Arbitration Commission with the appointment of one arbitrator from among the Panel of Arbitrators of the Arbitration Commission.

If the claimant or the respondent fails to make such appointment or entrustment within 20 days from the date on which the respondent's side receives the Notice of Arbitration, the appointment shall be made by the chairman of the Arbitration Commission.

Article 27

Any appointed arbitrator having a personal interest in the case shall himself disclose such circumstances to the Arbitration Commission and request a withdrawal from his office.

Article 28

A party may make a request in writing to the Arbitration Commission for the removal of an arbitrator from his office, if the party suspects the impartiality and independence of the said arbitrator, provided he states clearly the facts and reasons for his request for the withdrawal and evidence shall be given.

Request for withdrawal of an arbitrator shall be put forward in writing no later than the first oral hearing. If the factors supporting the withdrawal occur or are made known after the first oral hearing, the request for withdrawal may be made before the end of the last hearing.

Article 29

The chairman of the Arbitration Commission shall decide on the withdrawal of the challenged arbitrator.

Until the chairman of the Arbitration Commission makes a decision on whether the challenged arbitrator should be removed, the arbitrator shall proceed with his function.

Article 30

If an arbitrator cannot perform his duty owing to withdrawal, death, removal or other reasons, a substitute arbitrator shall be appointed in accordance with the procedure whereby the replaced arbitrator was appointed.

After the appointment of a substitute arbitrator, the arbitration tribunal has discretion to decide whether all or some of the previous hearings shall be repeated.

Section 3 Hearing

Article 31

An arbitration tribunal shall hold oral hearings when examining a case; however, the arbitration tribunal may examine a case and render an award only on the basis of documentary evidence, provided both parties request or consent to it. The arbitration tribunal may also consider an oral hearing unnecessary.

Article 32

The date of the first oral hearing shall be fixed by the arbitration tribunal in consultation with the Secretariat of the Arbitration Commission, and shall be communicated by the Secretariat to both parties 30 days before the date of the hearing. A party having justified reasons may request a postponement of the date of the hearing, provided his written request is communicated to the Secretariat of the Arbitration Commission 12 days before the date of the hearing. The arbitration tribunal shall decide whether to postpone the hearing.

Article 33

The notice of the date of the hearing subsequent to the first oral hearing is not subject to the 30 day time limit.

Article 34

The cases taken cognisance of by the Arbitration Commission shall be heard in Beijing, or may be heard in other places with the approval of the Secretary General of the Arbitration Commission.

Where the place of arbitration has been agreed on by the parties, the oral hearing of the arbitration case shall be held in the agreed place.

Article 35

The arbitration tribunal shall not hear cases in open session. If both parties request a hearing to be held in open session, the arbitration tribunal shall decide whether to hold the hearing in open session.

Article 36

Where a case is heard in closed session, no substantive or procedural matters of the case shall be disclosed to outsiders by the parties, their representatives, witnesses, arbitrators, experts consulted by or appraisers appointed by the arbitration tribunal and the relevant staff members of the Secretariat of the Arbitration Commission.

Article 37

The parties shall produce evidence for the facts underlying their claim, defence and counter-claim. The arbitration tribunal may undertake investigations and collect evidence on its own initiative, if it considers it necessary.

If the arbitration tribunal investigates and collects evidence on its own initiative, it shall in a timely manner inform the parties of this if it considers it necessary. Should one party or both parties fail to appear at the place, the investigation and collection of evidence by the arbitration tribunal shall be by no means affected.

Article 38

Evidence may be questioned by the parties at oral hearings, unless both parties agree to examine the case on the basis of documentary evidence or the evidence is questioned in writing.

Where a party submits, with the approval of the arbitration tribunal, supplementary written evidence after an oral hearing, the arbitration tribunal shall forward the evidence to the other party and give him the opportunity to comment.

Article 39

The arbitration tribunal may consult an expert or appoint an appraiser for their expertise or appraisal on special issues relating to the case. Such an expert or appraiser may be a Chinese or foreign organisation or a citizen.

The arbitration tribunal is entitled to require the parties to submit or produce for the expert or appraiser any materials, documents, property or goods related to the case for check-up, inspection and/or appraisal. The arbitration tribunal shall, after making duplicate copies or effective records of the evidence, return in a timely manner the original evidence submitted by the party.

Article 40

The report prepared by the expert or the appraiser shall be copied to the parties so that they may have the opportunity to give their opinions thereon. At the request of any party to the case and with the approval of the arbitration tribunal, the expert or appraiser may be present at the hearing and give explanations of their reports where the arbitration tribunal considers it necessary and appropriate.

Article 41

The evidence submitted by the parties shall be examined and approved by the arbitration tribunal. The adoption of the report prepared by the expert or the appraiser shall be determined by the arbitration tribunal.

Article 42

Should a claimant fail, without justifiable reason, to appear at an oral hearing that he has been informed of by a written notice, or withdraw in the course of a hearing without the approval of the arbitration tribunal, the arbitration tribunal may regard it as a withdrawal of the application for arbitration, and where the respondent has made a counter-claim, an award by default can be made. Should a respondent fail, without justifiable reason, to appear at a hearing that he has been informed of by a written notice, or withdraw in the course of a hearing without approval of the arbitration tribunal, an award by default may be rendered, and where the respondent has made a counter-claim, the counter-claim may be regarded as withdrawn.

Article 43

During the oral hearing, the arbitration tribunal may record and/or make tape recordings of the hearing. The arbitration tribunal may, after the hearing, make a summary of the record stating the main points of the hearing where it considers it necessary and ask the parties and/or their representatives, witnesses and/or other persons involved to sign and/or affix their seals to the summary record.

The record and the tape recording of the oral hearing are only for reference by the arbitration tribunal.

Article 44

The parties shall submit written documents and evidence in accordance with the requirements of the arbitration tribunal within the prescribed time; and the arbitration tribunal is entitled to decide whether to accept the documents and evidence submitted by a party after the prescribed time.

Article 45

Where a person other than the parties to the arbitration case considers he has a legal interest in the conclusion of the case in relation to the claim or counter-claim submitted by any of the parties, the person may, with the agreement of both parties, apply, with the approval of the arbitration tribunal, for participation as a party in the arbitration case.

Article 46

Where two or more arbitration cases involve the same matters, the arbitration tribunal may consolidate the cases, if the arbitration tribunal considers it appropriate, after obtaining the consent of all parties concerned. The presiding arbitrators of each case shall select a person from among themselves who will chair an oral hearing, while the awards for the case shall be made separately.

Article 47

The arbitration tribunal may, at the request of a party, decide to suspend the arbitration proceedings under one of the following occurrences:

(1) the parties are working for a settlement by themselves;

(2) the case under arbitration depends on the conclusion of another case which has not been decided;

(3) a party is unable to participate in the arbitration on account of *force majeure*; or

(4) other appropriate occurrences.

Article 48

If the parties to an arbitration case reach an amicable settlement agreement by themselves, they may either request the arbitration tribunal to conclude the case by making an award in accordance with the contents of their settlement agreement or request a dismissal of the case. The Secretary General of the Arbitration Commission shall decide on the request for a dismissal of the case if the request is made before the formation of the arbitration tribunal, and the arbitration tribunal shall decide if the request is put forward after the formation of the arbitration tribunal.

If the party or parties refer the dismissed case again to the Arbitration Commission for arbitration, the chairman of the Arbitration Commission shall decide whether to accept the reference.

If the parties reach a settlement agreement by themselves through conciliation without the involvement of the Arbitration Commission, any of them may, based on an arbitration agreement concluded between them providing for arbitration by the Arbitration Commission and their settlement agreement, request the Arbitration Commission to appoint a sole arbitrator to render legally an arbitration award in accordance with the contents of the settlement agreement.

Article 49

A party who knows or should have known that any provision or requirement of these Rules has not been complied with and yet proceeds with the arbitration proceedings without explicitly raising in writing his objection to non-compliance in a timely manner shall be deemed to have waived his right to object.

Article 50

If both parties desire conciliation, or one party so desires and the other party agrees to it when consulted by the arbitration tribunal, the arbitration tribunal may conciliate the case under its cognisance in the process of arbitration.

Article 51

The arbitration tribunal may conciliate cases in a manner it considers appropriate.

Article 52

The arbitration tribunal shall terminate conciliation when one of the parties requests a termination of conciliation or when the arbitration tribunal believes that further efforts to conciliate will be futile.

Article 53

If the parties have reached an amicable settlement outside the arbitration tribunal in the course of conciliation conducted by the arbitration tribunal, such settlement shall be considered as one which has been reached through conciliation by the arbitration tribunal.

Article 54

The parties shall sign a settlement agreement in writing when a settlement is reached through conciliation conducted by the arbitration tribunal, and the arbitration tribunal shall conclude the case by making an award in accordance with the contents of the settlement agreement unless otherwise agreed by the parties.

Article 55

Should conciliation fail, any statement, opinion, view or proposal which has been made, raised, put forward, acknowledged, accepted or rejected by either party or by the arbitration tribunal in the process of conciliation shall not be invoked by the other party as grounds for any claim, defence and/or counter-claim in the subsequent arbitration proceedings, judicial proceedings or any other proceedings.

Section 4 Award

Article 56

The arbitration tribunal shall make an award within nine months from the date on which the arbitration tribunal was formed. The Secretary General of the Arbitration Commission may extend this time limit at the request of the arbitration tribunal if the Secretary General of the Arbitration Commission considers the request justifiable and necessary. Where a decision is made by the arbitration tribunal suspending the arbitration proceedings, the time required for such suspension shall not be counted in the time limit.

Article 57

The arbitration tribunal shall independently and impartially make its award on the basis of the facts, in accordance with the law and the terms of the contract, with reference to international practices and in compliance with the principles of fairness and reasonableness.

Article 58

Where a case is heard by an arbitration tribunal composed of three arbitrators, the award shall be rendered in accordance with the opinion of the majority of the arbitrators and the minority opinion may be noted down and filed.

Where the arbitration tribunal cannot attain a majority opinion, the award shall be rendered in accordance with the presiding arbitrator's opinion.

Article 59

The arbitration tribunal shall state in the award the claims, the facts of the dispute, the reasons for making the award, the result of the award, the allocation of the arbitration fees and costs, and the date and place of the award. The facts of the dispute and the reasons for making the award may not be stated in the award if the parties have so agreed or the award is made in accordance with the contents of the settlement agreement reached by the parties.

Article 60

Unless the award is made in accordance with the opinion of the presiding arbitrator or the sole arbitrator, the award shall be signed by the majority of the arbitrators sitting on the arbitration tribunal. An arbitrator who has a dissenting opinion may or may not sign the award.

The arbitrators shall submit their draft award to the Arbitration Commission before signing the award. The Arbitration Commission may remind the arbitrators of any issue related to the form of the award provided that the arbitrators' independence in respect of making a decision is not affected.

The official seal of the Arbitration Commission shall be affixed to the award.

The date on which the award is made is the date on which the award comes into legal effect.

Article 61

The arbitration tribunal may, at any time in the course of arbitration before the final award is made, make an interlocutory award or a partial award on any issue of the case if it considers it necessary or agrees to such a request made by a party. Either party's failure to perform the interlocutory award does not affect the continuation of the arbitration proceedings or the making of the final award by the arbitration tribunal.

Article 62

The arbitration tribunal has the power to determine the arbitration fee in the award and other expenses to be eventually paid by the party or parties to the Arbitration Commission.

Article 63

The arbitration tribunal has the power to decide in the award that the losing party shall pay the winning party as compensation a proportion of the expenses reasonably incurred by the winning party in dealing with the case.

The amount of such compensation shall not in any case exceed 10% of the total amount awarded to the winning party.

Article 64

The award is final and binding upon both disputing parties. Neither party may bring a suit before a law court or make a request to any other organisation for revising the award.

Article 65

Either party may request in writing that a correction be made to the writing, typing, calculations and similar errors contained in the award within 30 days from the date of receipt of the award; if there is an error in the award, the arbitration tribunal shall make a correction in writing within 30 days from the date of receipt of the written request for correction. The arbitration tribunal may by itself make a correction in writing within 30 days from the date on which the award is issued. The correction in writing forms a part of the award.

Article 66

If anything that should be awarded has been omitted in the award, either of the parties may make a request in writing to the arbitration tribunal for an additional award within 30 days from the date on which the award is received.

If something which should be awarded is omitted, the arbitration tribunal shall make an additional award within 30 days from the date of receipt of the request in writing for an additional award. The arbitration tribunal may by itself make an additional award within 30 days from the date on which the award is issued. The additional award forms a part of the award which has been previously issued.

Article 67

The parties must automatically execute the award within the time limit specified in the award. If no time limit is specified in the award, the parties shall carry out the award immediately.

If one party fails to execute the award, the other party may apply to a Chinese court for enforcement of the award pursuant to Chinese law or apply to a competent foreign court for enforcement of the award according to the 1958 Convention on Recognition and Enforcement of Foreign Arbitral Awards or other international treaties that China has concluded or acceded.

Chapter 3 Summary Procedure

Article 68

Unless otherwise agreed by the parties, this Summary Procedure shall apply to any case in dispute where the amount of the claim totals not more than RMB 500,000 (exclusive of interest).

This Summary Procedure shall also apply to cases where the amount of the claim totals more than RMB 500,000 provided that one party applies for and the other party agrees to it.

Article 69

Where an application for arbitration submitted by a claimant to the Arbitration Commission is accepted after examination by the Arbitration Commission and the Summary Procedure is applicable, the Secretariat of the Arbitration Commission shall immediately serve a Notice of Arbitration to each of the parties.

Both parties shall jointly appoint or jointly entrust the chairman of the Arbitration Commission with the appointment of one sole arbitrator from the arbitrators on the Panel of the Arbitration Commission within 15 days from the date on which the Notice of Arbitration is received by the respondent. Should the parties fail to make such appointment or entrustment within the time limit, the chairman of the Arbitration Commission shall immediately appoint one sole arbitrator to form an arbitration tribunal to hear the case.

Article 70

The respondent shall, within 30 days from the date of receipt of the Notice of Arbitration, submit his defence and relevant documentary evidence to the Arbitration Commission; a counter-claim, if any, shall be lodged together with documentary evidence within the said time limit.

Article 71

The arbitration tribunal may hear the case in the way it considers appropriate. The arbitration tribunal has discretion to hear the case only on the basis of the written materials and evidence submitted by the parties, or to hold an oral hearing.

Article 72

The parties shall deliver written materials and evidence needed for the arbitration in compliance with the requirements of, and within the time limit given by, the arbitration tribunal. The arbitration tribunal is entitled to decide whether to accept documents submitted by the party beyond the time limit.

Article 73

Where a case is to be heard orally, the Secretariat of the Arbitration Commission shall, after the arbitration tribunal fixes a date for the hearing, inform the parties of the date of the hearing 15 days before the date of the hearing.

Article 74

If the arbitration tribunal decides to hear a case orally, only one oral hearing shall be held. However, the arbitration tribunal may hold a second hearing if necessary.

Article 75

Should one of the parties fail to act in compliance with this Summary Procedure during summary proceedings, such failure shall not affect the process of the proceedings or the power of the arbitration tribunal to render an award.

Article 76

Neither the modification of the claim nor the lodgment of a counter-claim shall affect the process of the summary proceedings, except where the amount of the modified claim or of the counter-claim contravenes the provisions of Article 68.

Article 77

Where a case is heard orally, the arbitration tribunal shall make an award within 30 days from the date of the oral hearing or from the date of the second oral hearing if any. Where a case is examined on the basis of documents only, the arbitration tribunal shall render an award within 90 days from the date of the formation of the arbitration tribunal. The Secretary General of the Arbitration Commission may, at the request of the arbitration tribunal, extend the said time limit if he considers such extension is necessary and justifiable.

Article 78

For matters not covered in this Chapter, the relevant provisions in the other Chapters of these Rules shall apply.

Chapter 4 Supplementary provisions

Article 79

The Chinese language is the official language of the Arbitration Commission. If the parties have agreed otherwise, their agreement shall prevail.

At the oral hearing, if the parties or their representatives or witnesses require language interpretation, the Secretariat of the Arbitration Commission may provide an interpreter for them or the parties may retain their own interpreters.

The arbitration tribunal or the Secretariat of the Arbitration Commission may, if they consider it necessary, request the parties to furnish them with corresponding translation copies in Chinese or other languages of the documents and evidential materials submitted by the parties.

Article 80

All arbitration documents, notices and materials may be served in person on the parties or their representatives, or by registered letter or express airmail, telefax, telex, cable or by any other means which are deemed proper by the Secretariat of the Arbitration Commission.

Article 81

Any written communication to the parties is deemed to have been properly served if it is delivered to the addressee or delivered to his place of business, habitual residence or mailing address; or if none of these can be found after making a reasonable inquiry, a written communication is deemed to have been served if it is sent to the addressee's last known place of business, habitual residence or mailing address by registered letter or by any other means which provide a record of the attempt to deliver it.

Article 82

Apart from charging arbitration fees from the parties according to the arbitration Fee Schedule of the Arbitration Commission, the Arbitration Commission may collect from the parties other extra, reasonable and actual expenses including arbitrators' special remuneration and their travel and boarding expenses for dealing with the case and the fees and expenses for experts, appraisers and interpreters, etc, appointed by the arbitration tribunal.

If a case is withdrawn after the parties have reached a settlement between themselves, the Arbitration Commission may charge a specified amount of payment from the parties in consideration of the quantity of work and the amount of the actual expenses incurred by the Arbitration Commission.

Article 83

Where it is explicitly stipulated by the parties to a maritime dispute in an arbitration agreement or an arbitration clause contained in the contract that arbitration is to be conducted by the China Maritime Arbitration Commission, or by its former name, the Maritime Arbitration Commission of the China Council for the Promotion of International Trade, or by the CCPIT/China Chamber of International Commerce, it shall be considered that the parties have unanimously agreed that the arbitration shall be conducted by the China Maritime Arbitration Commission.

Article 84

These Rules shall come into force as from 1 January 2001. For cases which have been taken cognisance of by the Arbitration Commission before the date on which these Rules become effective, the Rules of Arbitration effective on the date when the cases were taken cognisance of shall continue to apply; however, these Rules shall be applied thereto if the parties so agree.

Article 85

The power to interpret these Rules is vested in the Arbitration Commission.

PART 6

INSURANCE LAW OF THE PRC 1995

(Adopted at the 14th Session of the Standing Committee of the 8th National People's Congress on 30 June 1995 and effective as of 1 October 1995)

Table of Contents

Chapter 1 General provisions

Article 1

This law is formulated for the purpose of regulating insurance activities, protecting the lawful rights and interests of parties in insurance activities, strengthening the supervision and control of the insurance industry and promoting the healthy development of the insurance business.

Article 2

For the purposes of this law, the term 'insurance' shall refer to a commercial insurance act whereby a proposer pays a premium to an insurer in accordance with a contract while the insurer assumes liability for payment of insurance monies for property losses as a result of the occurrence of an event specified in the contract, or when the insured dies, becomes injured or disabled, falls ill or reaches the age or time limit as specified in the contract.

Article 3

This law shall apply to parties engaged in insurance activities within the People's Republic of China.

Article 4

Parties engaged in insurance activities must abide by the laws and administrative regulations and adhere to the principles of voluntariness, honesty and trustworthiness.

Article 5

Entities engaged in commercial insurance business must be insurance companies established in accordance with this law. No other organisation or individual may engage in commercial insurance business.

Article 6

Where legal persons and other organisations in the People's Republic of China need to take out insurance inside China, such insurance shall be proposed to an insurance company in the People's Republic of China.

Article 7

In developing their business, insurance companies shall adhere to the principle of fair competition and may not engage in unfair competition.

Article 8

The financial supervision and control department of the State Council shall be responsible for supervision and control of the insurance industry in accordance with this law.

Chapter 2 Insurance contracts

Section 1 General provisions

Article 9

An insurance contract is an agreement between a proposer and an insurer on the relationship of rights and obligations in respect of insurance.

The term 'proposer' refers to a person who concludes an insurance contract with an insurer and bears an obligation to pay a premium in accordance with the insurance contract.

The term 'insurer' refers to an insurance company which concludes an insurance contract with a proposer and assumes liability for payment of insurance monies.

Article 10

An insurance contract between a proposer and an insurer shall be concluded in accordance with the principles of equality, mutual benefit, consensus and voluntariness, and may not harm the public interest.

No insurance company or other undertaking may compel a third party to conclude an insurance contract, unless insurance is required by laws or administrative regulations.

Article 11

A proposer shall have an insurable interest in the insured subject matter.

An insurance contract shall be void where the proposer has no insurable interest in the insured subject matter.

The term 'insurable interest' refers to a legally recognised interest of the proposer in the subject matter of insurance.

The term 'insured subject matter' refers to property and its related interests or to the life or physical body of a person, as an object of insurance.

Article 12

An insurance contract shall be formed after a proposer has made an insurance offer and an insurer has agreed to accept such offer, with an agreement on the terms and conditions of the contract reached. The insurer shall issue a policy or other insurance certificate to the proposer in a timely manner and specify the contents of the contract as agreed between the parties in the policy or other insurance certificate.

If agreed by the proposer and the insurer following consultations, an insurance contract may be concluded in the form of a written agreement other than that specified in the preceding paragraph.

Article 13

A proposer shall pay a premium to an insurer upon formation of an insurance contract as agreed. The insurer shall begin to assume insurance liability from the time as agreed.

Article 14

Upon formation of an insurance contract, a proposer may rescind the contract, unless otherwise provided for by this law or such contract.

Article 15

Upon formation of an insurance contract, an insurer may not rescind such contract, except otherwise provided by this law or such contract.

Article 16

When concluding an insurance contract, an insurer shall explain the details of the terms and conditions of such contract to the proposer and may raise questions concerning relevant details of the insured subject matter, or of the insured. The proposer shall truthfully inform the insurer of such details.

The insurer shall have the right to rescind the insurance contract where the proposer, in bad faith, withholds facts and fails to perform his duty to truthfully inform the insurer of relevant facts or fails to perform such duty as a result of a mistake so that the failure influences the insurer's decision as to whether he will accept the insurance or raise the premium rate.

Where the proposer, in bad faith, fails to perform his duty to truthfully notify the insurer, the insurer shall not be liable for payment of insurance monies in connection with events insured against that occur prior to the rescission of the contract, and shall not refund the premium.

Where the failure of the proposer to perform his duty to truthfully notify the insurer as a result of a mistake has a serious impact on the occurrence of events insured against, the insurer shall not be liable for payment of insurance monies in connection with events insured against that occur prior to the rescission of the contract, but he shall refund the premium.

The term 'events insured against' shall refer to events within the scope of insurance liability specified in an insurance contract.

Article 17

Where an insurance contract contains terms and conditions providing for exclusion of the liability of an insurer, the insurer shall clearly explain such terms and conditions to the proposer at the time of concluding the contract. Where such terms and conditions are not clearly explained, they shall not be effective.

Article 18

An insurance contract shall contain the following particulars:

(1) the name and domicile of the insurer;

(2) the name and domicile of the proposer and the insured and in the case of a personal insurance contract, the name and domicile of the beneficiary;

(3) the insured subject matter;

(4) the insurance liability and exclusion of liability;

(5) the insurance period and time of commencement of insurance liability;

(6) the insured value;

(7) the insured sum;

(8) the premium and the method of payment thereof;

(9) the insurance money or method of payment;

(10) liability for breach of contract and settlement of disputes; and

(11) the date of concluding the contract.

Article 19

A proposer and an insurer may agree on other particulars concerning insurance in an insurance contract, in addition to those particulars provided for in the preceding Article.

Article 20

During the term of an insurance contract, the proposer and insurer may amend the relevant contents of such a contract after reaching an agreement through consultation.

Where the insurance contract is amended, the insurer shall endorse or attach an endorsement to the original policy or other insurance documents, or a written agreement on the amendments shall be concluded between the proposer and the insurer.

Article 21

Proposers, the insured or beneficiaries shall immediately notify insurers after learning of the occurrence of an event insured against.

The term 'insured' shall refer to a person whose property or physical body is covered by an insurance contract and who has the right to claim insurance monies. A proposer may be the insured.

The term 'beneficiary' shall refer to a person with the right to claim insurance monies, as designated in a personal insurance contract by the insured or the proposer. Proposers and the insured may be beneficiaries.

Article 22

Where insurance monies are claimed from an insurer in accordance with an insurance contract following the occurrence of an event insured against, the proposer, the insured or the beneficiary shall provide in good faith such documents and information confirming the nature and cause of such event and the degree of loss, etc.

Where the insurer considers relevant documents and information incomplete pursuant to the provisions of the insurance contract, he shall notify the proposer, the insured or the beneficiary of the requirement to provide the missing relevant documents and information.

Article 23

Upon receipt of a claim for insurance monies from the insured or the beneficiary, the insurer shall verify the claim in a timely manner. Where the claim comes under his insurance liability, he shall perform his obligation to pay insurance monies within 10 days of reaching an agreement with the insured or the beneficiary on the sum insured. Where the sum insured and the time limit for payment thereof are stipulated in the insurance contract, the insurer shall perform his obligation to pay insurance monies in accordance with such stipulations.

Where the insurer fails to perform his obligations as specified in the preceding paragraph in a timely manner, he shall indemnify the insured or the beneficiary for losses suffered as a result thereof, in addition to payment of the insurance monies.

No undertaking or individual may unlawfully interfere with the insurer's performance of his obligation to pay insurance monies or restrict the insured's or the beneficiary's right to obtain insurance monies.

The term 'sum insured' shall refer to the maximum amount of insurance monies for which an insurer assumes indemnity or payment liability.

Article 24

Where a claim for insurance monies received by an insurer from an insured or a beneficiary does not come under his insurance liability, the insurer shall issue a written notice of refusal of payment of insurance monies.

Article 25

Where an insurer is unable to determine the amount of insurance monies within 60 days of receiving a claim for insurance monies from the relevant documents and information, he shall first pay the minimum amount as can be determined on the basis of the existing documents and information. After determining the final amount of insurance monies, the insurer shall make up the difference in respect of such insurance monies.

Article 26

The right of an insured or a beneficiary to claim insurance monies from an insurer under insurance other than life insurance shall be extinguished if it is not exercised within two years from the date on which the insured or the beneficiary learned of the occurrence of the event insured against.

The right of the insured or the beneficiary to claim insurance monies from the insurer under life insurance shall be extinguished if it is not exercised within five years from the date on which the insured or the beneficiary learned of the occurrence of the event insured against.

Article 27

Where an insured or a beneficiary falsely claims that an event insured against has occurred before such event actually occurs, and submits a claim for payment of insurance monies to the insurer, the insurer shall have the right to rescind the insurance contract without having to refund the premium.

Where the proposer, the insured or the beneficiary creates, in bad faith, an event insured against, the insurer shall have the right to rescind the insurance contract and shall not be liable for payment of insurance monies and shall not refund the premium, except otherwise provided for in the first paragraph of Article 64.

Where the proposer, the insured or the beneficiary fabricates false causes of an event or overstates the degree of losses by means of forged or altered relevant documents, information or other evidence after the occurrence of such an event, the insurer shall not be liable for payment of insurance monies for the portion that is false.

The proposer, the insured or the beneficiary shall return the insurance monies or reimburse the expenses paid by the insurer as a result of any of the acts in the preceding three paragraphs performed by the said proposer, assured or beneficiary.

Article 28

Where an insurer transfers part of the insurance business he has undertaken to another insurer (reinsurer), such insurance is reinsurance.

At the request of the reinsurer, the reinsured shall disclose to the reinsurer relevant details of his own liability and the original insurance.

Article 29

The reinsurer may not demand payment of the premium from the original proposer.

The original insured or the original beneficiary may not submit a claim for insurance monies to the reinsurer.

The reinsured may not refuse to perform or delay the performance of his original insurance liability on the grounds of the failure of the reinsurer to perform his reinsurance liability.

Article 30

When a dispute arises between the insurer and the proposer, the insured or the beneficiary over the terms and conditions of an insurance contract, the People's Court or arbitration organisation shall interpret such terms and conditions in favour of the insured and the beneficiary.

Article 31

An insurer or a ceding reinsurer is obliged to maintain the confidentiality of the business and details of the property of the proposer, the insured or the reinsurer that he learns of in the course of handling the insurance.

Section 2 Property insurance contracts

Article 32

Property insurance contracts are insurance contracts in which property and its related interests are the subject matter of insurance.

In this Section, the term 'property insurance contract' is abbreviated to 'contract' unless expressly stated otherwise.

Article 33

An insurer shall be notified of an assignment of the subject matter of the insurance, and after the insurer agrees to continue to underwrite the insurance, the contract shall be amended according to other relevant laws, except in the case of contracts for insurance of the transport of goods and contracts that provide otherwise.

Article 34

After the commencement of insurance liability for a contract for insurance of the transport of goods or the journey taken by a means of transportation, the parties to the contract may not rescind such a contract.

Article 35

An insured shall abide by laws and regulations such as those concerning fire protection, safety, production operations and labour protection, etc, and shall maintain the safe condition of the subject matter of the insurance.

As agreed in the contract, the insurer may inspect the subject matter of the insurance as regards safety and submit a written proposal to the proposer or the insured requiring removal of unsafe factors and potential dangers.

Where the proposer and the insured fail to perform their due responsibilities for the safety of the subject matter of the insurance as agreed, the insurer shall have the right to demand an increase in the premium or to rescind the contract.

With the consent of the insured, the insurer may adopt preventive or safety measures to maintain the safe condition of the subject matter of the insurance.

Article 36

Where the degree of risk of the subject matter of the insurance increases during the term of a contract, the insured shall notify the insurer in a timely manner in accordance with the contract and the insurer shall have the right to demand an increase in the premium or rescind the contract.

Where the insured fails to perform his obligation of notification specified in the preceding paragraph, the insurer shall not be liable for indemnity in the case of the occurrence of an event insured against due to the increase in the degree of risk.

Article 37

Unless a contract provides otherwise, the insurer shall reduce the premium and refund the corresponding premium calculated on a daily basis under any of the following circumstances:

(1) if the degree of risk of the subject matter of the insurance has decreased materially as a result of the changes to the circumstances under which the premium rate was determined; or

(2) if the value of the subject matter of the insurance has decreased materially.

Article 38

Where a proposer demands rescission of a contract prior to the commencement of insurance liability, he shall pay a service charge to the insurer and the insurer shall refund the premium. Where the proposer demands rescission of the contract after the commencement of insurance liability, the insurer may charge the premium for the period from the date of commencement of insurance liability to the date of rescission of the contract, with the balance to be refunded to the proposer.

Article 39

The insured value of the subject matter of insurance may be agreed upon by the proposer and the insurer and be specified in the contract. Alternatively, such value may be determined on the basis of the actual value of the subject matter of insurance at the time of the occurrence of an event insured against.

The sum insured may not exceed the insured value. Where the sum insured exceeds the insured value, the portion exceeding the insured value shall be void.

Where the sum insured is less than the insured value, the insurer's liability to indemnify shall be in accordance with the proportion the sum insured bears to the insured value, unless the contract provides otherwise.

Article 40

Where a proposer takes out dual insurance, he shall notify each insurer of the relevant details of such dual insurance.

Where the total of the sums insured under dual insurance exceeds the insured value, the total amounts of indemnity of each insurer may not exceed the insured value. Each insurer shall assume liability to indemnify according to the ratio his sum insured bears to the total of the sums insured, unless the contract provides otherwise.

The term 'dual insurance' refers to insurance contracts that the proposer concludes separately with two or more insurers in respect of the same subject matter of the insurance, the same insurable interest and the same insured event.

Article 41

On the occurrence of an event insured against, an insured shall be responsible for using his best efforts to adopt the measures necessary to prevent or reduce losses.

Necessary and reasonable expenses paid by the insured after the occurrence of an event insured against in order to prevent or reduce losses in respect of the subject matter of the insurance shall be borne by the insurer. The amount of such expenses borne by the insurer shall be calculated separately from the indemnity for the losses in respect of the subject matter of the insurance, and the amount of the expenses shall not exceed the sum insured.

Article 42

Where a partial loss is suffered in respect of the subject matter of insurance, the proposer may terminate the contract within 30 days after the insurer has indemnified the proposer for such loss. The insurer may also terminate the contract, unless the contract stipulates that he may not do so. Where the insurer terminates the contract, he shall notify the proposer 15 days in advance and shall refund to the proposer the premium for the portion of the subject matter of the insurance in respect of which no loss was suffered, less the portion chargeable from the date of commencement of insurance liability until the date of termination of the contract.

Article 43

Where the sum insured has already been paid in full by the insurer and such sum is equal to the insured value following the occurrence of an event insured against, all rights to the subject matter of the insurance in respect of which loss was suffered shall be owned by the insurer. Where the sum insured is less than the insured value, the insurer shall take over some of the rights to the subject matter of the insurance in respect of which loss was suffered, according to the ratio the sum insured bears to the insured value.

Article 44

Where a third party damages the subject matter of the insurance, thereby leading to the occurrence of an event insured against, the insurer shall, from the date of payment of insurance monies to the insured, be subrogated to the insured's right to claim indemnity from the third party within the amount of indemnity.

Where an insured has already obtained indemnity from a third party following the occurrence of an event insured against as mentioned in the preceding paragraph, the insurer may, at the time of paying the insurance monies, deduct an amount equivalent to such indemnity obtained by the insured from the third party.

An insurer's exercise of his right of claim by subrogation in accordance with the first paragraph shall have no impact on the insured's right to claim indemnity from the third party for the portion which has not been indemnified.

Article 45

Where an insured waives his right to claim indemnity from a third party following the occurrence of an event insured against and prior to the insurer's payment of insurance monies, the insurer shall not be liable for the payment of insurance monies.

Where the insured, without the consent of the insurer, waives his right to claim indemnity from a third party after the insurer has paid insurance monies to him, the waiver shall be void.

Where the insurer is unable to exercise his right to claim indemnity by subrogation due to the fault of the insured, the insurer may make a corresponding deduction from the amount of indemnity.

Article 46

An insurer may not exercise his right to claim indemnity by subrogation against the insured's family members, except where the insured's family members cause an event insured against to occur as mentioned in the first paragraph of Article 44.

Article 47

When the insurer exercises his right to claim indemnity by subrogation against a third party, the insured shall provide the insurer with the necessary documents and relevant details known to him.

Article 48

Necessary and reasonable expenses paid by an insurer or an insured in order to investigate and establish the nature and cause of the event insured against and the degree of loss in respect of the subject matter of the insurance shall be borne by the insurer.

Article 49

In respect of damages caused to a third party by the insured under liability insurance, the insurer may pay insurance monies directly to such a third party, as provided for by law or in the contract.

The term 'liability insurance' refers to insurance where the subject matter is the insured's legal liability to indemnify a third party.

Article 50

Where arbitration or legal proceedings are instituted against the insured under liability insurance as a result of damages caused to a third party by an event insured against, the arbitration or court costs and other necessary and reasonable expenses paid by the insured shall be borne by the insurer, unless the contract provides otherwise.

Section 3 Personal insurance contracts

Article 51

The term 'personal insurance contract' shall refer to an insurance contract the subject matter of which is the life or physical body of a person.

In this Section, the term 'personal insurance contract' shall be abbreviated to 'contract' unless expressly stated otherwise.

Article 52

A proposer shall have an insurable interest in the following persons:

(1) himself;

(2) his spouse, children and parents; and

(3) members of his family and close relatives other than those in the preceding item who are raised or supported by him.

In addition to the persons mentioned in the preceding paragraph, the proposer shall be deemed to have an insurable interest in any insured person who agrees that the proposer may conclude a contract on him.

Article 53

Where the age of the insured as declared by the proposer is not true and his true age fails to meet the age requirements set forth in the contract, the insurer may rescind the contract and in this case, he shall refund the premium to the proposer after deducting a service charge, except when more than two years have lapsed from the date of conclusion of the contract.

Where the age declared by the insured is not true, so that the proposer pays a premium less than the premium payable, the insurer shall have the right to adjust the premium and demand the proposer to make up the premium, or pay insurance monies in accordance with the proportion of the premium actually paid to the premium payable at the time of paying such insurance monies.

Where the age declared by the insured is untrue, so that the proposer has actually paid a premium more than the premium payable, the insurer shall return the excess premium received to the proposer.

Article 54

A proposer may neither propose nor may an insurer underwrite personal insurance on a person without capacity for civil acts where the death of such a person whose life is insured is set as the condition for payment of the sum insured.

Proposals of personal insurance by parents for their minor children shall not be governed by the preceding paragraph, provided that the total sum insured payable upon the death of minor children whose lives are insured does not exceed the limit set by the financial supervision and control departments.

Article 55

A contract in which the death of a person whose life is insured is set as the condition for payment of the insurance monies shall be void where such contract has not been agreed by, and the sum insured has not been approved by, the insured in writing.

Policies issued for contracts in which the death of a person whose life is insured is set as the condition for payment of the insurance monies may not be assigned or pledged without the written consent of the insured.

Proposals for personal insurance by parents for their minor children shall not be governed by the first paragraph.

Article 56

Following conclusion of a contract, the proposer may pay the entire premium in a lump sum to the insurer or pay the premium by instalments as specified in the contract.

Where the contract provides for payment of the premium by instalments, the proposer shall pay the first instalment promptly upon conclusion of such contract and pay the remaining instalments according to schedule.

Article 57

Where the contract provides for payment of the premium by instalments and the proposer, after having paid the first instalment of the premium, fails to pay the second instalment within 60 days upon the expiration of the time limit thereof, the effect of the contract shall be suspended or the sum insured shall be reduced by the insurer as agreed in the contract, except as otherwise provided for in the contract.

Article 58

Where the effect of a contract is suspended pursuant to the preceding Article, such effect shall be restored after the insurer and the proposer have reached an agreement through consultations, and the proposer has made up the unpaid premium. However, where the parties fail to reach an agreement within two years from the date of suspension of such effect, the insurer shall have the right to rescind the contract.

Where the insurer rescinds a contract pursuant to the preceding paragraph and the proposer has been paying the premium for two years or more, the insurer shall refund the cash value of the policy in accordance with the contract. Where the proposer has been paying the premium for less than two years, the insurer shall refund the premium after deducting a service charge.

Article 59

An insurer shall not require a proposer to pay a premium for personal insurance by means of litigation.

Article 60

The beneficiary of personal insurance shall be designated by the insured or the proposer.

The consent of the insured shall be required when the proposer designates a beneficiary.

Where the insured is a person without capacity for civil acts or with limited capacity for civil acts, the beneficiary may be designated by his guardian.

Article 61

The insured or the proposer may designate one or several persons as beneficiaries.

Where there are several beneficiaries, the insured or the proposer may determine the sequence in which they shall receive benefits and the amount of benefits. Where the amount of benefits is not determined, the beneficiaries shall be entitled to an equal amount of the benefits.

Article 62

The insured or the proposer may change the beneficiary and in this case, he shall notify the insurer in writing. Upon receipt of a written notice of a change of beneficiary, the insurer shall endorse the policy.

A change of the beneficiary made by the proposer shall be subject to the consent of the insurer.

Article 63

Upon the death of the insured, the insurance monies shall become part of the insured's estate, and the insurer's obligation to pay insurance monies shall be performed in favour of the insured's successors under any of the following circumstances:

(1) where no beneficiary has been designated;

(2) where there is only one beneficiary, and such beneficiary dies prior to the death of the insured; or

(3) where there is only one beneficiary, and such beneficiary loses or waives his beneficiary right according to law.

Article 64

An insurer shall not be liable for payment of insurance monies where the proposer or a beneficiary causes, in bad faith, the insured to die, become disabled, injured or sick. Where the proposer has been paying the premium for two years or more, the insurer shall refund the cash value of the policy to the other entitled beneficiaries as provided for in the contract.

A beneficiary shall lose his beneficiary right where, in bad faith, he causes the insured to die or to become disabled or injured, or attempts to kill the insured but fails.

Article 65

In the case of contracts in which the death of a person whose life is insured is set as the condition for payment of the insurance monies, the insurer shall not be liable for payment of insurance monies where the insured commits suicide, except as provided for in the second paragraph hereof. However, the insurer shall refund the cash value of the policy in accordance with the policy in respect of premiums already paid by the proposer.

In the case of a contract in which the death of a person whose life is insured is set as the condition for payment of the insurance monies, the insurer may pay insurance monies in accordance with the contract if the insured commits suicide after two years from the date of conclusion of the contract.

Article 66

An insurer shall not be liable for payment of insurance monies where, in bad faith, the insured commits a crime causing injury, disability or death to himself. Where the proposer has been paying the premium for two years or more, the insurer shall refund the cash value of the policy.

Article 67

Where an insured covered by personal insurance suffers an event insured against, such as death, injury, disability or illness, etc, as a result of an act by a third party, the insured shall not have recourse against such third party after the insurer has paid insurance monies to the insured or the beneficiary.

Article 68

Where the proposer rescinds a contract and has been paying the premium for two years or more, the insurer shall refund the cash value of the policy within 30 days of receiving the notice of rescission of the contract. Where the insured has been paying the premium for less than two years, the insurer shall refund the premium in accordance with the contract after deducting a service charge.

Chapter 3 Insurance companies

Article 69

Insurance companies shall be organised in one of the following forms:

(1) company limited by shares; or

(2) wholly State owned company.

Article 70

The establishment of an insurance company must be approved by the financial supervision and control department.

Article 71

The following requirements shall be met for establishing an insurance company. The company must have:

(1) articles of association that conform to this law and the Company Law;

(2) the minimum amount of registered capital prescribed herein;

(3) senior management personnel with the professional knowledge of their positions and with working experience in the business;

(4) a sound organisational structure and management system; and

(5) a place of business that meets the requirements of the relevant laws and regulations, and other business-related facilities.

The financial supervision and control department shall take into consideration the needs for the development and fair competition of the insurance industry when examining an application for approval to establish insurance companies.

Article 72

The minimum amount of registered capital of an insurance company to be established shall be RMB 200 million.

The minimum amount of registered capital of an insurance company must be paid-up capital in currency.

The financial supervision and control department may adjust the minimum amount of registered capital of an insurance company according to the scope and scale of its business. However, such an amount may not be less than the minimum amount set forth in the first paragraph.

Article 73

The following documents and information shall be submitted in order to establish an insurance company:

(1) a written application for approval to establish the insurance company, stating the name, amount of registered capital, scope of business, etc, of such company;

(2) a feasibility study report; and

(3) other documents and information specified by the financial supervision and control department.

Article 74

After an application for approval to establish an insurance company has gone through preliminary examination, the applicant shall make preparations for the establishment of the insurance company in accordance with the provisions hereof and of the Company Law. Where the requirements for establishing an insurance company specified in Article 71 are met, an official application form and relevant documents and information listed below shall be submitted to the financial supervision and control department:

(1) the articles of association of the insurance company;

(2) the register of shareholders and shareholding owned by such shareholders, or the register of contributors and the amounts of their contributions;

(3) proof of creditworthiness and relevant information on the shareholders holding 10% or more of the shares;

(4) capital verification certificates issued by the statutory capital verification authority;

(5) resumés and qualification certificates of the senior management personnel who are to hold positions;

(6) business policies and plans;

(7) information on the business site and other business-related facilities; and

(8) other documents and information specified by the financial supervision and control department.

Article 75

The financial supervision and control department shall decide whether to grant or refuse approval within six months of receiving official application documents for approval to establish an insurance company.

Article 76

The approval authority shall issue a 'Permit for Insurance Business Operations' to an insurance company approved to be established. Such insurance company shall then perform registration procedures with, and obtain a business license from, the administration for industry and commerce on the strength of such permit.

Article 77

Where an insurance company fails to perform a company establishment registration without proper reason within six months of obtaining a 'Permit for Insurance Business Operations', its 'Permit for Insurance Business Operations' shall automatically become void.

Article 78

Upon establishment, an insurance company shall allocate 20% of the total amount of its registered capital as security, and deposit such security with a bank designated by the financial supervision and control department, and may not use it other than for paying the debts of the insurance company at the time of liquidation.

Article 79

The establishment by an insurance company of a branch office inside or outside the People's Republic of China shall be subject to the approval of the financial supervision and control department for the acquisition of a 'Permit for Insurance Business Operations of a Branch Office'.

Branch offices of an insurance company shall not have the status of a legal person, with their civil liability being borne by the insurance company.

Article 80

The establishment by an insurance company of a representative office inside or outside the People's Republic of China shall be subject to the approval of the financial supervision and control department.

Article 81

Any of the following changes in respect of an insurance company must be approved by the financial supervision and control department:

(1) change of the name;

(2) change in the registered capital;

(3) change of the place of business of the company or of any branch office;

(4) adjustment of the scope of business;

(5) division or merger of the company;

(6) amendment to the company's articles of association;

(7) change of capital contributors or shareholders holding 10% or more of the company's shares; or

(8) other changes specified by the financial supervision and control department.

Where an insurance company changes the director or the general manager, it shall submit his qualifications for the position to the financial supervision and control department for examination.

Article 82

The provisions of the Company Law shall apply to the organisational structure of insurance companies.

Article 83

Wholly State owned insurance companies shall set up a board of governors. A board of governors shall be composed of personnel from the financial supervision and control department, relevant experts and representatives of personnel working in the insurance company. The board of governors shall supervise the withdrawal of reserves, the minimum repayment capability as well as the preservation and appreciation of the value of State owned assets, etc, of the wholly State owned insurance company, and also supervise the senior management personnel of the company to see whether they carry out activities in violation of laws, administrative regulations or the articles of association, or whether such activities are harmful to the company's interests.

Article 84

Where an insurance company is divided or merged, or where a cause for dissolution of the company as specified in its articles of association arises, it shall be dissolved upon approval by the financial supervision and control department. The insurance company shall set up a liquidation committee according to law for carrying out liquidation.

Insurance companies with life insurance business may not be dissolved, but they may be divided or merged.

Article 85

Where the 'Permit for Insurance Business Operations' of an insurance company is legally revoked by the financial supervision and control department due to the company's violation of laws or administrative regulations, the company shall be liquidated according to law. The financial supervision and control department shall promptly organise a liquidation committee according to law for carrying out liquidation.

Article 86

Insurance companies that cannot pay debts upon maturity shall be lawfully declared bankrupt by a People's Court after the financial supervision and control department has given its approval. Where an insurance company is declared bankrupt, the People's Court shall arrange for relevant undertakings such as the financial supervision and control department, etc, and relevant individuals, to set up a liquidation committee for carrying out liquidation.

Article 87

Where an insurance company with life insurance business is closed down or declared insolvent according to law, its life insurance contracts and reserves must be transferred to another insurance company with life insurance business. Where no transfer agreement can be reached with another insurance company, the financial supervision and control department shall designate an insurance company with life insurance business to take over such contracts and reserves.

Article 88

Where an insurance company goes into bankruptcy according to law, the property involved in the bankruptcy shall be applied to repayment purposes in the following chronological order after being used first for payment of expenses involved in the bankruptcy:

(1) wages and labour insurance premiums owed to staff and workers;

(2) payment of insurance monies;

(3) taxes owed; and

(4) payment of the company's debts.

Where the property involved in the bankruptcy is insufficient to pay all the claims in chronological order, it shall be distributed on a pro rata basis.

Article 89

Insurance companies which terminate their business activities according to law shall have their 'Permits for Insurance Business Operations' cancelled.

Article 90

Matters concerning the establishment, dissolution and liquidation of, and changes in respect of, insurance companies that are not provided for herein shall be governed by the Company Law and other relevant laws or administrative regulations.

Chapter 4 Insurance business rules

Article 91

The scope of business of an insurance company is as follows:

(1) property insurance includes property insurance, liability insurance, credit insurance, etc; and

(2) personal insurance includes life insurance, health insurance, accident insurance, etc.

An insurer may not at the same time engage in both property insurance and personal insurance business.

The scope of business of an insurance company shall be approved by the financial supervision and control department. An insurance company may only engage in the insurance business activities within the approved scope of business.

The State Council shall formulate measures for division of business in accordance with the second paragraph in respect of insurance companies established prior to the implementation of this law.

Article 92

Insurance companies may, upon approval by the financial supervision and control department, engage in the following reinsurance business in respect of the insurance business mentioned in the preceding article:

(1) taking out of an insurance with another insurer; and

(2) acceptance of an insurance from another reinsurer.

Article 93

Insurance companies which engage in insurance business other than life insurance shall make allocations from their retained insurance premiums of the current year to a portfolio reserve. An amount of 50% of the retained insurance premiums of the current year shall be allocated and carried over.

Insurance companies which engage in life insurance business shall make allocations to a portfolio reserve on the basis of the whole net value of their effective life insurance policies.

Article 94

Insurance companies shall make allocations to an outstanding loss reserve on the basis of the amount of insurance monies already claimed and the amount of insurance monies not yet claimed in respect of events insured against that have already occurred.

Article 95

In addition to making allocations to reserves in accordance with the two preceding Articles, insurance companies shall make allocations to a common reserve in accordance with the provisions of the relevant laws, administrative regulations and State financial and accounting systems.

Article 96

In order to safeguard the interests of the insured and support the stable and sound operation of insurance companies, insurance companies shall deposit allocations into an insurance protection fund as prescribed by the financial supervision and control department.

The insurance protection fund shall be centrally managed and used in a unified manner.

Article 97

An insurance company shall possess the minimum solvency corresponding to its scale of business. The balance of the actual assets of an insurance company less its actual liabilities may not be lower than the amount prescribed by the financial supervision and control department. Where such balance is lower than the prescribed amount, its capital shall be increased to make up the difference.

Article 98

Premiums of the current year retained by insurance companies engaged in property insurance business may not be more than four times the sum of the paid-up capital and common reserve of such insurance companies.

Article 99

The liability of an insurance company for each risk, that is, the maximum coverage of loss that may be caused by an event insured against, may not be more than 10% of the sum of paid-up capital and common reserve of such insurance company. Any part exceeding the sum shall be reinsured.

Article 100

Insurance companies shall submit their methods for the assessment of risks and their arrangement plans for catastrophic risks to the financial supervision and control department for approval.

Article 101

Insurance companies shall, in accordance with the relevant State regulations, reinsure 20% of each insurance that they accept, except for life insurance.

Article 102

Where an insurance company needs to reinsure its own insurance business, it shall give priority to insurance companies within the People's Republic of China for reinsurance.

Article 103

The financial supervision and control department shall have the right to restrict or prohibit insurance companies from reinsuring their own insurance business with insurance companies outside the People's Republic of China, or from accepting reinsurance business from insurance companies outside the People's Republic of China.

Article 104

Insurance companies must employ funds in a stable and safe manner, and ensure the preservation and appreciation of asset value.

The employment of funds by insurance companies shall be limited to bank deposits, purchase and sale of government bonds and financial bonds, and other ways specified by the State Council.

The funds of insurance companies may not be used for the establishment of securities houses or investment in enterprises.

The funds applied by an insurance company and the specific percentage of funds for its specific projects out of its total assets shall be determined by the financial supervision and control department.

Article 105

An insurance company and its working personnel may not perform the following acts in the course of insurance business operations:

(1) deceiving a proposer, insured or beneficiary;

(2) withholding important details relating to an insurance contract from a proposer;

(3) hindering a proposer from performing, or inducing a proposer not to perform, his duty of disclosing the true details as specified herein; and

(4) promising a proposer, an insured or a beneficiary a rebate on the insurance premium or other benefits not provided for in the insurance contract.

Chapter 5 Supervision and administration of the insurance industry

Article 106

The basic insurance clauses and premium rates for the main types of risk in commercial insurance shall be formulated by the financial supervision and control department.

The insurance clauses and premium rates for other types of risk proposed by insurance companies shall be submitted to the financial supervision and control department for the record.

Article 107

The financial supervision and control department shall have the right to inspect the business situation, financial position and employment of funds by insurance companies, and require insurance companies to provide relevant written reports and information within a specified period.

Insurance companies shall be subject to supervision and inspection in accordance with other relevant laws and regulations.

Article 108

Where an insurance company fails to allocate or carry over funds to various reserves or handle reinsurance in accordance with the provisions of the law, or materially violates the provisions hereof relating to the employment of funds, the financial supervision and control department shall order the insurance company to rectify the situation within a specified period by adopting the following measures:

(1) allocating or carrying over the funds to various reserves according to law;
(2) handling reinsurance according to law;
(3) rectifying illegal employment of funds; or
(4) replacing responsible persons and relevant management personnel.

Article 109

Where an insurance company fails to rectify the situation within the specified period decided by the financial supervision and control department in accordance with the preceding paragraph, the financial supervision and control department may appoint insurance professionals and designate relevant personnel of the insurance company to form an organisation for restructuring the insurance company.

The name of the insurance company to be restructured, reasons for restructuring, restructuring organisation and term for restructuring shall be stated in the decision on the restructuring and shall be publicly announced.

Article 110

During the restructuring process, the restructuring organisation shall have the right to supervise the day-to-day business of an insurance company. The responsible persons and relevant management personnel of such company shall exercise their own functions and powers under the supervision of the restructuring organisation.

Article 111

During the restructuring process, the original business of an insurance company shall be continued; however, the financial supervision and control department shall have the right to stop new business overall or in part of the business, or to change the employment of funds.

Article 112

Where an insurance company being restructured returns to a normal business situation following correction of its acts that were in violation of the provisions hereof, the restructuring organisation shall issue a report and the restructuring shall be ended after approval from the financial supervision and control department.

Article 113

Where an insurance company violates the provisions hereof by damaging public interest so that the solvency of the insurance company may be or may have been seriously endangered, the financial supervision and control department may assume control over such company.

The purpose of assumption of control shall be to take necessary measures for an insurance company over which control is assumed for the protection of the interests of the insured and the resumption of normal business by such insurance company. The credit and liabilities of an insurance company over which control is assumed shall remain unchanged as a result of such assumption of control.

Article 114

The composition of the organisation assuming control and the method of assuming control shall be decided by the financial supervision and control department, and shall be publicly announced.

Article 115

The financial supervision and control department may decide to extend the term of control upon expiration of such term. However, the maximum term of control may not be longer than two years.

Article 116

Where an insurance company over which control was assumed has recovered its capacity for normal operations upon expiration of the term of control, the financial supervision and control department may decide to terminate control.

Where the organisation assuming control regards the property of the insurance company placed under control as insufficient for the full repayment of its debts, it may, upon approval by the financial supervision and control department, apply to a People's Court for a declaration of bankruptcy of such insurance company.

Article 117

Within three months after the end of each fiscal year, an insurance company shall submit to the financial supervision and control department a business report, financial and accounting reports and relevant statements for the preceding year, and publish the same according to law.

Article 118

By the end of each month, an insurance company shall submit to the financial supervision and control department statements of business statistics for the preceding month.

Article 119

Insurance companies engaged in personal insurance business must employ professional actuaries recognised by the financial supervision and control department, and set up an actuarial reporting system.

Article 120

The insurer and the insured may employ an independent evaluation organisation established according to law or experts with statutory qualifications to carry out evaluations and appraisals of events insured against.

Article 121

Insurance companies shall properly keep a complete set of account books, the original vouchers and information concerning their business activities.

The period for keeping a complete set of account books, original vouchers and relevant information mentioned in the preceding paragraph shall begin from the date of termination of an insurance contract, and shall not be less than 10 years.

Chapter 6 Insurance agents and insurance brokers

Article 122

Insurance agents are undertakings or individuals entrusted by an insurer to handle insurance business on behalf of the insurer within the scope of the insurer's authorisation and who charge an agency fee to the insurer.

Article 123

Insurance brokers are undertakings that provide intermediary services for the conclusion of insurance contracts between proposers and insurers in the interests of the proposers, and who charge a commission thereof according to law.

Article 124

An insurer shall be responsible for the acts of its insurance agents in handling insurance business on its behalf in line with its authorisation.

Insurance agents engaged in life insurance agency business may not accept entrustment by two or more insurers at the same time.

Article 125

Insurance brokers shall be liable to pay compensation for losses suffered by the proposer or the insured due to the fault of such insurance brokers in the course of handling insurance business.

Article 126

When handling insurance business, insurance agents and insurance brokers may not coerce or induce proposers to conclude, or restrict proposers in concluding, an insurance contract by taking advantage of their administrative powers and functions, the convenience provided by their positions or other unfair means.

Article 127

Insurance agents and insurance brokers shall meet the qualification requirements specified by the financial supervision and control department, obtain a 'Permit for Insurance Agency Business Operations' or a 'Brokerage Permit', register with the administration for industry and commerce, obtain a business licence and pay a deposit or take out professional liability insurance.

Article 128

Insurance agents and insurance brokers shall have their own places of business, special account books for recording the particulars of revenue and expenditure relating to insurance agency or brokerage business, and shall be subject to supervision of the financial supervision and control department.

Article 129

Insurance companies shall keep a register of their insurance agents.

Article 130

The provisions of Articles 105, 107 and 117 shall apply to insurance agents and insurance brokers.

Chapter 7 Legal liability

Article 131

Where a proposer, an insured or a beneficiary engages in insurance fraud by performing any of the following acts, and a criminal offence is committed, this shall be punished according to the law:

(1) taking out insurance for a fictitious subject matter of insurance in bad faith for the purpose of deceiving the insurer;

(2) falsely claiming that an event insured against has occurred before such event has actually occurred for the purpose of deceiving the insurer;

(3) causing in bad faith an event insured against to occur that involves property loss for the purpose of deceiving the insurer;

(4) causing in bad faith a personal insurance event, such as the death, injury, disability or illness of the insured to occur for the purpose of deceiving the insurer; or

(5) forging or altering documents, information or other evidence relating to an event insured against; instigating, abetting or bribing others to provide false documents, information or other evidence, so as to falsify a cause of the event or overstate the extent of the loss for the purpose of deceiving the insurer.

Where the circumstances of any of the acts set forth in the preceding paragraph are not sufficiently serious to constitute a criminal offence, an administrative penalty shall be imposed in accordance with the relevant State regulations.

Article 132

Where an insurance company or its working personnel withhold, in the course of insurance operations, important details relating to an insurance contract, deceive the proposer, the insured or the beneficiary or refuse to perform the obligation of paying insurance monies as stipulated in the insurance contract, and thus a criminal offence is committed, criminal liability shall be punished according to law. Where no criminal offence is constituted, the financial supervision and control department shall impose a fine of between RMB 10,000 and RMB 50,000 on the insurance company. Sanctions and a fine of no more than RMB 10,000 shall be imposed on the working personnel who committed the illegal acts.

Where an insurance company or its working personnel hinder proposers from performing, or induce proposers not to perform, their duty of disclosing true details, or promise the proposer, the insured or the beneficiary an illegal rebate on the insurance premium or other benefits, the financial supervision and control department shall order rectification and impose a fine of between RMB 10,000 and RMB 50,000 on the insurance company. Sanctions and a fine of no more than RMB 10,000 shall be imposed on the working personnel who committed the illegal acts.

Article 133

Where an agent or an insurance broker deceives the proposer, the insured or the beneficiary in the course of his business operations, the financial supervision and control department shall order rectification and impose a fine of between RMB 10,000 and RMB 50,000. Where the circumstances are serious, the 'Permit for Insurance Agency Business Operations' or the 'Brokerage Permit' shall be revoked. Where a criminal offence is committed, criminal liability shall be punished according to law.

Article 134

Where the working personnel of an insurance company fabricate an event insured against which never occurred and make a sham settlement in bad faith by taking advantage of their positions, thereby deceiving the insurer of insurance monies, their criminal liability shall be punished according to law.

Article 135

Where the provisions of this law are violated by establishing an insurance company without authorisation or by illegally engaging in commercial insurance activities, criminal liability shall be punished according to the law, and the financial supervision and control department shall ban the company or the activities. Where the circumstances are not sufficiently serious to constitute a criminal offence, an administrative penalty shall be imposed.

Article 136

Where this law is violated by engaging in insurance operations exceeding the approved scope of business, the financial supervision and control department shall order rectification and the return of the insurance premiums received and where there is illegal income, confiscate the illegal income and impose a fine of one to five times the amount of the illegal income; where there is no illegal income, it shall impose a fine of between RMB 100,000 and RMB 500,000. Where rectification is not made within the specified term or serious consequences are caused, it shall order the suspension of business for rectification or revoke the 'Permit for Insurance Business Operations'.

Article 137

Where this law is violated by making a change without authorisation in particulars such as the name, articles of association or registered capital of an insurance company, the place of business of an insurance company or a branch office, etc, the financial supervision and control department shall order rectification and impose a fine of between RMB 10,000 and RMB 100,000.

Article 138

Where any of the following acts are committed in violation of this law, the financial supervision and control department shall order rectification and impose a fine of between RMB 50,000 and RMB 300,000; where the circumstances are serious, it may restrict the scope of business, order cessation of the acceptance of new business or revoke the 'Permit for Insurance Business Operations':

(1) failure to pay a deposit in accordance with regulations or use of such deposit in violation of regulations;

(2) failure to allocate or carry over funds to the portfolio reserve or outstanding loss reserve in accordance with regulations;

(3) failure to make allocations to the insurance protection fund or common reserve;

(4) failure to reinsure an insurance in accordance with regulations;

(5) employment of insurance company funds in violation of regulations;

(6) establishment of a branch office or representative office without approval; or

(7) division or merger without approval.

Article 139

Where any of the following acts are performed in violation of this law, the financial supervision and control department shall order rectification and where rectification is not made within the specified term, impose a fine of between RMB 10,000 and RMB 100,000:

(1) failure to submit relevant reports, statements, documents and information in accordance with regulations; or

(2) failure to submit the insurance clauses and premium rates for the proposed types of risk.

Article 140

Where any of the following acts are performed in violation of this law, the financial supervision and control department shall order rectification and impose a fine of between RMB 100,000 and RMB 500,000:

(1) provision of sham reports, statements, documents or information; or

(2) refusal or hindrance of lawful inspection and supervision.

Article 141

Where any of the following acts are performed in violation of this law, the financial supervision and control department shall order rectification and impose a fine of between RMB 50,000 and RMB 300,000:

(1) providing coverage in excess of the insured sum; or

(2) underwriting insurance for a person without capacity for civil acts where the death of such person is set as the condition for payment of the insurance monies.

Article 142

Where this law is violated by illegally engaging in insurance agency or brokerage activities without having obtained a 'Permit for Insurance Agency Business Operations' or a 'Brokerage Permit', the financial supervision and control department shall ban such activities, confiscate the illegal income and impose a fine of five to ten times the illegal income. Where a criminal offence is committed, this shall be punished according to the law.

Article 143

Where senior management and other personnel of an insurance company are directly responsible for acts in violation of this law that do not constitute a criminal offence, the financial supervision and control department may, depending on the circumstances, issue a warning, order a replacement of such personnel and/or impose a fine of between RMB 5,000 and RMB 30,000.

Article 144

Where damages are caused to others as a result of violation of this law, civil liability shall be incurred according to the law.

Article 145

Where applications for establishment of an insurance company that fail to meet the requirements specified by this law are approved or where applications of insurance agents or insurance brokers who fail to meet the requirements are approved, administrative sanctions shall be imposed; where the circumstances are serious enough to constitute a criminal offence, criminal liability shall be pursued according to law.

Article 146

Where personnel of the financial supervision and control department abuse their power, or are involved in graft or dereliction of duty in the course of supervision and control of the insurance industry, so that a criminal offence is committed, criminal liability shall be punished according to law; where no criminal offence is committed, administrative sanctions shall be imposed.

Chapter 8 Supplementary provisions

Article 147

Marine insurance shall be governed by the relevant provisions of the Maritime Code. Matters not provided for in the Maritime Code shall be governed by the relevant provisions of this law.

Article 148

The establishment of insurance companies with foreign equity or the establishment of branches in the People's Republic of China by foreign insurance companies shall be governed by this law. Where laws or administrative regulations provide for otherwise, the provisions of such laws or administrative regulations shall apply.

Article 149

The State shall support the development of insurance business for agricultural production. Agricultural insurance shall be separately provided for by laws or administrative regulations.

Article 150

Insurance organisations of a nature other than insurance companies provided for in this law shall be separately provided for in laws or administrative regulations.

Article 151

Insurance companies established upon approval in accordance with State Council regulations prior to the implementation of this law shall be maintained. Those which do not meet all the requirements provided herein shall meet the requirements provided herein within a specified time limit. Specific procedures shall be provided for by the State Council.

Article 152

This law shall be effective as of 1 October 1995.

PART 7

THE SHIP REGISTRATION REGULATIONS OF THE PRC 1994

(Promulgated by the 155th Order of the State Council of the People's Republic of China on 2 June 1994)

Table of Contents

Chapter 1 General provisions

Article 1

These Regulations are enacted for the purpose of strengthening the supervision and control over ships by the State, and to safeguard the legal rights and interests of the parties involved in the registration of ships.

Article 2

The following ships shall be registered in accordance with the provisions of these Regulations:

(1) ships owned by citizens of the People's Republic of China whose residences or principal places of business are located within the territory thereof;

(2) ships owned by enterprises which are legal persons established under the laws of the People's Republic of China and whose principal places of business are located within the territory thereof, provided the proportion of registered capital contributed by Chinese investors is not less than 50% where foreign capital is invested in such legal persons;

(3) public service ships of the government of the People's Republic of China and ships owned by other institutions which are legal persons; and

(4) any other ships whose registration is deemed necessary by the competent authority of the People's Republic of China.

Military ships, fishery ships and sports crafts shall be registered in compliance with other relevant laws and regulations.

Article 3

Ships are allowed to sail under the national flag of the People's Republic of China after being registered and granted the nationality of the People's Republic of China. No ship may sail under the national flag of the People's Republic of China without being registered.

Article 4

A ship shall not have dual nationality. A ship registered abroad shall not be granted Chinese nationality unless the former registration has been suspended or cancelled.

Article 5

The acquisition, transfer or extinction of ownership of a ship shall be registered at the Ship Registration Administration. An acquisition, transfer or extinction of ownership shall not be valid against a third party unless it is registered.

Where a ship is jointly owned by two or more individuals or legal persons, the joint-ownership thereof shall be registered at the Ship Registration Administration. The joint-ownership shall not be valid in action against a third party unless it is registered.

Article 6

The establishment, transfer or extinction of a ship mortgage or demise charter shall be registered at the Ship Registration Administration. No mortgage or demise charter shall be valid against a third party unless registered.

Article 7

Ships of Chinese nationality shall be manned by Chinese citizens. If it is necessary to recruit foreign seafarers, their employment shall be approved by the competent authority of transport and communications under the State Council.

Seafarers on board ships of Chinese nationality who are required to possess certificates of competency shall hold the appropriate certificates of competency issued by the People's Republic of China.

Article 8

The Bureau of Harbour Superintendency of the People's Republic of China is the competent authority in charge of the registration of ships. The Harbour Superintendency Administration (referred to as the 'Ship Registration Administration' in these Regulations) at a local port is the proper agency conducting ship registration. The scope of authority of the Ship Registration Administration shall be defined by the Bureau of Harbour Superintendency of the People's Republic of China.

Article 9

The port where a ship is registered shall be the port of registry of the ship.

The owner of a ship may choose a port close to his residence or his principal place of business as the port of registry, but he is not allowed to choose two or more than two ports as the port of registry.

Article 10

Each ship shall have only one name.

The name of a ship shall be checked and approved by the Ship Registration Administration at its port of registration. A ship's name shall not be the same as one already registered, neither in wording nor in pronunciation.

Article 11

The Ship Registration Administration shall establish a ship registration book, which shall be accessible to those having an interest therein.

Article 12

The provisions of these Regulations concerning shipowners shall apply to legal persons who operate State owned ships.

Chapter 2 Registration of ownership

Article 13

An owner applying for registration of a ship shall produce to the Ship Registration Administration at the port of registry the documents evidencing his legal status, and submit the originals and copies of the documents evidencing his ownership over the ship and the technical information thereof.

For the registration of ownership of a ship purchase, the following documents shall be submitted:

(1) seller's invoice, sales contract and delivery document;

(2) a document issued by the ship registration authority at the original port of registry certifying the deletion of the ownership;

(3) a document evidencing that the ship is not under mortgage or that the mortgagees agree to the transfer of the mortgaged ship.

For the registration of ownership of a newly built ship, the contract of ship construction and the delivery document shall be submitted.

For the registration of ownership of a ship under construction, the contract of ship construction shall be submitted.

For the registration of ownership of a ship procured through inheritance, gift, auction under legal process or court judgment, a document with appropriate legal effect evidencing the ship's ownership shall be submitted.

Article 14

The Ship Registration Administration, having examined and verified the application for registration of ownership, shall issue to the shipowner whose application meets the requirements of these Regulations a Certificate of Registration within seven days of the date of receipt of the application, whereupon an official registration number shall be granted to the registered ship and the following particulars shall be recorded in the register of ships:

(1) ship's name and its call sign;

(2) port of registry, official registration number and identification mark of the ship;

(3) name and address of the shipowner and name of his legal representative;
(4) way in which the ship's ownership was procured and the date of procurement;
(5) date on which the ship's ownership was registered;
(6) name of the shipbuilder, and time and place of building;
(7) value of the ship, material of the ship's hull and the ship's main technical information;
(8) original name and port of registry of the ship and the date of deletion or suspension of its original registration;
(9) information about joint-ownership if the ship is owned by two or more owners;
(10) name and address of the demise charterer or ship operator, and name of his legal representative, if the shipowner is not the one who operates or actually controls the ship; and
(11) information about the effecting of a mortgage, if any.

The Ship Registration Administration shall inform the shipowner in writing of any non-compliance of his application with these Regulations within seven days of the date of receipt of the application.

Chapter 3 Nationality of ships

Article 15

A shipowner applying for the nationality of a ship shall, in addition to the Certificate of Registration of Ship's Ownership, submit the following documents according to the ship's navigation zone:

(1) For ships engaged in international voyages, the valid technical documents of the ship issued by an authorised organisation for survey of ships in accordance with the type of the ship:
   (a) Tonnage Measurement Certificate;
   (b) Loadline Certificate;
   (c) Cargo Ship Safety Construction Certificate;
   (d) Cargo Ship Safety Equipment Certificate;
   (e) Certificate of Number of Passengers Authorised to Carry;
   (f) Passenger Ship Safety Certificate;
   (g) Cargo Ship Safety Radiotelegraphy Certificate;
   (h) International Oil Pollution Prevention Certificate;
   (i) Ship Safety Navigation Certificate; and
   (j) other relevant technical certificates.
(2) For ships engaged in domestic voyages: the ship survey book issued by an authorised organisation for survey of ships; and other valid technical certificates according to the type of the ship.

A shipowner applying for the Chinese nationality of a ship of foreign nationality purchased abroad which still has the foreign nationality, shall, in addition, submit a certificate issued by the ship registration authority at the former port of registry to the effect that the former nationality has been deleted or that the former nationality will be immediately deleted at such time as the new registration is effected.

The Ship Registration Administration shall issue a Certificate of Ship's Nationality to the ship whose application has been examined and approved to be in compliance with these Regulations.

Article 16

Subject to its approval, the Ship Registration Administration shall issue a Certificate of Ship's Nationality to a ship registered under Article 13. The validity period of the Certificate of Ship's Nationality shall be five years.

Article 17

For a ship built in this country and sold overseas, the owner shall apply to the Ship Registration Administration at the place of construction for a Provisional Certificate of Ship's Nationality by submitting the document evidencing the ownership of the ship and the valid technical certificates thereof.

For a newly built ship purchased from overseas, the owner shall apply to the local embassy or consulate of the People's Republic of China for a Provisional Certificate of Ship's Nationality by submitting the document evidencing the ownership of the ship and its valid technical certificates.

For a ship built in a place of this country other than its intended port of registry, the owner who needs a Provisional Certificate of Ship's Nationality shall apply for the certificate by submitting the contract of the ship's construction and its valid technical certificates.

For a ship built overseas, the owner shall apply to the local embassy or consulate of the People's Republic of China for a Provisional Certificate of Ship's Nationality by submitting the contract of the ship's construction, the delivery document and the valid technical certificates of the ship.

For a ship demise chartered overseas, the demise charterer shall apply to the Ship Registration Administration for a Provisional Certificate of Ship's Nationality by submitting the demise charter-party and the certificate issued by the ship registration authority at the former port of registry to the effect that the former nationality of the ship has been suspended or deleted, or that the former nationality of the ship will be suspended or deleted immediately at such time as the new registration is effected.

The Ship Registration Administration or the local embassy or consulate of the People's Republic of China, having examined and verified that the application is in compliance with these Regulations, shall issue a Provisional Certificate of Ship's Nationality to the ship.

Article 18

The validity period of a Provisional Certificate of Ship's Nationality shall generally not exceed one year.

For a ship which is demise chartered overseas, the validity period of the Provisional Certificate of Ship's Nationality can be determined according to the charter period, but shall not exceed two years. Where the charter period exceeds two years, the charterer shall, within the period of validity, apply to the Ship Registration Administration at the ship's port of registry for the renewal of its Provisional Certificate of Ship's Nationality.

Article 19

A Provisional Certificate of Ship's Nationality shall have the same legal effect as a Certificate of Ship's Nationality.

Chapter 4 Registration of ship mortgage

Article 20

Where a mortgage is effected with respect to a ship of 20 tons gross tonnage or over, the mortgagee and the mortgagor shall apply to the Ship Registration Administration at the ship's port of registry for the registration of the ship mortgage by submitting the following documents:

(1) written application signed by both mortgagee and mortgagor;

(2) Certificate of Ship's Ownership or contract of ship's construction; and

(3) contract of ship mortgage.

If there are other mortgages effected, the relevant certificates shall be submitted.

Where a mortgage is effected on a jointly owned ship, the joint-owners shall, in addition, submit a document evidencing the agreement by the joint-owners holding more than two-thirds or otherwise agreed proportion of shares thereof.

Article 21

After the application has been examined and verified as being in compliance with these Regulations, the Ship Registration Administration shall, within seven days of the date of receipt of the application, record matters regarding the mortgagee, the mortgagor and the ship as well as the date of mortgage registration in the register of ships and the Certificate of Ship's Ownership, and issue the Certificate of Registration of Ship's Mortgage to the mortgagee.

Article 22

The registration of a ship mortgage shall specify the following items:

(1) name and address of mortgagee and name and address of mortgagor;

(2) name and nationality of the mortgaged ship, the number and title of the administration that issued the Certificate of Registration of Ship's Ownership; and

(3) amount of debt secured, interest rate and pay-off period.

The Ship Registration Administration shall make the information about the registration of the ship mortgage available to the public.

Article 23

In the case of transfer of a mortgage, the mortgagee and the transferee shall apply to the Ship Registration Administration at the ship's port of registry for registration of the mortgage transfer by submitting the contract of ship mortgage transfer.

After the application has been examined and verified to be in compliance with the requirements of these Regulations, the Ship Registration Administration shall record the transferee as the mortgagee in the register of ships and in the Certificate of Registration of Ship's Ownership, issue to the transferee a Certificate of Registration of Ship's Mortgage, and close the former Certificate of Registration of Ship's Mortgage.

The mortgagee shall notify the mortgagor of the mortgage transference prior to its registration thereof.

Article 24

Where two or more mortgages are effected on the same ship, the Ship Registration Administration shall register the mortgages in sequence of the dates on which the applications were registered, and indicate the dates of registration in the register of ships.

The date on which the application is registered shall be the date of registration. Where two or more applications are made on the same day, the dates of registration shall be the same.

Chapter 5 Registration of demise charter

Article 25

In any of the following cases, the shipowner and the charterer shall apply for the registration of the demise charter-party:

(1) a ship of Chinese nationality demise chartered to a Chinese enterprise;

(2) a ship of foreign nationality demise chartered to a Chinese enterprise; or

(3) a ship of Chinese nationality demise chartered overseas.

Article 26

Where a ship is chartered within the territory of this country, the shipowner and the charterer shall, prior to the commencement of the charter, apply to the Ship Registration Administration at the ship's port of registry for the registration of the demise charter by submitting the Certificate of Registration of Ship's Ownership, the Certificate of Ship's Nationality and the original and a copy of the demise charter-party.

After the application has been examined and verified as being in compliance with the requirements of these Regulations, the Ship Registration Administration at the port of registry shall record the main points of the demise charter-party in the Certificate of Registration of Ship's Ownership and the register of ships respectively, and issue the Certificate of Registration of Demise Charter to the shipowner and the charterer.

Article 27

Where a ship is demise chartered overseas, the shipowner shall apply to the Ship Registration Administration at the port of registry for registration of the demise charter by submitting the documents specified in Article 26.

After the application has been examined and verified as being in compliance with the requirements of these Regulations, the Ship Registration Administration shall suspend or delete the nationality of the ship in accordance with Article 42 and issue to the applicant the Certificate of Registration of Demise Charter in duplicate.

Article 28

Where a ship is demise chartered from overseas, the charterer shall choose the port of registry for the ship according to Article 9 and shall apply, prior to the commencement of the charter, to the Ship Registration Administration for registration of the demise charter by submitting the following documents:

(1) the original and a copy of the demise charter-party;

(2) the ship's valid technical certificates issued by an authorised organisation for ship surveys; and

(3) a certificate issued by the ship registration authority of the former port of registry to the effect that the former nationality of the ship has been suspended or deleted, or that the former nationality of the ship will be suspended or deleted immediately when the new registration is effected.

After the application has been examined and verified as being in compliance with the requirements of these Regulations, the Ship Registration Administration shall issue the Certificate of Registration of Demise Charter and the Provisional Certificate of Ship's Nationality in accordance with Article 17, and shall record the original country of registration in the register of ships.

Article 29

Where the demise charter period is to be extended, the shipowner and the charterer shall, 15 days prior to the expiration of the charter period, apply to the Ship Registration Administration for the renewal of the demise charter registration by submitting the original and the copy of the Certificate of Registration of Demise Charter and the document for extension.

Article 30

During the period of a demise charter, the charterer shall not apply for the registration of a sub-charter unless agreed by the shipowner in writing.

Chapter 6 Ship's marking and company flag

Article 31

A ship shall be marked as follows:

(1) ship's name in Chinese on both sides of the stem and at the stern;

(2) port of registry below the name at the stern;

(3) the corresponding Chinese phonetic alphabets below the ship's name and port of registry;

(4) draft scale on both sides of the stem and at the stern; and

(5) loadline mark at midship, on both sides.

Where a ship being constrained by its type and size is unable to be marked as above, it shall be marked with its name and port of registry in an easily seen position.

Article 32

A shipowner may apply to the Ship Registration Administration at the port of registry for registration of the ship's funnel mark and its company flag by submitting the drawings of the standard design in compliance with the relevant regulations.

Article 33

Ships belonging to one company shall use the same funnel mark and the same company flag.

The funnel mark and the company flag of a company shall be examined by the Ship Registration Administration at the port of registry.

The funnel mark and the company flag of a company shall not be the same as or similar to those which have been registered previously.

Article 34

The Ship Registration Administration shall publicise the funnel marks and company flags which have been approved and registered.

The registered funnel mark and company flag shall be used exclusively by the applicant and shall not be used by other ships or companies.

Chapter 7 Alteration and deletion of registration

Article 35

In case of any alteration to the particulars entered in the ship registration, the shipowner shall apply to the Ship Registration Administration at the port of registry for the registration of such alteration by submitting the relevant documents of ship registration and those evidencing such alteration.

Article 36

Where a ship's port of registry is changed, the shipowner shall apply to the Ship Registration Administration at the former port of registry for registration of the change by submitting the ship's Certificate of Nationality and the document evidencing such a change. After the application has been examined and verified as being in compliance with the requirements of these Regulations, the Ship Registration Administration at the former port of registry shall indicate the change in the 'Alteration' column in the Certificate of Ship's Nationality and deliver the entire file of the ship's registration to the Ship Registration Administration at the new port of registry.

Article 37

Where there is any change of joint-ownership, the shipowner shall apply to the Ship Registration Administration at the port of registry for registration of the change by submitting the Certificate of Registration of Ship's Ownership and the document evidencing such a change.

Article 38

Where the contract of ship's mortgage is changed, the mortgagee and the mortgagor shall apply to the Ship Registration Administration for registration of such a change by submitting the Certificate of Registration of Ship's Ownership, the Certificate of Registration of Ship's Mortgage and the document evidencing such a change.

After the application has been examined and verified as being in compliance with the requirements of these Regulations, the Ship Registration Administration at the port of registry shall indicate the change of the mortgage contract in the Certificate of Registration of Ship's Ownership, the Certificate of Registration of Ship's Mortgage and the register of ships.

Article 39

In the case of a transfer of a ship's ownership, the former owner shall apply to the Ship Registration Administration at the port of registry for the registration of deletion by submitting the Certificate of Ship's Ownership, the Certificate of Ship's Nationality and other relevant documents.

After the application has been examined and verified as being in compliance with the requirements of these Regulations, the Ship Registration Administration at the port of registry shall delete the registration regarding the ship's ownership and other relevant entries in the register of ships, withdraw the certificates of registration concerned, and issue a certificate of deletion of the ship's registration to the shipowner. If the ship is sold overseas, the Ship Registration Administration shall issue a certificate to the effect that the ship's nationality has been deleted, or that the ship's nationality will be deleted immediately when the ship is registered anew.

Article 40

Where a ship is lost (scrapped or sunken included) or is missing, the owner shall, within three months after the ship is lost or missing, apply to the Ship Registration Administration at the port of registry for the registration of deletion by submitting the Certificate of Registration of Ship's Ownership, the Certificate of Ship's Nationality and a document evidencing that the ship has been lost or is missing. After the application has been examined and verified as being in compliance with the requirements of these Regulations, the Ship Registration Administration shall delete the ship's registrations in the register of ships, withdraw the certificates of registrations concerned, and issue a certificate of deletion to the shipowner.

Article 41

Where a contract of mortgage is terminated, the mortgagee and mortgagor shall apply to the Ship Registration Administration at the port of registry for the registration of deletion by submitting the Certificate of Registration of Ship's Ownership, the Certificate of Registration of Ship's Mortgage and the document signed by the mortgagee evidencing the termination of the mortgage contract. After the application has been examined and verified as being in compliance with the requirements of these Regulations, the Ship

Registration Administration at the port of registry shall delete the registration of the ship's mortgage in the Certificate of Ship's Ownership and the register of ships.

Article 42

Where a ship is demise chartered overseas, the shipowner shall, in addition to applying for registration of the demise charter in accordance with Article 27, apply for registration of suspension or deletion of the ship's nationality. The Ship Registration Administration at the port of registry shall seal up the original Certificate of Ship's Nationality and issue a certificate of suspension or deletion of the ship's nationality. Under some special circumstances, the Ship Registration Administration may issue a certificate to the effect that the ship's nationality will be deleted immediately at such time as the ship is registered anew.

Article 43

Upon the expiration of a demise charter-party or the termination thereof, the shipowner shall, within 15 days after the date of such expiration or termination, apply to the Ship Registration Administration at the port of registry for registration of deletion of the demise charter by submitting the Certificate of Registration of Ship's Ownership and the demise charter-party or the document evidencing such termination.

If the ship is demise chartered overseas, the shipowner shall, in addition, submit a certificate issued by the ship registration authority at the charterer's place of business to the effect that the ship's nationality has been deleted or that the ship's nationality will be deleted immediately at such time as the ship is registered anew.

The Ship Registration Administration at the port of registry, having approved of the application, shall delete the registration of demise charter in the Certificate of Registration of Ship's Ownership and the register of ships, and return to the shipowner the original Certificate of Ship's Nationality.

Article 44

Where a ship is demise chartered, the charterer shall, within 15 days of the expiration or termination of the demise charter, apply to the Ship Registration Administration at the port of registry for registration of deletion by submitting the demise charter-party or the document evidencing such termination.

If the ship is demise chartered from overseas, the Provisional Certificate of Nationality shall be submitted as well.

The Ship Registration Administration at the port of registry, having approved of the application, shall delete the ship's registration of demise charter in the register of ships, withdraw the Provisional Certificate of Nationality, and issue a certificate of deletion of the demise charter and a certificate of deletion of the provisional certificate of the ship's nationality.

Chapter 8 Renewal and reissue of certificates

Article 45

The owner of a ship shall, within one year prior to the expiration of the Certificate of Ship's Nationality, apply to the Ship Registration Administration at the port of registry for the renewal of the certificate by submitting the Certificate of Ship's Nationality and the valid technical certificates.

Article 46

Where the Certificate of Registration of Ship's Ownership or the Certificate of Ship's Nationality is defaced, damaged or rendered useless, the shipowner shall apply to the Ship Registration Administration at the port of registry for the reissue of the certificate.

Article 47

Where the Certificate of Registration of Ship's Ownership or the Certificate of Ship's Nationality of a ship is lost, the shipowner shall apply to the Ship Registration Administration at the port of registry for the reissue of the certificate, stating the reasons in writing and submitting appropriate documents as evidence.

The Ship Registration Administration at the port of registry shall make a statement in the local newspaper that the lost certificate is null and void.

Article 48

Where the Certificate of Ship's Nationality is lost, defaced or damaged in a foreign country, the shipowner shall apply to the local embassy or consulate of the People's Republic of China for a Provisional Certificate of Ship's Nationality, but shall, as soon as the ship arrives at the first Chinese port of call, apply to the Ship Registration Administration at the port of registry for the reissue of the Certificate of Ship's Nationality.

Chapter 9 Legal responsibility

Article 49

A ship in respect of which the nationality of the People's Republic of China is falsely assumed and which illegally sails under the flag of the People's Republic of China, shall be confiscated by the Ship Registration Administration according to the relevant laws.

The provisions of the above paragraph shall be applicable to a Chinese ship that falsely assumes foreign nationality and illegally sails under the flag of a foreign country.

Article 50

Where the registration of a ship made at home or overseas is concealed, which results in dual nationality, the Ship Registration Administration at the port of registry shall annul the Certificate of Ship's Nationality and impose the following penalties, depending on the circumstances of the case:

(1) a fine of RMB 2,000 up to RMB 10,000 for a ship of 500 tons gross tonnage or below;

(2) a fine of RMB 10,000 up to RMB 50,000 for a ship of 501–1,000 tons gross tonnage;

(3) a fine of RMB 50,000 up to 200,000 for a ship of 10,001 tons gross tonnage or above.

Article 51

The Ship Registration Administration at the port of registry shall, according to the seriousness of the case, punish any of the following violations against these Regulations by giving a warning, imposing a fine of 50% of the amounts specified for ships of different gross tonnage as set out in Article 50, or withdrawing the ship's registration certificates:

(1) concealing the true facts and providing false information for registration;

(2) concealing the fact of registration, resulting in dual registration; or

(3) forging or altering certificates of ship's registration.

Article 52

The Ship Registration Administration shall order those who fail to apply for the alteration or deletion of registration under these Regulations or those who use expired certificates of nationality or provisional certificates of nationality to go through the formalities for the registration concerned, and if the case is considered serious, may impose a fine of 10% of the amounts specified for ships of different tonnage as set out in Article 50.

Article 53

The Ship Registration Administration at the port of registry shall order those who violate these Regulations by employing without approval foreign seafarers or using a funnel mark or company flag registered by others to rectify such matters, and shall impose a fine of 10% of the amounts specified for ships of different gross tonnage as set out in Article 50 against those who refuse to rectify, and, if the case is serious, shall withdraw the Certificate of Ship's Nationality or the Provisional Certificate of Ship's Nationality.

Article 54

Any person working in the Ship Registration Administration who abuses his power, practices graft, ignores his duty, or grossly neglects his responsibilities shall be punished by the Administration, or shall be liable to have criminal proceedings brought against him if the offence constitutes a crime.

Article 55

A person or party concerned who refuses to accept the actions taken by the Ship Registration Administration may apply for a review of the case or bring the case to court in accordance with the provisions of relevant laws or administrative regulations.

Chapter 10 Supplementary provisions

Article 56

For the purpose of these Regulations:

(1) 'ship' means any self-propelled or non-self-propelled vessel and any other mobile unit on water with the exception of life boats and life rafts equipped on board ships and boats or rafts of less than five metres in length;

(2) 'fishery ship' means any vessel engaged in fishing or any vessel belonging to the fishing industry and serving the purpose of fishery; and

(3) 'public service ship' means any vessel serving the administrative purposes of the government.

Article 57

With the exception of public service ships, ship registration fees shall be levied by the Ship Registration Administration in accordance with the relevant rules. The levels and rules concerning the levy of ship registration fees shall be formulated by the financial department and the department in charge of commodity prices under the State Council in consultation with the competent authority of transport and communications under the State Council.

Article 58

The forms of the register of ships, the Certificate of Ship's Nationality, the Provisional Certificate of Ship's Nationality, the Certificate of Registration of Ship's Ownership, the Certificate of Registration of Ship's Mortgage, the Certificate of Registration of Demise Charter, the applications and other certificates shall be solely formulated by the Bureau of Harbour Superintendency of the People's Republic of China.

Article 59

These Regulations shall enter into force on 1 January 1995.

INDEX